Praise for *Let Your Light Shine*

"Honesty, raw and inspiring wisdom, a powerful blend of deep insights into the real world we live in and the practical tools to build individuals and communities—these are brilliantly woven into the narrative tapestry of this book. *Let Your Light Shine* is a compelling invitation to dig deep and love broadly. Written by three co-authors and illuminated throughout by Uncle Will as mentor and spiritual guide, this book is not organized with the typical topic, discussion, and application structure. Instead, it is, like life itself, an open conversation between these gifted mindfulness teachers, with their long history creating and running the Holistic Life Foundation, and us, the readers who will so powerfully benefit from these visionaries' courage, tenacity, and wisdom that shines through every one of these real pages of a story that we are so fortunate they took the time to create—in this book and in our world. We will all be better for the brilliance of Ali, Andres, and Atman that shines through in this wonderful contribution to our collective lives."

—Daniel J. Siegel, MD, executive director, Mindsight Institute; founding co-director, UCLA Mindful Awareness Research Center; and *New York Times* bestselling author of *IntraConnected: MWe (Me + We) as the Integration of Self, Identity, and Belonging*

"When we think about the most oppressed and marginalized group in the world, most of us would never guess that this could be young people 18 and under. Young people struggle with a range of obstacles, from the stress of a fast-moving technology age to the trauma of surviving various forms of violence in schools, in their communities, and at home. It is no easy feat making it out of early adolescence into adulthood. The Holistic Life Foundation, with its founders Ali Smith, Atman Smith, and Andres Gonzalez, have offered young people a path of healing and resilience founded in deep care, love, and a commitment to understanding that young people are not the violence they survive. *Let Your Light Shine* is an important contribution toward building a society that centers the healing of young people so that they are able to enter into their adulthood offering the same healing back to others around them."

—Lama Rod Owens, teacher and author of
Love and Rage: The Path of Liberation Through Anger

"*Let Your Light Shine* captures the originality, insight, and, most importantly, the brother-love that make Ali, Andy, and Atman's work so vital and effective. Blending wisdom from their own Baltimore-based Black community and family with 2,500-year-old teachings originally offered in India, this trauma-sensitive, engaging book is just the contribution to the mindfulness movement that we need right now."

—Rhonda V. Magee, MA, JD, author of *The Inner Work of Racial Justice*

"Ali, Atman, and Andres, with so much heart and in the true spirit of collective care, have written a book that teaches us the important practice of healing and loving our whole self, and that in doing so, we cannot help but extend that healing and love to ALL. This, they express, is how we mend collectively, and move toward a more connected, self-realized, and compassionate society that benefits and supports everyone equally and with grace. Through personal narratives, social insights, and mindfulness practices, they explore how the deep complexities of trauma—developmental, generational, ancestral, cultural, and systemic—impact our body and consciousness, inform our reality, and perpetuate the belief systems that keep us feeling separate, rather than interdependent. This separation is the fractured foundation that births racism, injustice, and all forms of oppression; the true sickness in our society. *Let Your Light Shine* is the medicine we can all use right now as it not only shares the essential insights and practices necessary to aid in individual healing but also invites us to pass on all that we learn to others, especially children. As a student and teacher of yoga, I found this book an excellent, informative, and inspirational resource that I know I will turn to again and again."

—Seane Corn, author of *Revolution of the Soul* and co-founder of Off the Mat, Into the World

"Simply put, this is one of the most important books on yoga that has been written in many years. It captures the absolute, true spirit of yoga, which is the removal of suffering and the experience of knowledge within. There are not too many places in America with greater levels of suffering than the streets of Baltimore, the home of Atman, Ali, and Andres. They have taken their spiritual practices, taken their learnings, and put them to the test on those very streets. To combat intergenerational trauma, systemic racism, and lack of opportunity and resources, they bring a message of hope and practical tools to awaken the sense of sovereignty in the hearts and minds of young people. Yoga in America has all too often been overtaken by consumerism. These brothers, though, without a doubt are restoring the essence of the equitable power of yoga through their brilliant work, and this book will take you on a journey through a side of America that much of the yoga world rarely talks about or experiences. It will inspire you, sadden you, turn your head upside down, encourage and empower you. It puts the spiritual burden of racism front and center and shows how we can use ancient tools to transform and remake ourselves and society. Please read this book. It's the future of yoga in America."

—Eddie Stern, ashtanga yoga teacher and author of *One Simple Thing*

Let Your Light Shine

How Mindfulness Can Empower Children and Rebuild Communities

Ali Smith, Atman Smith, and Andres Gonzalez

Foreword by Bessel A. van der Kolk, MD

A TarcherPerigee Book

tarcherperigee

an imprint of Penguin Random House LLC
penguinrandomhouse.com

Most TarcherPerigee books are available at special quantity discounts for bulk
purchase for sales promotions, premiums, fund-raising, and educational needs.
Special books or book excerpts also can be created to fit specific needs. For
details, write SpecialMarkets@penguinrandomhouse.com.

Library of Congress Cataloging-in-Publication Data

Names: Smith, Ali (Mindfulness educator), author. | Smith, Atman, author. |
    Gonzalez, Andres (Mindfulness educator), author.
Title: Let your light shine: how mindfulness can empower children and
    rebuild communities / Ali Smith, Atman Smith, Andres Gonzalez.
Description: [New York]: TarcherPerigee, an imprint of
    Penguin Random House LLC, [2022] | Includes index.
Identifiers: LCCN 2022018534 (print) | LCCN 2022018535 (ebook) |
    ISBN 9780593332283 (hardcover) | ISBN 9780593332290 (epub)
Subjects: LCSH: Cognitive therapy for children—Popular works. |
    Mindfulness (Psychology)—Popular works. | Meditation for children—
    Popular works. | Hatha yoga for children—Popular works. | Minority
    youth—Mental health services—Maryland—Baltimore.
Classification: LCC RJ505.C63.S65 2022 (print) | LCC RJ505.C63 (ebook) |
    DDC 618.92/891425—dc23/eng/20220727
LC record available at https://lccn.loc.gov/2022018534
LC ebook record available at https://lccn.loc.gov/2022018535

Printed in the United States of America
1st Printing

Book design by Shannon Nicole Plunkett

We dedicate this book to Uncle Will,
Smitty, and Cassie for planting the seeds for
this journey and nourishing us with love, light,
knowledge, and support along the way.

Contents

Foreword

Walking the Walk, Talking the Talk, and Learning to Live in Stillness

Innumerable people in our society live with a legacy of violence within their families, on their streets, in their schools and institutions, and in society at large. Living on streets infested with violence, unresolved grief, anger, and hatred results in a range of trauma-related problems, including PTSD. Our brains and identities are shaped by the realities to which we are exposed early in our lives, and chronic exposure to violence and neglect inevitably results in minds and brains that specialize in the detection of danger—brains that shut down in the face of challenges and misinterpret minor stresses as catastrophes.

Traumatized children and adolescents have great difficulty feeling safe and often have serious problems with impulse control, attention, concentration, and forming trusting relationships. All too often, educators and psychologists, rather than focusing on how these kids can be helped to feel safe, connected, and worthwhile, label the behavioral effects of trauma in these children as proof that they are "bad" and that they need to be brought in line and punished for their behavior.

Punitive teachers, a lack of solid mentors and of schools that are safe, clean, and warm all further compound the challenge of growing up as a goal-directed, focused, competent, and compassionate human being. Frightened and angry people cannot learn, and for many of these kids, school systems, rather than serving as safe havens in a violent and unpredictable world, become mere confirmations of how meaningless and terrifying life is, reinforcing how inadequate, bad, and damaged these children are.

People who are born into a world of deprivation, violence, and unpredictability did not create that world; it's not their fault that they are immersed in adversities from the very start, or that their view of themselves and the world around them is profoundly shaped by these life experiences. Add to this systemic racism, domestic violence, overcrowding, poverty, and massive levels of incarceration, and we cannot help being stunned by the overwhelming magnitude of the misery. The challenges are pervasive and intergenerational: parents and families often have to work multiple jobs to make ends meet; others may survive by selling drugs or being addicted to them; they may be in jail, or too traumatized to be able to provide consistent care and protection. The resulting chronic terror, deprivation, grief, and humiliation are transformed into anger and hatred. Yet one of the rewards that keeps us going in our efforts to alleviate these problems is getting to know so many extraordinary individuals who can cobble together loving and productive lives despite having grown up with these horrendous obstacles.

For more than two decades, the brothers Atman and Ali Smith, together with their friend Andy Gonzalez, have created and run an extraordinary program in Baltimore, the Holistic Life Foundation (HLF), that works with kids who live in the kind of circumstances so poignantly portrayed in the HBO series *The Wire*. They help kids leave the devastated world they grew up in by supplying them with profoundly new experiences. They call this process of helping kids cultivate their relationship with their inner selves "involution." As a neuroscientist, this resonates with me, since scientific research has shown that the most powerful way of getting control over one's emotions and sensations is by activating the interoceptive pathways of the brain—i.e., by sensing and cultivating awareness of one's inner reality and the state of one's being, and practicing ways to regulate one's arousal.

Traumatized people often become rigid and unbending, and they are likely to look up to, and place their hopes in, the toughest, most intimidating people in their world. Ali, Atman, and Andy are none of these things—they are gentle, thoughtful, and passionate embodiments of compassion, stillness, and non-reactivity.

How do a bunch of guys teaching yoga and meditation in the hood overcome the natural resistance to such weird and alien practices? By modeling involution. By listening, holding space, and reminding kids of their true selves, unburdened by social media stupidity, and by giving them the tools to help keep themselves on their own path. When you get to know these guys, it is immediately obvious that they walk the walk and talk the talk.

Yes, we can focus on all the injustices and systemic racism that perpetuate the misery, and we should, but even if we manage to fundamentally change the social realities that children today live with and improve their collective opportunities, this can only do so much. It also is necessary to get in touch with the sources of their anger and distrust. Understanding why you are messed up is important, but it rarely solves the problem because the understanding parts of our brains only have a tenuous communication with our emotional reactions.

The fundamental challenge for traumatized kids and adults is to explore how their rage and humiliation still affect them and the community they live in. What they can *do* to change their automatic reactions. After all, when you're living in a traumatized body, you are stuck in a constant state of fight or flight. It's difficult to focus and sustain your attention, it's impossible to listen to other points of view, you cannot control your agitation or your inner sense of deadness. And it is almost impossible to learn from experience. When you live in an enraged or terrified body, there's no time to draw a breath, to relax, and to heal.

Brains shaped by chronic fear or worry change how you respond to ongoing stresses and challenges. In the long run, this manifests itself in explosive anger, cognitive impairment, and chronic depression. The body keeps the score, and the ongoing secretion of stress hormones may feed a host of physical disabilities, including hypertension, diabetes, and chronic pain. In a study done in Washington, DC, inhabitants of Chevy Chase turned out to enjoy three decades' longer life expectancy than those who lived in Anacostia.

The Holistic Life Foundation works with children, adolescents, and adults to help them develop their inner resources in order to transform their agitated inner bodily world into a safe space. They do this by fostering a sense of inner peace, and its leaders aspire to be living examples. I've always felt that part of being a good teacher or therapist is to aspire to being a model of what we advocate for others and to open the possibility for our students, clients, and patients to feel "when I grow up, I want to be just like him." That sure was my reaction when I first met Andy, Ali, and Atman at a yoga conference at the Omega Institute in Rhinebeck, New York: "I wish I could be more like them."

Mirroring people we admire, and feeling seen by and connected with predictable, safe, and competent people, is central to the process of healing. So the folks at HLF directly confront the internal residues of having witnessed the death and murder of their peers as well as the trauma of not having been heard and believed that they have carried for such a long time. This is a complex and arduous process. After all, trauma keeps on hurting from generation to generation: grandparents who were flogged and beaten pass on that trauma, that lack of love, to their kids and grandkids, compounded by too much alcohol, too many opiates, and too little affection. The premise is that it is almost impossible to shed the legacy of so much trauma unless we can help people to establish an inner sense of tranquility, regardless of the chaos all around them. To be able to turn inward during times of intense stress or trauma.

The fundamental work of the Holistic Life Foundation is based on the idea of giving traumatized people the room they need simply to breathe—through yoga and meditation. Once kids can share what's bothering them, they are invited to participate in breathing exercises and to sit quietly together in silent contemplation. A staff member invites them to notice where in their body they register their memories and experiences and guides them through observing their physical signals of stress as indicators to practice their deep breathing, which helps them to feel more calm and focused.

Helping kids to transform their bodies into safe spaces is an important step to releasing trauma and to envisioning a bigger, more capacious world, one that welcomes and supports them rather than rejecting and hurting them. I had the privilege of conducting the first NIMH-funded studies of yoga for the treatment of PTSD, which had surprisingly positive results. Those studies established yoga as an "evidence based" intervention for PTSD. In fact, yoga appears to be more effective than any of the most commonly prescribed psychiatric medications.

Yoga involves practicing being aware of your thoughts and intentions and letting that awareness shape more kind and loving thoughts. Yoga helps children build self-awareness and self-regulation at the same that it promotes a communal feeling of connection and a model of what relationships can be. Of course, HLF had to be flexible and translate alien yoga-related Sanskrit words and phrases into words that the kids could relate to: *kaki* breath became taco breath, and *sitali* breath became burrito breath. You've gotta speak the language of the folks you work with.

As you read this marvelous book and absorb its lessons, you'll travel the country, meeting up with folks who are finding their own way to foster the "involutionary" spirit in their own homes and communities. It shares the strategies that have given thousands of kids that edge that allows them to survive and succeed: be it love, support, self-confidence, or simply a friendly ear at a moment when no one else is listening. More importantly, this book shows you how this love, support, and empathy needs to be consistent and reliable, thereby finally adding a degree of stability to these young people's lives. Too many underprivileged and traumatized people have been let down innumerable times before. It's better to consistently show up once a month than renege on a weekly commitment.

This book shares the details of their breakthrough program for fortifying the spirit, finding peace, and fueling the righteous anger that will be required to break through to the next level of physical and spiritual emancipation. It will explain the importance of working with people who look like them as well as the importance of consistency and commitment. This program has given thousands of kids who grew up under the most adverse of circumstances skills and tools to deal with their anger, trauma, and lack of focus. In addition, it's given kids the chance to learn self-regulation and tools to get back to center.

The foundations of the Holistic Life Foundation are critical: you cannot do this work by yourself. It is essential to have a strong support system to help you to see, tolerate, and accept your limitations; healthy, loving acceptance and nonattachment are essential for your own sanity and well-being.

Bessel A. van der Kolk, MD
President, Trauma Research Foundation

Dr. Van der Kolk is the author of the *New York Times* bestseller *The Body Keeps the Score: Brain, Mind, and Body in the Healing of Trauma.*

I'm Not a Teacher, I'm a Reminder

It's spring 2022, and the world is on fire, in more ways than one. In DC, the first woman vice president is in the White House. In the streets, communities are still grappling with the effects of COVID-19. Two years on from the protests of 2020 we are still *saying their names*—change seems so possible—and yet daily, more young Black and Brown people join the ranks of the shot-down, murdered, and ended people.

So, we have hope, but forgive us for being skeptical.

Justice in this country is like the foxtrot, or some other old-time dance. We take one step forward, two steps back. Voters in Florida overwhelmingly passed a resolution giving former felons their votes back. The Republican governor tacked on the requirement that those former inmates have to pay all court fees, going back as far as the '60s or '70s. Dig deeper, and you'll find it is impossible to track down, let alone pay, how much is owed. What seems like an easy win for justice turns into a twenty-first-century poll tax.

If you were paying attention to this story, you might have been surprised by just how smoothly the bureaucratic machine moved to neutralize what seemed to be a minor civil rights milestone. But this is America, and this is how it's always been. Abraham Lincoln signed the Emancipation Proclamation: his successor, Andrew Johnson, reinstated many of the Confederate leaders who assumed they were going to the gallows. Congress proposed the Thirteenth, Fourteenth, and Fifteenth Amendments: the Southern states delayed ratifying them, or found ways around them. Black Americans boarded trains for the North during the Great Migration: White police officers tore up their tickets and arrested them for vagrancy. "Vagrants" were released to White plantation owners, who paid their fines and took their repayment in months or years of field labor. Black women in the South were arrested if they refused employment—at minimal wages—in White homes, leaving their own daughters and sons uncared for while they raised their employers' children instead. In 1964, the Twenty-fourth Amendment banned the use of poll taxes to deny voters their ballot: much good it did the 100,000 Floridians petitioning for their right to a vote five decades later. In Andy's parents' home of Puerto Rico, the American government conducted numerous illegal, deadly, and secret medical experiments, infecting islanders with cancerous cells and sterilizing women. They also dropped bombs on the island of Vieques for *fifty-five* years, leading to multigenerational PTSD, and cancer rates 27 percent higher than off the island.[1]

We're not cynical. We've got hope. We see it every day with the kids we work with. We see the power of active, engaged love, rather than fear. Our love stays strong, but let's just say that our hope is tempered by an awareness of history. Atman and Ali's father, Smit, and our godfather, Uncle Will—our spiritual mentor—were both members of the Black Panthers. Uncle Will used to tell us: "I'm not a teacher, I'm a reminder. I'm just reminding you guys of what you forgot. The stuff you don't even realize you used to know. I haven't taught you a damn thing. I am just a conduit of energy and information."

Uncle Will was talking about our spiritual path, and we'll get to that in a moment. But this sentiment—"I'm a reminder"—sits with us today. We all know this stuff. Us, living in Baltimore, working with the most vulnerable, underserved, ignored kids in America. You, wherever you are now, reading this book and dipping into a world outside of your own. Politicians, policy makers, teachers, parents, kids. Even if we don't all know all the details, we feel the facts of American history in our bones and see them reflected back to us, in the societies we live in. So what now?

Just like Uncle Will, we see ourselves as reminders rather than teachers. Sometimes, when one of our brand-new students slips right into an effortless *pranayama* practice, or a deep meditation, we'll look at each other and say, "This isn't her first time!" But whether you believe in past lives or not, there's truth to the idea that we all carry a kind of knowledge of our past, encoded in our genes.* When we fight to survive, our body suppresses genes that aren't related to survival, and doubles down on expressing genes that help keep us alive just one more day. These adverse childhood experiences (ACEs)

---

* Transgenerational trauma is a fascinating concept, and one we won't touch too deeply on in this book. If you come from a lineage of generational trauma—whether it's slavery or the Holocaust or other genocides—it's worth researching and studying to see if it applies to you.

rewire brains: Years later, when the trauma is supposedly over, our genes are still operating as if we are in a daily fight to live. Our kids can inherit this genetic predisposition, and even though they haven't personally experienced that old trauma that shaped their parents, grandparents, or great-great-great-grandparents, they feel, think, and act as if they have, even before they experience trauma themselves. Kids who don't exhibit signs of this multigenerational, genetic trauma may still experience ACEs that can derail their emotional, mental, and behavioral development.

The children of the Holocaust or the Cambodian genocide survivors, for instance, understand this. So do Black Americans, who are dealing with the double whammy of systemic racism and the denial of this systemic racism by White people (even well-meaning White people). You can't talk this shit out. And for most Black Americans, trying to talk this shit out can be actively toxic to our emotional, mental, physical, and spiritual well-being. Over the course of this book we will share our story, and how we began to heal our own wounds and the wounds of the people around us.

This book is based on our program, designed to help underserved youth and communities all over the planet. We started with our home first. And because Baltimore is so segregated, "home" was originally the Black youth who lived in West Baltimore. Eventually it spread to Baltimore as a whole. This program is universal, however, and applicable for anyone feeling the intense strain of life today. It allows for deep healing on a somatic level—and who doesn't need that these days?

This program eventually became known as the Holistic Life Foundation (HLF), and it reaches thousands of the most vulnerable kids in Baltimore, and America as a whole, every year. Our program is designed to work with young children, tweens, teens, and young adults, teaching them mindfulness practices that serve as a circuit breaker and reset from the stress and trauma of their lives. As they learn, they also become teachers, sharing their knowledge with their family members and eventually teaching other kids under our supervision. Our goal is to give them the tools to survive and thrive in situations of intense stress and trauma, and to teach them other healthful habits—eating veggies, exercising, talking shit out—that will help them create a joyful life, full of possibility, and on their own terms.

Most of us think it takes a revolution to spur big change, but revolution is often a violent and painful process. Instead, we prefer to follow the peaceful path of evolution, but not in the way Darwin defined it. Instead of changing the body, we're looking at something deeper: the inner change that allows us to not just survive but thrive in the face of challenges. We call our philosophy and program Involution. Involution was another Smit and Uncle Will–ism. Uncle Will defined it as: "To change the outside world you have to go within and change yourself first." The way he saw it, our real gurus were inside of us. The real learning is in going deeper and deeper into yourself and, if you're very lucky, breaking through to experience the expansive, unending, infinite self within each of us. This is a profound concept for someone who's lived within the spiritual community or explored different practices over the years. Now imagine being eight or nine years old, from the worst part of Baltimore, and your life is on the edge of falling apart. It's not surprising we get some blank looks on the first day of class.

We see involution in people like Freddie Gray, a kid who could have been straight out of one of our programs. We see it in Elijah McClain, the self-taught violinist who played to shelter cats to calm them down. Or in Sandra Bland, driving cross-country solo to hit that next rung on the career ladder. We see it in Stephon Clark, holding an iPhone in his grandma's backyard. We see involution in the mega celebrities like Beyoncé, shining a light on HBCUs at Coachella. We see involution in urban gardeners like Ron Finley in Los Angeles, turning food deserts into blossoming oases of free food for local communities. In this book, we'll travel the country, meeting up with folks who are finding their own way to foster the involutionary spirit in their own homes and communities. Even more importantly, we'll stay close to home, digging deep on twenty years of intensive work in our community, to share the strategies that have given thousands of kids that edge that allows them to survive and succeed—be it love, support, self-confidence, or simply a friendly ear in a moment when no one else is listening. Crucially, we'll ensure this love, support, and empathy are consistent and reliable, adding stability to young people's lives.

The problem is so clear to us: young Black people living their lives seem suspect, dangerous, or in some way "disordered" to Karens dialing 911 or police at the other end of a gun or Taser. There are plenty of books out there breaking down racism in all its forms, uncovering how it persists today, and guiding White people to be better allies. There aren't that many books about healing the spiritual burden that comes with racism, for all people—Black, Brown, and White. In the next pages, we'll share our breakthrough program for fortifying the spirit, finding peace, and fueling the righteous anger that will be required to break through to the next level of physical and spiritual emancipation.

How Do You Achieve Inner Peace When Your Outer Life Is Chaotic?

So, let's clear up one thing before we go any further. Who are we? There's three of us. Ali and Atman are brothers who grew up on North and Pulaski in West Baltimore, the corner that *Time* magazine photographed as the worst drug corner in America. Nonetheless, they were lucky to have hippie parents who fed them hearty vegan food and meditated with them every day. It's not every Black kid who attends weekly meditation meetings on the serene grounds of the Divine Life Church of Absolute Oneness (part of the Self-Realization Fellowship organization founded in 1920 by Paramahansa Yogananda to teach scientific methods of meditation and principles of spiritual living). Atman and Ali feel blessed to have had the opportunity; at the same time, they attended the Quaker Friends School of Baltimore. All throughout school, they went to "meeting for worship." If the spirit moved you, you got up and shared and then sat back down and reflected on it. If the spirit moved you again, you could speak again. If nothing happened, it was just a time for silence and stillness to see what was coming up inside. Silence was valued there. Before the students did pretty much anything—a class, an assembly, a visiting speaker, a game—there was a moment of silence. It influences their work to this day.

And Andres? Well, Andy likes to say that Atman and Ali meditated him into existence, right when we needed that third element to our triad (always the strongest and most stable structure, FYI). That's pretty self-effacing of Andy, and not true at all.

If Ali and Atman got their spiritual kick-start from their Quaker school, and their dad and uncle's yogic beliefs, then Andy got his from his mom and aunts' access to dream worlds, and their spiritual history of growing up in Puerto Rico. Andres's ancestors came from a tradition of Caribbean spirituality called *espiritismo*. Like his ancestors, Andres feels the good and bad spirits that surround us and shape our lives, tweaking our luck and shaping our destinies in ways we can't always see, understand, or predict. If Andy tells you he dreamed that you need to stay off the roads tomorrow, well, you better stay off the roads tomorrow. Now, most of us aren't tapped into this kind of deep spirituality. But let's translate it to the secular world: Who among us doesn't feel that unseen good and bad actors, or some kind of invisible, all-powerful force, are steering our lives? And who would say no to a system that allows us to regain some control over this sense of exterior forces shaping our world?

Andy may not be blood, but he is family. And this philosophy is a big part of who we are. We are not bound by blood ties. We see everyone as family and look beyond the physical to see that spiritual connection that unites all of us. So, throughout this book you are going to hear references to our dad, Smit; our Uncle Will; our family; our home. Understand that Andy is family. Smit may not be his dad, but he was always a father figure to Andy. Ditto Uncle Will. Andy may not have grown up in the hood, but he's been here long enough for it to become home, and to become a place he is deeply and passionately committed to.

We're lucky that we have each other, and our parents, and Uncle Will. Their influence built us up to be strong, empathetic men, with the ability to navigate a uniquely difficult and often dangerous world. Their lessons made us resilient to the stress around us. And that stress is everywhere, because, let's get real: This country was built on trauma.

The people who suffer most from this trauma are the ones descended from slaves, Indigenous peoples, and all folks deemed "lesser" by the powers that be.[2] When you're living in a traumatized body, you are in a constant state of fight or flight. There's no time to draw breath, to relax, to heal. All you have is that moment you're living in, and the choices you have to make in that second—choices that can in the worst-case scenario define the rest of your life. Our work is based on the idea of giving these traumatized people—kids mostly, but young adults too—the spaciousness they need within to just breathe. If we can help these kids to make their bodies safe spaces, then that can be the first step in releasing trauma, or learning to take that extra second. To be responsive, rather than reactive. To envision a bigger, more expansive world, one that welcomes and supports them, rather than rejecting and hurting them.

And it's not just the oppressed who are traumatized. Everyone out there resisting change, retreating in fear to some old vision of "how things used to be," well, they're traumatized too. It's a different kind of trauma, because it's the trauma that comes from knowing you benefited from the evil actions of your ancestors. It's the trauma that comes from holding on tightly to the past, because you can't face the accountability of the present. It's the trauma of finding any way—no matter how convoluted—to justify unjustifiable belief systems. They're the people waving guns at peaceful protestors or pouring water on a child's chalk drawings celebrating the Black Lives Matter movement, all the while spreading rumors and innuendo about people doing the actual hard work of social justice. We meet these people in some of our private and corporate work. Even though they are often initially resistant to us and our ideas, we are usually able to break through with them. How? By modeling involution to them: in the ability to listen, to hold space, and reminding them of their true selves, unburdened by social media stupidity, and giving them the tools to help themselves on their own involutionary path.

Now think of centuries of transgenerational trauma, passed down from parent to child, written in our genes, and felt so deeply that it feels like part of you. Think of the Black child, living with the weight of ancient pain, constricted in her soul and her body. And her White counterpart, rigid and unblinking in his belief that his parents' beliefs have to be right, because how will he define himself if they are wrong? There's a reason that trying to talk this shit out can only go so far. If we want to heal the psychic wounds of our country, if we want to fortify the oppressed, and forgive the oppressors, we need to go deeper than platitudes, slogans, and good intentions.

How to Use This Book

Involution might sound like a lot of work. Well, yes. In one sense it is work. Involution means you are willing to let go of some pretty deep stuff. It means surrendering a broken part of yourself that nonetheless feels safe and familiar. This can be scary stuff for a little kid, so mostly we don't use this kind of language for them—and if you're guiding a child through involution, you won't either. But at the same time, involution is effortless. Think of it like waking up after a lifetime of physical pain, to find that your head no longer hurts, or your leg no longer limps. Suddenly you can think clearly and walk easily.

Being able to think clearly and walk easily is always important, but right now, it's doubly essential. Who knows what the next few years are going to deal us. We're two years into the 2020s, and we've already seen a global pandemic; a civil rights resurgence and a patriarchal, White supremacist backlash; an international depression; and multiple climate change catastrophes. It's a lot.

Part One is what's going on. In it, we will break down the environment: home, school, the natural world. What does it mean to live in a community that either nurtures or actively ignores its residents? Baltimore is a living, breathing example of what happens when trauma is institutionalized on a massive scale: both in size and time. You want to know what happens when multiple generations of people are told, "This is as good as it's going to get"? Well, come here and you can see the ramifications of this play out in real time. We'll look at what's happening in the homes, the schools, and the green spaces (or lack of them). How small choices reverberate throughout a community. How even seemingly well-intentioned policies like desegregation can reverberate with terrible consequences.

We'll travel to communities like the Mohawk Nation in the Akwesasne territory in northern New York to find out what happens when communities throw themselves into loving, nurturing, and fortifying their youth. There's a lot to learn, including the concept of tribal sovereignty—something that has allowed the tribes to educate, heal, and police their people on their own terms.

Part Two is our adult involution intensive, followed by techniques to help the children in your lives. The adult techniques will help you work on yourself and become the image of what you want the world to be. They are a series of clear, simple steps that allow the mind to rest and blossom, the soul to relax and breathe, and the body to begin to heal itself. The goal of this program is to give everyone an opportunity to see how it could be. Practice solo, with your kids, or with other adults.

And finally, Part Three is our vision of the future. We'll look at ways that communities are pushing back against the narrative of American life, and establishing a new, bold future for themselves and their children.

We look forward to walking this path with you.

Part One

Our Path

CHAPTER ONE

Wipe the Dust Off and Let Your Inner Light Shine Out

We travel a lot. We regularly jump on planes to visit schools or private companies, where we give keynotes, hold workshops, teach, or simply share ideas. As we do every summer, at the beginning of June 2021, the three of us flew up to the Akwesasne territory, part of the Mohawk Nation, on the border of the United States and Canada, west of Montreal. This is an intensive program: over a five-week period fourteen young Mohawks participate in over eighty hours of intensive yoga and mindfulness training. When they graduate, they are fully trained in our Mindful Leader program—and ready to share this knowledge with other young Mohawks. That's not all: We also partnered with local community educators to provide mental health awareness training, guidance in managing a classroom, and traditional Haudenosaunee cultural education. We also teach basic skills essential for any future career path: managing finances, becoming confident at public speaking, building a strong résumé, and resolving conflicts. These newly minted young leaders get a weekly stipend too, which helped many of them financially over the pandemic. Now these young people are employed and earning as well as learning, providing relief during the unexpected challenge presented by the COVID-19 pandemic, and allowing trainees to fully prioritize their training. There are multiple reasons we do this, but the primary one is our belief that struggling communities all over America—and the world—need to learn from each other, support each other, and work collaboratively together to design new ways of living to elevate their kids' prospects and uplift their communities in a joyful, hopeful way. At the end of the book you'll read about how we encourage our students in Baltimore to become teachers themselves or, at the very least, actively share what they've learned with their family and friends. This is very purposeful. There's only three of us, and if we had to teach every class, or mentor every kid, our program would have run out of gas years ago. Our goal is to seed communities all over the country, and eventually the world, with the techniques that will empower them to thrive and blossom in a way that conventional society, education, policing, and government policies actively squash.

Uncle Will (hold on, you'll hear all about him in a few pages) always told us that you have to "wipe the dust off, and let your inner light shine out." On an individual level this is easy to understand: If you've ever had a deep meditation, you've experienced that sensation of clarity, calm, acceptance. But it has bigger implications too: We interpret this as a light that has the potential to sweep across the world, like a lighthouse illuminating a rough sea. This light is less about us swooping in and doing the work than it is about highlighting the talent and energy and potential already in these local communities. We share our knowledge, and support—but once these groups are up and running, they need us less and less.

This trip to the Akwesasne would probably be one of our last—at least in a formal capacity—as the program was rapidly evolving into a self-sustaining model. It was primarily a working trip, but frankly after a solid year of negotiating COVID, we needed a break. It was a relief to fly north over the vast, unbroken forests of upstate New York and look down on land that—in appearance at least—comes as close as you can to uncolonized in the continental United States. Our hosts, of course, have a different perspective.

Our hosts in the Akwesasne territory are members of the Mohawk Nation. The name *Akwesasne* means "land where the partridge drums." And in their language they call themselves Kanien'kehá:ka, or "people of the flint."

Like most First Nations or Native Americans, the Mohawk had a complex relationship with the early European settlers. In the 1500s, the Dutch arrived. Initially relations were good. The Dutch suggested they were the "fathers" and the Mohawk were the "sons." Unsurprisingly, the Mohawk objected to this, and said the two groups were instead "brothers." The Mohawk created a wampum belt, with two rows of purple beads that represented the Mohawk canoes and the Dutch ships sailing through the world in kinship. However, as the Dutch expanded into Mohawk territory, their relationship frayed. In the seventeenth century, Christian missionaries began to convert some of the Native tribespeople. Later, the Roman Catholics did the same. The French and English alternated between allying themselves with and fighting against the tribes. During the American Civil War, the tribes allied themselves with the British against the American settlers. When the British lost, the tribes were forced to give up most of their land, and they relocated to the land they live on now.

In the nineteenth century, Richard Pratt founded the first off-reservation boarding school for Native American children in Pennsylvania. He thought himself a good man. After all, popular opinion often called for genocide against the tribes. He merely believed that you needed to "kill the Indian, and save the man."[1] Thousands of children disappeared, and for over a hundred years these schools insisted that the children had run away. Shortly after our visit, sonar and excavations revealed the horrific truth these schools had hidden for a hundred-plus years.

Is it surprising that we see some parallels between our world and theirs?

Throughout the twentieth century, the Mohawk had to fight to preserve what was theirs: In the 1990s things got heated when White Canadian developers tried to build a golf course on tribal lands. The mother of one of our Mindful Leaders—while pregnant with him—almost died in a shootout over it. The Canadian Army sent thousands of troops, but the Mohawk blocked off a bridge into Montreal, protesting the incursion and refusing to back down. For a minute it looked like the blood was going to flow (and two people did die). In the end, the land was purchased by the government but never actually returned to the Mohawk people.[2]

This protest was both good and bad: It caused even worse strife and division in the tribe, and divided many people against each other, yet it also literally gave birth to the young activists we work with today. When we sit down on that green Mohawk grass with our students it's inspiring as hell: The residential schools might have tried to destroy their language and culture, even erased it from their grandparents' and parents' lives. But the young people are embracing being Mohawk fearlessly. They are learning their language, renaming themselves with Mohawk names, re-creating lost traditions, and relearning lost ceremonial practices, piece by piece. One of our teachers, Steven, moved off the reservation when he was six, with his family. He was unable to process the aftereffects of generational trauma (it was his mother who almost died at the protest) and lost years of his life to opiates. Eventually he returned to Akwesasne and struggled to get clean.

The Bear Clan Mother (Wakerakas:te, also known as Louise Herne) encouraged him to complete the six-week ceremonial Ohero:kon, or rites of passage, along with seventy other young people, eventually fasting silently and alone in the forest for four days. He told us, "Being out there you don't have your partner, parents, there is no one out there. No cell phone, no video game, no food, no water, no distractions, just you and yourself. You get inside yourself. Inside your own thoughts, your own mind and heart. You come out of this ancient ceremony with a lot of gratitude for all that you have in your life. It was a pivotal moment in my life filled with so much healing."

Steven's grandfather, even into his eighties, can't help saying the Hail Mary he was forced to learn and recite, over and over again, in the residential school, even as his soul rejects the colonizers' religion and yearns to spiritually rejoin the

Longhouse, where his true ancestors are. Knowing yourself, and being free of the voice of your oppressor, is a gift no one should take for granted. Today Steven and his grandfather are learning the traditional opening address of the Mohawk culture, reclaiming their true selves word by word.

You might be wondering why a book that is mostly set in Baltimore is taking a swerve into upstate New York. Well, here's one reason: We've learned over the last twenty years that we have to roam far and dig deep to find the resources to help our kids. And equally, we've been drawn to spread what we know to other communities. Once you've seen young people's lives dramatically improved in your backyard . . . well, it's hard to keep that news to yourself. This kind of learning is always a two-way street, however. We've learned even more about how to rebuild a struggling community from the Mohawk than they've learned from us—especially in the ways that the tribe has embraced its matriarchal structure.

It's not an easy matter to travel to upstate New York in the middle of a global pandemic, but it's not an easy matter to get help from close at hand either. Sometimes you have to step outside of your world to see what is broken in it. And once you've reached a place of insight, you need to share what you've figured out. Look at our world today: We are all in varying states of crisis, all struggling to find answers to similar problems. Think how much faster we would find solutions if we shared our discoveries. We believe there's no point in solving your problems if you can't also help other people solve theirs. It's a holistic approach, and one that we've embraced for twenty years. We don't have all the answers, but we have some of them. Same with the Mohawk: they don't know everything, but what they know is valuable, and applicable to every struggling community.

The Akwesasne territory isn't some perfect place. The Mohawk deal with a ton of racism and resentment from both America and Canada. (The reservation crosses the border.) They are still recovering from their own version of Jim Crow, when Indigenous peoples were banned from places like bars and bowling alleys and discriminated against when it came to voting or getting good jobs. They are—still—confronting prejudice and discrimination when they deal with the world outside of the reservation. They had to fight two hundred years for compensation from the last time land was stolen from them* and as late as 2009 Canadian border guards moderating a customs dispute interrogated every member of the tribe who left their home or attempted to return to it.

The Mohawk also have the trauma of not being heard and believed. Everyone knew that something happened to their children, but it took decades of fighting and protesting to get permission to bring ground-penetrating sonar onto church property. That generational trauma keeps on hurting: grandparents who were whipped and beaten and worse at residential schools pass on that trauma, that lack of love, to their kids and grandkids. There's sometimes too much alcohol, too many opiates, and too little affection. Yet things are changing.

The tribe are fighting like hell for their children. Sure, their youth struggle with the same existential despair of any

---

* The Dundee land claim, which was settled thirty-seven years after the case was first filed, and almost two hundred years after the land was first leased by non-Indigenous settlers.

kid growing up in an isolated or impoverished area with low wages and limited prospects. And yet the tribe has rallied together as a people. They have a deep connection to family and community, and a shared identity as a tribe and a culture. They are Mohawk first, everything else second. Within the common identity as Mohawk they have reemphasized the clan structure, giving their children an added layer of identity and belonging.

They have a connection to their heritage and their ancestors that is missing in American culture in general, but especially in Baltimore. You'll read about how Baltimore has lost all the social structures, like mentors, weak ties, social networks, and rites of passage, that are being reinvigorated in the Akwesasne territory. What's more, the Mohawk have held on to a core truth about themselves that many Americans have forgotten: at the very core of the tribe they are fully realized citizens.

The word *sovereign* is something we'll refer to throughout this book, but let's get something out of the way right now: We reject the way various right-wing cults or other questionable groups use the term. We don't use the word in the sketchy, fake-license-plate, "sovereign citizen" kind of way,[3] but in a way that suggests a path forward for other struggling communities. Nor is *sovereign* a code for beliefs in various conspiracies or an excuse for antisocial behavior.

Our definition of *sovereignty* is more aligned with the kind of practices we've seen on the Mohawk reservation. They have the right to govern themselves and determine their own way of life, their own traditions and rituals, and in many cases, their own laws. They teach, feed, heal, police, and judge themselves. They often feel unloved, unwanted, and unprotected by the American and Canadian cultures that surround them. Because of this they fight every day to preserve the right to determine the ethos under which their community lives. This feels familiar to us: Our dad, Smitty, often talked about how the segregated Baltimore he grew up in was "self-contained," and how much better this version of the city was. We'll get to that in a bit.

Part of the difference between the Akwesasne territory and society outside of the reservation is that the Mohawk embody a more matriarchal social structure. The clan leaders are women. They oversee the community and select the male members of the Haudenosaunee Council (the group of tribes more commonly known as the Iroquois Confederacy). The tribe's lineage carries on through the women. Steven is only Bear Clan because his mom was Bear Clan. The clan mothers control who leads the community in each clan. They give names out too. Steven's Mohawk name was given to him by a clan mother. When a man and woman marry, the man moves into the woman's family's longhouse; their children become members of her clan. This emphasis on the matriarchy has ebbed and flowed, but now, as the Mohawk embrace it as the means of organizing their community, their community is stronger than ever.

The Mohawk care for their children the way that moms care for their kids—from the beginning of their lives to the end. They also understand that when their kids act out or mess up it is a reflection on the society the elders have created for the kids to live in. Instead of punishment, they have compassion and understanding for the circumstances of the child's life.

By the time we left, the late summer heat was through the roof. As the elders gathered to say goodbye, they were also coordinating the distribution of air conditioners to all families on the reservation. It was, as they noted, the first time in the tribe's history that the temperature was so dangerously high. Dry too: It hadn't rained for weeks. Those air conditioners were expensive—no doubt something else in the tribe's budget had to give for them to make the purchase. But the health and well-being of the most vulnerable members of their group—the very old among them—was an undisputed priority. At the same time, the elders were busy trying to figure out Wi-Fi hotspots and tablets for the kids in summer school. They understood that their kids were already dealing with all-too-limited resources. Making sure their young people didn't fall even further behind was critical.

As we hurtled along the Burlington runway, on our flight heading home, we were all thinking along the same lines. The matriarchy—and the sense of sovereignty it encourages—is where it's at. The powers that be could give a damn about them, so these communities, discarded by said powers, have to reject everything about the (traditional) power structure to provide for their young and thrive for themselves.

The tribe saw their elders as a treasure, the key to how their culture and society have been able to endure all the oppression. In struggling hoods like Philly, Detroit, and Baltimore, drained of the big industry jobs that used to support them, there is a very antagonistic relationship between old and young people, and the youth don't get to benefit from that wealth of knowledge.

Even as we visited the reservation, Andy was still processing the betrayal and abandonment of his island after Hurricane

Maria. Like the Native American tribes, his people have constantly been invaded and taken over by the Spanish, English, and Dutch. Their history has been splattered with atrocities and colonizers, but their pride and honor are something that these colonists can not and will not ever take from them. Puerto Ricans, and Indigenous people, have been constantly lied to and taken advantage of but they still push forward knowing that one day they will once again gain their independence.

We knew that we were bringing something invaluable back to Baltimore and to other underserved communities, whether hood communities or poor White communities: a belief that we need to take care of our own, and others we empathize with, because no one is going to do it for us. And, even more importantly, proof that it is possible to resist the domination of a culture that doesn't care about us, and create a community that does.

Our next observation, and the thing that kept us talking all the way home, was simple. How can we apply what we've learned here, about the importance of having a culture to connect to, when the culture that defines most of our kids, Black culture, was almost destroyed both by the original sin of slavery and the successive sins of Jim Crow, incarceration, and desegregation? And what would it mean if the people of Baltimore could teach, heal, police, and judge themselves?

Back Home

$550 million. That was the Baltimore Police Department's budget for 2020.[4] Sure, it's down a bit. $7 million was sliced from the officer overtime fund. Another $2.4 million was cut from the mounted and marine divisions. Here's the funny part, though. When you actually ask the residents of Baltimore what they would like their tax dollars spent on, they say youth programs, affordable housing, small business and neighborhood development.

No shit.

Policing came in fifth, behind that list of other, perennially underfunded services. Here's another problem: Every jurisdiction in Maryland has the authority to require its senior police officers to live within the district they serve. There's only one exception to that rule. Guess which?[*5] Why do we care about this? Because the police who roll through the streets of Baltimore don't understand the neighborhoods they serve. Some of them can't even understand the Baltimore accent or have the willingness or ability to filter out the sometimes aggressive speaking tone to hear the actual words being said. They don't understand the context of these kids' lives, and they don't know the kids they pull over for minor, or nonexistent, infractions. The residents of Baltimore don't trust their police, and vice versa.

Being a cop is a power trip. Sure there are good ones. We've met some. But there are more of the other kind. Up until 2020, cops in Baltimore could roll through the neighborhood in unmarked cars wearing bulletproof vests under plain clothes. When they saw a young Black man walking to a store—or school—they'd slow their roll, lean out the window, and tell him to stop. Now, everyone in Baltimore has heard the stories of what these cops do and exactly how they treat young Black men, so nine times out of ten the kid would take

---

* Baltimore, but we know you got that already.

off running, cops following. If the cops catch up, they drag the kid into the alley and lay into him, punching him in the guts and the jaw. When the kid objects—and this has happened to every eleven-year-old we know—the cops would tell them, "Go and tell your parents."[6] Translated, they were telling him, "No one's gonna believe you, and no one's going to care. Take your licks and shut the f**k up."

Ra'Mon—one of our former students turned mentor and teacher—says, "Every time the cops did shit like this it closed my heart down a little bit more, made me a little harder and a little angrier." This hardness, or rigidity, is like a calcification that has cracked and broken the old communities of Baltimore. Imagine a community full of young men who are treated like criminals more or less as soon as they hit double digits, and who know that no one believes them, trusts them, or has any interest in listening to them. Ra'Mon is one of the most thoughtful, responsible, and passionate young people we know. Not that the cop punching him in his then-twelve-year-old guts gave a damn to get to know him.

This isn't a Baltimore problem. It's an America problem. Ask any resident of any "troubled" city or neighborhood: the police don't make them feel safe. The best-case scenario is that calling the cops might be the lesser of two bad outcomes. Might. This isn't a new problem either: Smitty came up in a Baltimore neighborhood called Turner Station in the '50s. He and his friends would gather under the streetlight on the corner to sing doo-wop, right up till the moment they saw the police heading up Fleming Drive and Main Street toward them. They knew it didn't matter that they were only eleven or twelve, or that they came from strict, disciplined, and matriarchal families, or that they spent their Saturdays crushing it in the (segregated) Little League. They knew the only thing the cops were going to see was threatening young Black men up to something that cops didn't recognize or understand. Smitty and his friends would scatter into the dark, making their way home to safety. After all, there was a reason they called the cops "body snatchers." Any Black male knows this dynamic of when he crosses the threshold of cute to threatening. Most of our kids join us when they are still in single digits, yet as they head toward ten or eleven and start sprouting, people stop thinking of them as kids. They become threatening, even to officers who most likely have tweens and teens of their own at home.

We've got thoughts about the police. We think that police officers who know the people they serve, and understand the complexities of those peoples' lives, will do a better job than cops who swoop in for a few shifts a week. Back in the day, there were beat cops, who patrolled on foot, and who were often Black and local, and knew the citizens they served. Police corruption and bad behavior were less problematic, because they were accountable to the neighborhood. But police unions disagree with this approach—and they have a grossly disproportionate power that overwhelms the desires of the people who live in the cities they serve.

We've had plenty of dealings with the cops too, starting young. One night, when Ali was in seventh grade, our dad, Smit, woke up in the middle of the night. He'd heard something outside the window of his bedroom on the second floor, looked out, and saw a person trying to break in. Smit being Smit, he grabbed a pillow, wrapped it around his fist, and punched the guy in the face through the window. The guy screamed and fell one story to the ground, then hobbled away. Our dad ran into our room madder than we had ever seen him to try to see which way the guy went.

Smit's girlfriend called the police and in that moment we felt some sense of relief, because in our young minds, the police would come help find the person. The police showed up over an hour later and were rude as hell, condescending assholes about the entire situation. That was when our idea of Officer Friendly, helping Black people, died. And it was when a lifelong string of mostly negative interactions started with the police in our lives.

Have you ever seen an eleven-year-old sitting on the curb, handcuffed, because he "looked suspicious"? Now imagine that same interaction if the police officer knew the kid, understood his background, was familiar with his family, and had empathy for his or her experience. Different, right?

This is also a book about resources, and how they are distributed among the competing populations both on a local level and a national or even global one. The Akwesasne have very limited resources, yet what they have is used to uplift all members of their community, starting with the most desperate. Our kids—living through the coronavirus in Baltimore—spent 2020 and some of 2021 walking to bus stops every Monday morning to pick up printed packets of schoolwork. Forget laptops, forget hot spots, forget Zoom: the lucky kids might be sharing one tablet between multiple siblings. When they got home, if they had a home to get to, they were mostly on their own, educating themselves the best they could. Some teachers went above and beyond, taking work to students' houses and working with them one-on-one virtually. More didn't.

Meanwhile, in Los Angeles, a survey of Black parents found they were more likely to keep their kids home, and prolong online learning,[7] because of the ongoing fear of COVID *and* a belief that their kids did better away from their peers and instructors and experienced less bullying and racism at home than on campus. This stuff is complicated and multifaceted. There's no one good answer.

The System and Who It Serves (Or, Am I Going to Believe You or My Lying Eyes?)

Baltimore should work. If you've never visited, then jump on Google Maps, punch in Turner Station or Sparrows Point or North and Pulaski and look around. Beneath the decay and the blight are wide streets and boulevards, some punctuated with small green parks, others shaded with trees, sometimes dying from neglect. The residential streets are lined with small two- or three-story rowhouses, built in successive waves of style from the late 1700s on (our childhood home was most likely built in the early twentieth century), some exposed red brick, others refinished with formstone, which mimics a stone veneer, even down to the mortar joints. Baltimore rowhouses are often narrow and deep, sometimes with a very small garden out back, and an alley running behind the block. (You'll see similar homes in other eastern cities like Philly or Pittsburgh.) Most have a basement, adding a utility room or maybe a den to the home. The older homes are famous for the marble steps leading up to the front door, and if you're lucky a porch with an awning, which your grandparents might sit on and while away an afternoon. In the afternoon, the wives would scrub the steps, making that marble shine, taking pride in what it meant to own those steps, and that house.

Many of these old houses are now being torn down in the name of blight reduction. Sometimes their old Baltimore molded bricks are sold to developers in places like Southampton, New York, or Washington, DC, where their patina and "made in America" heritage lend instant history to beach houses and faux-historic lofts alike. The latter will no doubt appeal to Amazon executives coming to Washington after the capital won a nationwide battle to house their new headquarters. Don't even get us started on the cynicism of that whole endeavor. (But let's just say *our* city leadership put a lot of time and money into trying to win that bid. Yet is anyone really surprised that the eventual winners were cities that frankly didn't need the help?)

The city is in a prime location on the Eastern Seaboard. You can commute to DC if you choose. We have an international airport, a kick-ass aquarium, a historical port, and access to the ocean and national parks. Those little houses should have helped create intergenerational wealth for the Black families who once owned them. Parents should be using the equity in their homes to get college loans for their kids, or fund repairs on the houses, or go on vacation. The tax base should be flourishing with communities enjoying all the benefits of a large, vibrant city. This should be a good place to live, and for many, many years, it was.

Here's where we are going to get controversial: We believe that desegregation was a terrible thing for Baltimore and the Black families who lived there. When we were growing up in the '80s, our dad would talk about how desegregation killed Black communities. We really couldn't understand that as kids: Desegregation was good, right? That's what we learned, at least. Didn't the NAACP fight for decades to get Black kids into White schools? Didn't groups like the American Civil Liberties Union (ACLU) fight for the end of racist social engineering policies like redlining? We had gone to a Quaker school, Friends, so we were isolated from the lingering aftereffects of segregation. But Smit kept pushing us to think deeper and understand more. We'd come home with history books depicting the Egyptians as White-ish or Christopher Columbus as a hero. He'd shut his own book, look at us sternly, and say, "Black history is more than running around the jungles of Africa, then slavery, then the civil rights movement." He'd point out that Caucasian-ifying the Pharaohs was dubious to say the least. Claiming that any irrefutably great Black figure was really kinda, sorta White, when you thought more about it, was a classic colonialist tool of oppression. He'd tell us how Alexandria was the seat of knowledge in the ancient world, and humanity and civilization were born in Africa. He schooled us on the genocide that followed Columbus wherever he went.* (Did you know that the original population of the Bahamas— the Lucayans—were enslaved and exterminated within twenty years of being encountered by him?)* Smitty didn't stop there. He pointed out that most of our Black peers still didn't have the opportunities that we did. We were lucky to be getting an exceptional education, and once we grew up we needed to do something with it.

---

* The Nazis used this kind of contorted wishful thinking to claim the Burmese and Tibetans as "Aryan."

Talking about desegregation as a bad thing is a loaded subject in the Black community. Even in our family: Some of our elders and loved ones disagree *strongly* with this opinion. Defenders of desegregation rightly point out that life was unjust, brutal, and incredibly hard for Black people during segregation. Black businesses in the early twentieth century operated with almost no legal or civil rights.[8] (No one was ever arrested or charged for the Tulsa massacre, or the Rosewood massacre in Florida.[9]) The police forces and district attorneys had zero interest in defending Black individuals—or prosecuting the White individuals who harmed them. (Most Southern police forces were essentially the old slave patrols, lightly rebranded post–Civil War. In the North, the primary function of one of the original "night watch systems" was controlling Indigenous and slave populations.[10]) Lynchings, either obvious or "disguised," were commonplace.* Black lives—even the lives of children—had no value. Their murders went uninvestigated and unpunished. The Black neighborhoods in most cities were forcibly overcrowded and often essentially slums. Black neighborhoods often paid more in taxes proportional to their income and received substantially less investment in their schools. Yet people like Smit and Uncle Will rebut this all with the simple fact that in segregated times, Turner Station—and Baltimore itself—held together. After desegregation it fell apart.

Our dad was angry. It was important to him that we understood what Baltimore had been. He'd talk to us about growing

---

* And arguably still are. From 2018 to 2020, there was a spate of seemingly happy, healthy, young Black men "hanging themselves," including the son of one prominent BLM activist.

up in Sparrows Point and Turner Station,[11] and how the families that moved there during the Great Migration had strong, matriarchal bonds. The grandmothers held shit down: church on Sunday, then a sit-down meal for every family member who was physically able to get there. The children were in their best clothes. "Yes, ma'am" and "No, ma'am" were the law . . . and often the only words out of the kids' mouths. (OK, so we don't think this part sounds so great for the emotional and mental health of the children.) And it was strictly Black folks sitting around the table.

Creating such a tight-knit community wasn't easy. Leaving the South was traumatizing, terrifying, and often deadly. (We know male elders who had to play dead and leave the South as "corpses" in coffins on trains—it was that dangerous.) The companies that needed and wanted to hire this influx of Black labor heading up North for jobs and the hope of safety had no interest in helping them find housing. Turner Station is now a community of modest two-story homes on a small peninsula sticking into the bay. But it was originally built piece by piece by newly arrived families who were desperate enough to buy up parcels of swampy land, build basic shacks, and call it their own.

Still, these new arrivals started to pull a community together, based around the twelve churches and the strict, no-messing-around culture that the women of Turner Station (and frankly the women of most Black communities) established. Smit's mom and grandmother bought their groceries at a Black-owned grocer. They bought their insurance at a Black-owned agency. When the kids were lucky, they saw a double feature at a local Black-owned cinema. There were three cab companies and multiple boutiques and barbershops and nightclubs and pool halls and gas stations and newspapers. There was a flourishing underground numbers racket. All told, these businesses generated money, and that money stayed in the community, and the community prospered as much as it could.

Turner Station and Sparrows Point were self-contained, and happy to be that way. Not because people lacked motivation or ambition to move up in the world into bigger homes or "better" neighborhoods, but because they recognized that their community was sovereign. People owned homes. Their kids were safer (but certainly not *safe*) from the roiling White rage that was causing death, trauma, and indescribable horror farther south. The schools lacked the facilities that the White high schools had: Smit remembered long bus rides to get to the Black high school, during which they would pass numerous White high schools. But once the kids made it there, they were surrounded by teachers who understood them and accepted them.

This wasn't just Baltimore. Most large cities had their Black Main Street or Wall Street that crumbled (or was plain crushed) out of existence during the twentieth century. Miami had Liberty City.[12] Los Angeles had multiple areas like Crenshaw, South Central, or Leimert Park. All these formally functional Black communities collapsed with desegregation, the rise of crack cocaine, and absentee landlords who swooped in to buy up distressed properties and rent them back to now-struggling Black families.* As the social structures frayed,

---

* LA's Black middle-class neighborhoods—filled with large, jaw-droppingly beautiful, craftsman homes—was effectively destroyed when the city built the Interstate 10 freeway right through it. The other potential path had been through the White upper-class neighborhood of Beverly Hills.

policing got more aggressive and the communities' anger boiled over into riots. Those carefully nurtured communities, and the discipline, respect, and politeness that created the social bonds, died along with the grandmas who had enforced them. Families who could afford to leave, did, moving to more gentrified homes in formerly all-White neighborhoods. Those who were left behind could not support the Black-owned businesses, which eventually withered away. Finally, the heroin epidemic of the late '60s, the crack epidemic of the '80s, and the disproportionate arrest rate and punishment for Black drug users sealed the deal.

Now, you might not have heard about this side of desegregation before. In America we generally assume that desegregation was a good thing for the Black community. We look at images of Ruby Bridges being escorted into her first day of school, and believe that this was a wholly positive thing. But we have a different perspective. We have to wonder if, like our students, Ruby was met with blank—or worse—faces, and teachers who had no understanding of, or empathy for, her life and her experiences. Ask yourself why Ruby had to be so brave, and why that weight was placed on such small shoulders to begin with. We think Ruby was another in a long line of Black women forced to carry outsize burdens disproportionate to their age, position, and wishes.

As our dad continued to educate us about the effect desegregation had on the Black community, he pointed out other things we hadn't really noticed, or considered. We all know about slavery, but the twentieth century was just as cruel: as we learned more, it was hard to avoid the conclusion that America has never loved Black folks. Our dad laid out the

Red Summer of 1919, when social tensions after WWI led to an explosion of White-on-Black violence and murder. He taught us about the Tulsa massacre, and how hundreds of Black-owned businesses were systematically destroyed—and hundreds of people murdered—by an enraged White mob. He schooled us about Ossian Sweet, a doctor in Detroit in the 1920s, whose life and family was destroyed simply because he wanted to move his family from the slums to a home in a "better" (i.e., White) neighborhood, befitting of a successful professional.* We learned how in the '80s the city of Philadelphia murdered six adults and five children—members of the MOVE Organization—by bombing their house with a satchel bomb (a combat weapon used to demolish buildings during war).[13] Black self-empowerment was seen—and still is seen—as threatening. And of course we witnessed things like Ferguson and Freddie Gray for ourselves. Now, Baltimore, unlike Tulsa, has never been razed to the ground in one frenzied night of purposeful, orchestrated violence, but we'd argue we've suffered an even worse massacre, just one that happened slowly, over time, and in such a way that it got minimal attention from the outside world.

We can't begin to explain the anger and the rage that fuels these murders and atrocities. We'll leave that to the historians, the psychologists, and the sociologists. What we can do is investigate how this rage still affects our communities today, and

---

* We can't read too deep on Ossian; it hurts too much even for people with no direct connection to him. His family did everything they could to get him out of the South, keep him safe, get him educated, and help him create his own "American Dream." The White community of suburban Detroit couldn't take it, and rallied a thousand armed men to surround his house the night he moved in.

what we can do to push back against it. When our hearts are truly stirred, we think the only option is to follow the path of the Mohawk tribe, and abandon this world to create our own. We have elders in our lives who are exhausted, done: They talk about taking Ghana up on its offer of citizenship for the descendants of slaves.[14] Those who have visited West Africa describe the palpable sense of relief when the plane's wheels touch the tarmac in Accra. For some it's the first time they've breathed easy in their life. They imagine living in a country where they are welcomed, wanted, and frankly, wealthy. Others push back. There's no way in hell they are getting chased out of a country their ancestors built for free.

A term you'll read about in this book is *trauma-informed reality*. We use this term to describe the long-term effects of multiple generations of people growing up in an environment that is inherently unsafe, un-nurturing, unloving, and unforgiving. Every member of our family knows that before you pull your car out of the parking spot, you look for the police cruising down your street. Every member of our family knows that you keep your registration and insurance in the sun visor, not the glove compartment. If you're smart, you stick your license up there too for the duration of your drive. We know that managing the primal, emotional response of a White police officer to a Black man is mostly our responsibility. The bigger question for us is what made that environment, and what can we do to change things?

There is a lot of talk about how the people of Baltimore—and other struggling communities—have to take responsibility for themselves. But we'll counter with our extended family's experience that right when the Black community was most successful, most self-reliant, most ambitious . . . it fell apart. It's easy to feel conspiratorial about the forces that came together to do this. But if you doubt that sinister forces were sabotaging Black communities, think about what those forces were doing to Black bodies at the same time: Henrietta Lacks, the Tuskegee experiments, and Emmett Till come to mind. Why is it so hard to believe that entities invested in White supremacy would hobble Black communities in the same way they abused Black bodies? It wasn't as though the citizens of our home collectively decided they just didn't care anymore. The decline of neighborhoods like Turner Station is about forces bigger than any individual and baked into a system as old as this country itself.

Systems aren't built to support people they don't really care about. Sometimes they're actively set up to break them down and break down the economy they live in. Often the rules of the social welfare system actively contradict the stated goals of that system. Up until 1968, the "man in the house" rule meant a mother could not live with an "able-bodied man" and still collect benefits—even if that man was not related to the child and not supporting either of them. These days, families often receive *less* support if the parents live together, despite the fact that every piece of scientific or sociological research points to the importance of having two parents at home (unless one or both are violent or abusive). Now think about what happens in a city like Baltimore, or Detroit, or any of the Rust Belt towns when industries pack up and disappear overnight—and stay gone for decades after. Those formerly employed dads might not have wanted to leave their homes, but if it's a choice between living at home or feeding their kids, they went. Those kids—boys especially—needed that male presence in their life, for the big stuff and the little, even stuff as seemingly obvious as remembering to wash between your balls when you shower.

Baltimore has plenty of police, but no justice. Ra'Mon has lived through the murders of *twenty-five* of his friends and family members. None of those crimes have ever been solved. Ask him what should happen to police departments and he says, "Defund them till they get the proper training!" Now fentanyl is killing. "If Larry Hogan cared, they would figure out how fentanyl is getting into the city and they'd stop it. They can stop crack cocaine, they can hunt guns, but you won't see them hunt the big problem now, fentanyl."

Ali and Atman grew up in this world, but Andy moved into it. His first impression when he moved into West Baltimore was shock. He'd lived twenty-five minutes away and couldn't believe the poverty that some of the families were living in. Andy grew up in a Baltimore suburb called Severn, but his mom grew up in the tropics. He was used to bugs and rodents from visits back to the island, but the thing that amazed him the most was how drastically different the living conditions were compared to people who were living in other neighborhoods in Baltimore.

Ask Andy about it and he'll tell you that when he first moved into the neighborhood, he was constantly asked one of two questions: *What'chu need?* or *What precinct do you work at?* (Because the local residents assumed he was an undercover cop.) He'll tell you how he vividly remembers visiting his old neighborhood and talking with his mom and friends about how crazy it was that just down the road there were neighborhoods with people who were living like they were in a developing country. He'd tell them, "This is America. We are policing the world and helping people in all these other countries but there is so much wrong still going on here at home. We always try to take care of everyone else before we take care of ourselves."

These days, there is less overt White supremacist mass murder (thank you, Southern Poverty Law Center [SPLC]; thank you, ACLU; thank you, livestreaming) and more reliance on the old standbys like city ordinances, over-policing, incarceration, Republican DAs and judges with lifetime appointments, welfare rules, and low wages to keep Black folks in their place. (As we edit this book, the Supreme Court has upheld an obvious racial gerrymander in Alabama on the basis that it would be too hard to change. Thanks, Brett.) Let's look at our hometown. Our experience of living in primarily African American communities is this: As soon as any type of money or funding comes in, it goes right out to other people's communities. The police, and the tax dollars they siphon off to wealthy bedroom communities, are prime examples. But so is the demise of small businesses, like the Black-owned corner stores that were gradually replaced by budget liquor outlets (themselves run by new Korean immigrants, grinding hard to get their kids into college).

The idea that Black communities could be self-reliant and sovereign withered as well. You doubt this is true? Well, let's give you a firsthand example. Recently someone from the Baltimore City Public Schools office took the idea behind our Mindful Moment program and limited us from being able to fully partner with them in the program without any explanation. That's our life. That's our work. That's everything we've invested in both our community and ourselves, and our ability to earn money, hire at-risk youth, create a support structure for the community, and support our families.

Let's jump back to the Mohawk for a minute. The tribe fights every day to regain its culture and repair the family bonds that were ripped apart by residential schools. Just as slave owners purposefully split up Black families in the nineteenth century, weakening family bonds and leaving individuals alone and adrift and surrounded by strangers (and just as the prison system perpetuates that strategy today, keeping one out of three Black men apart from their families for at least some part of their lives), so the Indigenous tribes were forcibly separated from their children at these residential schools.

It was dangerous to speak Mohawk there. If the teachers heard you speak it, you'd be beaten. You had to hide who you were, try to forget where you came from if you wanted to survive. It was that important to the teachers that they made you forget what kept you together and made you one. You had to hide who you were to survive. You had to keep your head down and get along.

Today all our young volunteers are on fire to keep their traditions alive. Steven doesn't just go by his salt water people name, he also goes by his Mohawk name, Kentsienó:ron. Translated, it means "valuable fish," or as he interprets it, "one who carries a message." He lives his name with every breath, fighting for his tribe and tribes all over the country. The students are using the HLF techniques to help process the generational trauma that they, their parents, and their ancestors have experienced. One of our Mindful Leaders, a young woman called Kanatires, put it best. She shared: "Growing up in a community that has felt so much grief generation after generation, it is an amazing gift to carry this knowledge and the ability to access the tools we have learned. The important thing now is to share these things with our families, our loved ones, and with all of the Akwesasne so we might use those practices to collectively heal . . . and so we don't continue the cycle of hurt in our youth."

These days the tribe works hard to bring together members from across the diaspora—whether they are hosting an occasional event called Kaienerakowa (where the tribes gather to tell an oral history of the creation of the Iroquois Confederacy) or more frequent gatherings of smaller groups. It's hard work. It takes effort to get these peoples together. It takes work to get the less motivated youth off their phones and into traditional culture. But it's essential. At its very core the tribe, as an entity, recognizes that the only thing that holds them together is a sense of group identity. The minute they lose that, they are done.

When we reflect on Baltimore, we see people who are kinfolk with the Mohawk and struggling against the same obstacles they do. We are not given much and we are expected to be law-abiding citizens. Some of our peers have—perhaps unsurprisingly—fallen into the trap of drugs, dealing, and crime. But we understand: we see people who make their way in a place where Maslow's hierarchy is a dream, yet it is supposed to be a baseline. In our opinion, Baltimoreans thrive or tread water in a situation that we are set up to fail by design. We would love some of these policy makers to live in the situations that our kids and families come from, and see how quickly they too would succumb to the strains and strife that they are so quick to turn their nose up at and judge.

Something is missing in Black communities these days. It's partly resources, partly hope. There's an excess of trauma, felt by multiple generations living in fear for their lives, knowing that even a nine-minute video of your murder will be denied and disputed by anxious White people in suburbs across the country. There's a lack of long-term roots and kinship. Homeowners have been replaced by renters, and no one leaves their front door unlocked anymore. We don't have all the answers, but we think we have some. It starts with finding some kind of inner peace among the chaos. It continues with us—like the Mohawk—continuing the fight to reclaim our culture and resurrect our pride in it. And it concludes with a radical decolonization of our minds.

On our last night in the Akwesasne territory, our friend and soul sister Jennifer Hutchins (the person who made the connection for us with the Akwesasne to begin with) decided that these three city guys needed to get lost in some deep nature. As the sun went down behind the casino hotel where we were staying, we jumped in an old, creaking 4x4 and drove ninety minutes into the dark, softly stirring forests full of maple, beech, birch, and old grandfather oaks and black walnuts towering silently above us. The birds were singing their last flurry of song before they bedded down for the night. Deer and fawns trotted alongside the road, looking for somewhere safe from coyotes and cars to call home till dawn. We parked at Jennifer's friend's house and were welcomed by a guy playing a guitar and by his wife, who ran over and hugged all of us. Together, we walked through the woods, past a spooky, old, abandoned steel mine that creaked gently in the breeze. We stopped on a pitch-black road to do some Bigfoot breaths—a pranayama technique called *sitkari* that our students named the Bigfoot breath because they said the noise you make when you inhale sounds like a Bigfoot mating call—to see if we could have a Sasquatch encounter. No luck. When we got to the top of the mountain, the scale of the wilderness around us made us feel like we were straight out of *Return of the Jedi*, walking through the unending desert on Tatooine, past deep vales and gullies that reminded us *Star Wars* nerds of the sarlacc pit. We came to the edge of the mountain, with a two-hundred-foot drop-off, with all the stars, the Milky Way, and Comet NEOWISE dangling right above our heads, sparkling against the darkness of the sky.

CHAPTER TWO

The Tsunami of Love

Hare Krishna, Hare Rama, Tat Tvam Así,
Aham Brahma Asmi,
So hum so hum so hum, Paramatman . . .

There's something missing from this story so far: love. You might think that the Smith brothers, and later Andy Gonzalez, would be pretty pissed off about the stuff that went on outside our stoop every day, but you'd be wrong. We might have been the most blissful people in Baltimore. Given that we moved back into the hood in the immediate aftermath of 9/11, it's possible we were also the *only* blissful people in America. There are a lot of reasons why we woke up every day, in our humble house, on one of the most dangerous corners in Baltimore or, as a matter of fact, America, feeling happy. It was partly our devotion to our practice, and our passion for the idea that would become HLF. Our belief that we were going to do something transformational for the kids on our block put smiles on our faces. But the main reason for the joy was an old man wearing a brightly patterned '80s dad sweater, a short white 'fro, and a smile: Uncle Will.

Uncle Will was a former Black Panther, a lifelong yogi, our dad's best friend from college, and—along with Smitty—our spiritual teacher. Uncle Will didn't ask for too much in exchange for his wisdom. After we got off from work, we'd call him up and ask if he wanted company, and he'd say, "Sure, you want to bring me a bang?" Bang was a half pint of Crown Royal. Add in a six-pack of Heineken and a few hours and you had the beginnings of a pretty deep conversation. Uncle Will would throw open the door and throw open his arms. The three of us would line up, and one by one would get the best hug in the world, as Uncle Will mashed together a whole bunch of mantras in welcome:

Hare Krishna, Hare Rama, Tat Tvam Así, Aham Brahma Asmi, So hum so hum so hum, Paramatman . . .

Uncle Will was adamantly positive. Atman's name is Atman Ananda, or Atman Bliss. Uncle Will adopted the second name for Andy because, he said, "You're always happy, you're always blissful. I can feel the love." Uncle Will, along with Smitty, were our mentors. Smitty initially taught us to meditate, but after we graduated college, he handled more of the practical parts: getting us into the house on Smallwood, telling us he'd cover our costs if we took advantage of the time and built a business. Uncle Will took care of the more esoteric stuff: keeping us up late into the morning, drinking bang and Heineken, and singing his jam, "This Little Light of Mine." Around midnight or so, Will would ask, "Want to get another bang?" and one of us would go to the store and pick up another

Crown. The funny thing is, while we were in Uncle Will's presence we felt sober and alert as judges, but the minute we stepped out of the house . . .

Here's the thing, though. Uncle Will was a peaceful person, and a joyful person. He was a powerful person. He believed that life is a tsunami of love and that it was all our jobs to spread it to as many people as possible. He was a man who loved life in all its elevated and otherwise ways. Hell, he even used to tell us that he loved George W. and, later, Trump. When we asked why the hell he was wasting his love on them he told us, "They need it more than most." He was also a hustler who wasn't about being oppressed and being a victim. He'd tell his son Oba, "You do the economics!" He was always into his money, doing whatever it took: shining shoes, serving in the military, grinding as an insurance salesman.

Uncle Will was also a man who recognized that many—if not most—of his brethren didn't recognize their own joy or power. He had the perspective that allowed him to shed fear and practice acceptance. But he knew that outside of his doors most everyone was afraid. As much as he wanted to laugh, he wanted to teach. He wanted us to continue the work he'd begun in the Panthers and could no longer continue as his health started to fail. He'd tell us: "Let your light shine through, the light within us is covered with so much dust. We need to remove the dust so we can realize our infinite self."

Physically he was tough. Mentally he was tough. He had a tough spirit, and it took a tough spirit to join an organization like the Panthers, which had a target on its back. There was no cover for him. There was no one standing up for them. He didn't back down from something that most people's spirits would back down from. And he was serious about his practice. He would kneel on his porch, shirt off, summer and winter, doing breath of fire while the guys on the corner paused their hustle and stared in disbelief.

At night he'd turn off the lights in the house and light a candle in the kitchen, practicing *ujjayi* breathing so loud that it sounded like a wolf howling. Oba—a little kid then—would creep down the stairs, scared at first at the noise, but the energy and vibration that came off him was calming and soothing. Soon young Oba was practicing beside him.

Young Will

Our Uncle Will had charisma. As a young man, he was a rebel, but a rebel who could navigate the conventional world when he needed to, or it suited him. He had come up in East Baltimore and graduated from high school in the late '50s and gotten into Maryland State. Part of the deal was that he had to join ROTC. Now, given that Will would soon join the Black Panthers, you can imagine he wasn't the type to mess with the military. He didn't show up for drills. Or when he did, his uniform was so wrinkled it looked like he'd slept in it. Eventually the officers just told him to stay home.

Meanwhile, Will and Smit had joined the Student Nonviolent Coordinating Committee. They signed up for a Freedom Ride demonstration in Cambridge, Maryland. Smit told us, "I never saw so many angry White people. They were calling us names, spitting on us. And we were from the mean streets of Baltimore! We'd gotten into plenty of little tribal fights. We could take care of ourselves." The famous Rap Brown, later

Jamil Abdullah Al-Amin, was there, rallying the students: "We are poor people, we don't have a lot of money, all we have is a penny. What can a penny buy? Matches! Burn this m****rf****r down . . ."

For whatever reason, this was too much for our dad and Will, at least in that moment. They were still teenagers after all, and both shook with the anger they saw. For now, they wanted to enjoy the relative safety of the college in Maryland State, join a frat, meet some girls, have some fun. Will wasn't one for studying, and he dropped out after the first year. The two lost touch for a bit, but when they met back up Will had joined the Panthers. He was still keeping one foot in the straight world, selling insurance. But the rest of the time he was hanging at the Aquarian Age bookstore underneath the Green Earth health food store. He was vegetarian, practicing folk medicine, and engrossed in learning all he could about herbs, radical politics, and yoga. At night he'd hang out at home, reading *Autobiography of a Yogi* and meditating. When Dad and Will met up again, in their late twenties, Smit was struggling with some health stuff and frustrated by the way his doctor seemed to dismiss his concerns. Will took over our dad's care, prescribed some yoga poses, and our dad got better. From that day onward they were both convinced that yoga offered a solution to the stress and trauma of just getting by in the hood.

Hippies in the Hood

If you're not from Baltimore, or you're not involved in the larger, older yogic community, you probably don't know how deep the roots of true yoga are on the East Coast. Pre-Instagram, pre-Lululemon, yoga was something that strange old vegetarian dudes like Will did, rather than an influencer-friendly exercise program available on every chic city block. After Will helped Smit recover from his health problems, the two of them became doubly committed to exploring everything they could about this new (to them) way of life.

Together, they consumed books like the *Complete Illustrated Book of Yoga* and *Life and Teaching of the Masters of the Far East*. These books resonated. Not only was yoga a way to heal your body and your mind outside of the mainstream medical tradition (a tradition that then as now wasn't super worried about the health and well-being of Black bodies to begin with), it was a path to spiritual liberation, and maybe, one day, social liberation too. Smit and Will knew that all in all, they had it OK. They were healthy. They were employed. They were loved. Plenty of the people who made up the community of Turner Station were starting to struggle, even then, in the late '60s and early '70s, as the community began its long, bitter fracturing under the forces of desegregation, drug use, and wrong-headed policing.

Compared to these folks, Will and Smit had a degree of financial and social stability. But they were also very aware that they were constrained in some ways. Neither of them was free to do exactly what they wanted in life. Both of them had to deal with the reality of being Black in a world that wasn't inclined to be kind to Black folks—especially when those folks wandered outside of the established structures of the local Black community. So, even as they understood that they were fortunate in many regards, these limitations would rankle them for years. Later, Smit and our mom, Cassie, would move mountains to make sure we had more expansive horizons.

Yoga was beginning to make more sense than the traditional church that Smit grew up in, with its focus on, as he termed it, some "icy arthropod in the sky." Yoga literally felt more grounded. Of course, this caused some tension in Smit's life. There was a radical disconnect between our family and his new beliefs. All the elders in our family—our grandparents and great-grandparents and aunts and uncles—were Methodists. The church had been one of the backbones of their community. Like the grandmas who guarded the stoops and kept an eye out for the neighborhood kids, the church was always there, watching, for both good and bad. The Black experience is rooted in churches, so walking away was more complicated than simply making a lifestyle change. In some ways it was a repudiation of one of the pillars that had held Black Baltimore together.

Cassie, Smit, and Will joined a church called the Divine Life Church of Absolute Oneness—an offshoot of the Self-Realization Fellowship. The DLC placed a big focus on *kriya yoga*: a combination of mantras and meditation and movement and pranayama. "Kriya" means physical and spiritual work, but most of what we learn is internal work: mind, energy, and soul. Smit and Will spent their weekend afternoons working on the property, building staircases and paths through a wooded area behind the church, and trying to improve the look of what was a pretty modest little building. After doing the physical work to strengthen the body, they would turn to the more important internal work. Together they would sit and practice breathwork to purify their energy. Us Smith kids went to Divine Life Church from the time we were born. There are pictures of Ali there before he could walk. There are pictures of him at spiritual ceremonies with one of their teachers, again before he could walk. Even Ali's and Atman's names come from yogic philosophy. We were born into the practice.

Every Sunday, we (Ali and Atman) would wake up early, gather up armfuls of Transformers and action figures, and creep past Smit practicing his headstand in the living room, to the old black-and-white TV that sat on the kitchen counter. We'd flip it on, at the lowest possible volume, and watch *Ma and Pa Kettle* or *The Three Stooges* till we heard Smit starting to breathe heavily from the exertion of staying up on his forearms. It seemed like he'd be up there for hours, balancing on the old, green, all-purpose army blanket that he used for a yoga mat. In a minute, we'd hear his feet hitting the floor— our signal to turn up the volume and start laughing out loud. Cassie would throw together some breakfast and then we'd be out the door to Sunday school. Unlike a lot of kids, we were excited to go to Sunday school. We'd get to hang with other kids who meditated. If nothing else, it was much-needed evidence that we weren't totally weird.

Achariya Peter

The church wasn't a church in the way we think of them. It was less about worshipping a deity, more about improving yourself through the practice of *karma yoga*—or service work. And at the heart of this service work was one of our spiritual fathers, Achariya Peter.

Achariya Peter had the biggest, brightest smile on the planet. He gave amazing hugs. You could feel his energy and his light when he walked into a room. Humor was always integrated into his spiritual talks. When people didn't laugh because something was slightly off-color but was a part of a spiritual lesson he would always say—a little lovingly, a little mockingly—"Oh, I feel so sorry for you, your God is so serious. My God is hilarious!" And then he'd burst out laughing.

That love, that humor, came from a life that was also full of pain. Achariya Peter was born into a German family that didn't support Adolf Hitler. At age five, his family sent him to boarding school in the south of Germany. He never saw any of them again: By the time the war was over, his family was dead. Because of this, he understood, more than most, how joy and despair go hand in hand throughout life. He got that you have to find the beauty in the moment you are in, and in the place you are standing. He realized that you have to learn to love the people who surround you instead of waiting for "better" ones to show up.

Achariya Peter was good at reading energy. He'd give a sermon, and his eyes would dance around the room as he made comments or insights, and in the moment you could tell he was talking directly to you. No matter what was going on he was rooted in the light. He'd tell us about the weekends he spent in the mountains of West Virginia and coming across a bear on his path. The bear stared at him; Achariya Peter stared at the bear. Each saw the other's light and moved on.

Achariya Peter always pushed us to dig deeper, spiritually. He'd tell us, "Whatever is going on outside happens, but you're still a spiritual being and that is where you have to stay no matter what. You have to find a way to translate your spirit into the world." Being based in the spirit is a hard thing to do! We have all manifested as humans this time around, yet you have to remain connected to that part of you that transcends this form. As Achariya Peter spoke, we'd look at a quote painted on the wall of the church: "Truth is One, men call it by various names." Achariya Peter would always say that the underlying truths in all religions were the same; they were packaged differently to cause separation. Then he would pull a reading from the Bible before moving on to other spiritual texts: the Gita, the Koran, and some Native American spirituality to show that truth was one. He'd tell us again and again: "Look at what it is actually saying instead of how it is packaged."

When Peter died, his obituary said "no immediate survivors," which was crazy. We were all his immediate survivors. And along with Smit and Uncle Will, Achariya Peter is one of the people who have left their physical body but are still with us, every day.

Eventually our dad and our godfather left the church. They still practiced, though—and it was a point in time when all the renowned gurus were coming through. The two of them attended lectures by Bhagwan Shree Rajneesh. They studied under Achariya Peter's guru, Swami Premananda from the Self-Realization Fellowship. Premananda's guru was Paramahansa Yogananda. Everything they learned was more philosophical than physical: *bhakti yoga*, *karma yoga*, and *kundalini yoga*.

As for us, well, we thought it was all pretty weird. We were children living in the hood—one street over from Pulaski, one of the most infamous drug corners in the world. Atman would jokingly say that their parents were the "hood hippies." We kept the fact that our dad and uncle were yogis under wraps; we didn't want our friends to think we were any stranger than they already did. Will and Smit didn't shout about their practice either, but they shared it with people who were receptive.

And that's how it was for years. Will and Smit kept their practice to a few friends. They didn't go through the community actively advocating yoga, although eventually they developed a closer circle of yogis. They both lost some friends over their new habits and beliefs. Maybe not surprising when you consider how they were beginning to see traditional religion as divisive, destructive, and dogmatic. To them religion felt less like a positive force and more like a cult. As Smit used to say, the appeal of yoga is not sectarian.

Smit didn't press our family to accept his new beliefs, but once Ali and Atman were five and three, he taught us to meditate every morning before we would go to school. We'd watch Smit practicing as we ate our cornflakes, until we'd pile into his old car and listen to NPR on our way to school.

CHAPTER THREE

Friends

Our mom, Cassie, moved to Baltimore in the late '60s. Her family settled on a street called Smallwood. Back then, the neighborhood was full of young—mostly White—families. Every day she would get dressed in a "cute little dress" (as she calls it), and her mom would do her hair. She'd walk a block to school 142 (later to be called Robert W. Coleman). The decline and fall of Coleman Elementary, from a community school where Black kids felt safe and nurtured to a place struggling to provide the bare minimum to a traumatized and angry student body, is a story in itself. By the time we were old enough to attend Coleman it was unrecognizable from our mom's memories of it. And it's still unrecognizable to our mom. She works with us now, mentoring kids and coordinating our after-school programs, and though she doesn't talk about it too often, we know it hurts her to see that "her" kids aren't getting the level of love and support that she did.

So when Cassie's kids—Ali and Atman—were ready for kindergarten there was simply no way she was sending them there. Even though Cassie and Smit had both attended and worked in the Baltimore City Public School System, they knew they would do anything to keep us out of it. The schools were fast falling apart. Smit was coaching and teaching basketball at Southern High School. His students called him Smit the Grit, because he was that tough. He was that tough because he had to be. And he didn't want us going somewhere that required that toughness just to get through the day.

Our mom and dad had a series of big discussions about whether they were going to move to the county or stay in the city and send us to private school. They wanted us to have the experience of living in the city and the realness and the grounding of living in Baltimore city. At the same time there was a program called B.E.S.T. (Baltimore Education Scholarship Trust), where Black kids from Baltimore who could handle the transition to private school got financial help to go. This transition was multifaceted: The academics were harder, and it would be most Black kids' first experience of sitting and studying alongside White kids—a rougher and more stressful experience than most well-meaning White people could comprehend.

We got a partial scholarship to Friends School, but it was still a big struggle for our parents to afford it. There were all types of students there: Filipino, Native American, European. Most of them were very affluent, but there were kids from poorer neighborhoods. Most of our friends from home were going to very homogeneous, segregated schools. We had computer labs when most of our friends from home had only seen computers in movies. You could go in and use them like it was nothing; they were there and no one even thought it was a big deal. There were so many opportunities. Sometimes we would come home upset, frustrated about having hours of home-work, when our friends were playing outside because they had no homework. Damn, come on!

Here's another way that Friends School kept us grounded. We were used to White people by the time we moved on to college. We'd been around enough shit with some of the kids from Friends to guess what was likely to happen once we got to college. We knew that White people who seemed OK at first would show different sides of themselves—let their mask slip—when they felt comfortable and safe enough to do so. When we went to Friends parties, and our White class-mates would have a few drinks and start using the N-word, it sucked—and it ended plenty of friendships—but it got us straight about what to expect as we moved on through life. The kids who stayed in the neighborhood and managed to go on to college got broken by their first experiences of being around White people. Hearing a White person calling them the N-word was crushing for them. They were unprepared for the anger and vitriol that a lot of White people feel toward Black people who enter traditionally White worlds—even supposedly progressive, decent White people.

This was all part of the balance that Cassie and Smit were determined to build in us. We didn't play Little League base-ball with White kids near Friends; we played it in the NW Little League with all the other Black kids. And there were White kids looking for balance of their own. In elementary school there were only certain kids who could come to our house. One was this kid Brian Hamilton, one of Ali's best friends from school. Brian was a tough kid. His family was originally from Indiana but had moved to Baltimore so his dad could work at Hopkins. They lived over the county line, but every so often they would drive into the city and drop Brian off for the weekend. Cassie and Smit would stand at the window, looking at Mr. and Mrs. Hamilton pulling up with their kid sitting in the back of the station wagon, like it was no big thing. They'd look at each other, shaking their heads, and ask each other, "Who the hell are these White parents?" Brian was a tough but good kid, and it still tickles Cassie to this day that his parents would come drop him off in the hood for the weekend.

Being Black at Friends is an experience: You're not going to get treated the same as everyone else. You're going to deal with racism everywhere you go, but you're going to deal with more of it at private schools (less at Friends because of the progressive people who were drawn to enrolling their kids there, but still). Ali and Atman were blessed compared to our neighbors, though. We were sent to Friends, where they taught a global view, and not a neighborhood view. It was worth the occasional f**ked-up moments.

Our parents reinforced this at home by making sure that we were taught the potential for unity in diversity and that, though people call it by various names, truth is one and we had a duty to help others—people who look like us and people who don't—and to lead by example. Learning from your mistakes is part of the human experience.

Our parents had already started to disagree on a lot of stuff. They'd soon get divorced. But they always agreed that they had to work together to thread an incredibly tight needle to give us the lives they wanted us to have. They knew they wanted a better education for us than the Baltimore City Public School System could provide. They also knew we were unprepared for life in a predominantly White world. They were determined to have their sons grow up to be adept at living both "in the streets and in the suites."

There were some places where we would be with our dad and we'd be like, "What are we doing here?" Now, Smit was tough as shit. It's not like we were ever worried when we were out with him. He was six foot two and weighed 220 pounds of solid muscle. Most people were afraid of our dad, so we weren't worried when he piled us into his car and took us out to visit with his friends and take care of things that needed taking care of.

While Cassie focused on getting us into better and better educational opportunities, Smit put his attention to making sure Ali and Atman and various cousins and friends saw the full expanse of the Black experience. Part of this was a place called Rhythm Skate—one of Smit's best friends, Melvin Washington, owned it and he would go help out as muscle and backup at big events. All the teens in Baltimore went there to hang. As kids we saw New Edition, Janet Jackson, and Run-DMC play there. These were huge names, showing up at a neighborhood venue, because it was back when White promoters thought Black acts couldn't make money. Later, when the show was over, we'd fall asleep in the back office till Smit and his friend who owned the place finished counting the money, and leave early in the morning, as the sun came up over the Baltimore skyline.

Later, when we were in middle and high school, Smit would drive us and this same group of kids to school on a regular basis. As he drove, he would lecture us—Ali and Atman, our godbrother Ellis, and our friend Joey—while we rode along in the back seat of the car.

In Atman's freshman year, Ellis "borrowed" a B+ paper from a White friend. Ellis retyped and turned it in. He got a C– and lots of red marks on it. Smit was mad that Ellis had cheated, but he was even madder that the teacher had graded Ellis lower than a White kid for the exact same work. He was mad that we were naive enough to think that we were treated the same as our White friends, or that attending Friends meant we were insulated from the shit our neighborhood friends had to deal with. Our dad would lecture us on what was in store for us as Black men, and that our experience in the Friends environment was not the same as we'd experience once we'd graduate.

> *You guys are going to have to work twice as hard to get a good grade as a White kid.*
>
> *You have to be on point.*
>
> *You cannot think that Friends is the real world.*
>
> *You cannot think that your experience there is how all White people are going to treat you.*
>
> *Your friends might seem like good people, but I can guarantee that at least some of them think that Black people are only good to f**k, fight, sing, or dance.*

We'd be sitting in the car listening to a Smit lecture about race and justice. We'd want to listen to music, but now we realize we wouldn't trade those rides for anything. They kept us grounded. And when things like Ellis's paper happened, we weren't surprised. We were prepared to handle it.

CHAPTER FOUR

The Path

By the time we graduated from Friends and were getting ready to head off to the University of Maryland, we had stopped meditating or following the tenets of holistic living. We were eating meat—Cluck-U was our favorite restaurant. Who can blame us for forgetting our practice? After all, we had real passions.

All three of us have loved *Star Wars* since we were little kids. The idea of intergalactic battles and beings from all over the universe hanging out at a bar was pretty mind-blowing for a young kid. Then you add the amazing special effects, spaceships, speeders, light sabers, laser guns, and telekinesis/telepathy with the Force and we were all-in. Fast-forward to us growing up—and getting into our practice and realizing our infinite selves—and *Star Wars* became even more badass because the Force was so similar to the way (the Tao). The light that Uncle Will always talked about was the Force: It existed everywhere and in everything. The powers that the Jedi had were basically the siddhis. All the Jedi were basically master yogis! So f**king awesome! Plus you add the hero's journey to all that and how could one not love *Star Wars*?

We were also born at a perfect time to be part of the video game world. We were around for the first computer games, playing *Dig Dug* on our godbrother Ellis's Atari, and went from Atari, ColecoVision, Nintendo, and Sega to Turbo Grafx-16 and beyond. This world allowed our imaginations to run wild. It allowed us to be heroes: to start off as a regular person and to build up to become the one who saves the world. Video games were egalitarian. You didn't have to start off with superpowers; you just had to be willing to work hard and give it your all in order to succeed and bring justice to the bad guys. Playing video games is a form of meditation. It allows us to go to our own little world and not think about all the outer turmoil and sensory overload that comes from the external. Being able to be in the shoes of a powerful hero whose responsibility was to save the world was an amazing experience. It is a big part of why when we saw all the suffering going on in the world it was so easy for us to be like, "We got this!" or, "We are going to save the world!" Because we had done it so many times when we were playing our video games.

And finally, hip-hop. To understand why, we need to go way back to the days when slaves were creating work songs in the fields. These slaves would create lyrics that were making fun of the slave owners except the words and meaning were hidden to them. The slave owners just assumed that they were singing to keep up their morale, but really they were using the music to talk about their struggles—all while secretly making fun of their captors.

Using music to describe the trials and tribulations that Black people were facing was a huge part of the Jazz Age too.

You could feel it not only in the lyrics but in the sound itself. Hip-hop is an extension of all this. It is a medium that allows people to bring up issues that need to be discussed, especially those that the mass media is trying to push under the rug: things like oppression, racism, injustice, and the extended history of these atrocities that White people continue to get away with. It is an art form that not only allows one to be creative but also allows a release.

Andy uses hip-hop as therapy. The beat is like a psychologist, and his lyrics are what he would say if he was lying on their sofa. As he puts it: "Things that I am not comfortable saying directly to people I can put in my lyrics and it allows me to get it off my chest. I have written over three hundred songs and you can hear the splatter of emotions from love, happiness, bliss, and togetherness to doubt, anger, frustration, and loneliness. I learned so much from hip-hop in terms of history and the state of the world. I love how these gems are often hidden in the metaphors, similes, and double entendres. The fact that you have to really look into it to understand is very similar to looking deeper into the ancient texts and looking deeper into yourself. You can't just take it at face value."

These three passions have shaped us in ways that go beyond pop culture or simple entertainment. Growing up in a rough part of the world, they told us that there were realities beyond West Baltimore—we just had to find a way to get there. As much as we might hope to wake up at Resistance Headquarters, it wasn't going to be on D'Qar. We would have to work our own version of the Force—and the Rebel Alliance—here on Earth instead.

When we were little kids, we thought Uncle Will was kind of a weird dude. He was always trying to get us to do yoga or pranayama. But as we got older it started to resonate. About the time we were graduating from UM, it suddenly clicked that we had our very own Yoda, sitting quietly in his own Dagobah system, right there, waiting for his students to appear, if we were willing to learn. In our last few months of college we finally asked Uncle Will to be our teacher, and he told us, "If you are interested, come to my house at 4:30 tomorrow morning. I don't want no devotees, and I'm not teaching students, I'm teaching teachers." We showed up the next morning after drinking beer with him all night. And we studied with him for years.

Now, in our post-college years, yoga and meditation have become a truly integral part of our lives, thanks to Will and Smit. We saw the benefits in our life, every day, as we struggled to get our first post-grad careers off the ground. We were resilient and optimistic. Our stress levels were way down compared to the other people our age in our neighborhood. We were non-reactive—we were able to survive in an incredibly violent and dangerous area because we stayed outside of the drama. We could observe our emotional states and respond in a detached way to them. Our executive functions were up. We could focus and pay attention in ways we couldn't have without yoga. And, maybe most importantly of all, we felt a sense of peace about ourselves: in other words, we were experiencing self-love, or self-worth.

Our years at a privileged high school and UM meant that

we had one foot in the hood and one foot in a privileged, safe, and comfortable world of places like Friends. Because of this we'd developed two kinds of survival skills. As Smit had always hoped, we could handle ourselves "in the streets and in the suites." We had an opportunity to access and leverage our "suite" skills and do something with them to help those kids left behind on the "street."

Our two mentors had worked together to get us to this place of being a bridge between two worlds. If Uncle Will was our spiritual guide, then Smit was the practical mastermind. He was the one urging us to grow deep roots in our community and our practice, with the goal of building something lasting. When we graduated college, he told us that he'd cover the cost of living in our old family house on Smallwood if we built a business: ideally in real estate (which showed his foresight, given the current boom in home prices everywhere except the hood). Smit didn't want us investing our energy in a nonprofit, but he was very clear on one point: Whatever business we built had to be about more than taking care of the three of us. It had to be something that would throw a lifeline to the people in our community who had no jobs, no opportunities, and no hope. Over and over he'd tell us, "Don't earn a check, BE the check." He'd seen enough Black folks and families thrown into chaos as manufacturing moved overseas or recessions throttled spending. He knew that we needed to be our own bosses. And he knew it wasn't enough that we succeed; we had to help all the kids around us who didn't have a Smit or an Uncle Will in their lives to support and believe in them.

That kept us going all the way through to that day in 2001, when we finally graduated, rolled up to the house on

Smallwood, stepped out of Atman's Toyota Corolla, and looked at a little row house that was now home.

The House on Smallwood

The house on Smallwood was a few houses down from the corner. The old-time residents remembered Ali and Atman from growing up there. But the newer residents didn't. They were the ones on the corner, hanging out. They knew pretty quickly that we weren't interested in buying. And because of that, and the fact that we can more than handle ourselves, they more or less ignored us. Eventually we had to tell them to pick a different corner.

We kept a clean and tidy house, but the rats and the roaches were in the walls, traveling along the row from the abandominiums, or the decrepit homes that should have been abandoned but weren't. No matter how hard you tried to make a home on that street, you couldn't keep the reality of Smallwood at the door. Whether it was dealers hanging on the stoop, or the rodents eating your groceries, or the rain coming through the ceiling, or the next-door house sagging and rotting around you—you always felt the weight of North and Pulaski on your shoulders.

Here's the thing, though: That house was in our family for almost sixty years. Our great-grandmother, Ada Alexander, moved to Baltimore from North Carolina and bought the house in 1955, part of her relentless drive to make something of herself, and make something of her family. When we talk about both the power of matriarchy and the destruction of Black wealth, our house on Smallwood is a perfect example of both. Ada brought her husband and her kids with her. Buying the house on Smallwood was a big deal: They had arrived in a safe and desirable neighborhood. They were one of only two Black families on the block, and a short walk down from a White-only girls' school. One day her husband left, rarely to be seen again. Nonetheless she kept grinding. She always instilled in her children and her grandchildren: "You must go to college, you must get a degree, *you must be somebody*. A doctor, a lawyer, a firefighter. Just be somebody." Cassie's paternal grandfather had lived these words: He became a lawyer and minister in the 1880s in Michigan—an impressive feat for a Black man originally from the South.

For almost sixty years the house on Smallwood was our stronghold, and it was a good house. It had marble steps, a porch for sultry summer nights, and just enough room for a growing family. When Cassie got home from school, her mother would send her upstairs to nap and bathe and change into "afternoon clothes." Then she'd come back down and run around the block to find her friends and play in the street or run to the park.

By the late '60s, Baltimore was full of social activist groups. Will and Smit were members of the Student Nonviolent Coordinating Committee, but there were dozens of other groups, like the Mother Rescuers from Poverty, CORE (Congress of Racial Equality), and U-JOIN (Union for Jobs or Income Now). The *Baltimore Afro-American* newspaper wrote in 1966 that the Mother Rescuers represented "the new mood creeping slowly through the Black ghetto of Baltimore like sunlight at an early dawn—a mood that demands rights and respect and a chance for a decent life as the natural birthright of all."[1]

The newspaper, published daily, was full of accounts of how multiple groups and individuals were advocating and fighting for civil rights within Baltimore.

Yet, as active as these groups were, so was the White establishment. After Martin Luther King Jr. was assassinated, the then-governor Spiro Agnew invited Black community leaders to meet on April 9, 1968. He proceeded to lecture them about their culpability for the unrest sweeping Baltimore. Most walked out in disgust. In 1971, when Baltimore elected the first Black congressman from a Southern state since reconstruction—Parren Mitchell (a vocal critic of the police)—the Baltimore PD illegally bugged his house. He was in office for three years before they stopped.

By the early '70s Cassie and Smit had met and married and made the house their own. But around the time Ali was born, in 1976, they started noticing things changing. Those lifelong residents started moving out, and renters moved into the vacant properties. Some of these new families were struggling. Cassie talks about how their kids were "hungry and looking for something. Not food so much as love and attention and respect." Their parents had problems, be they financial, emotional, or social. They couldn't provide structure, even when they wanted to. Their kids gravitated to Cassie and Smit, and our parents did the best they could to parent them too. But eventually Cassie and Smit also moved, saying goodbye to the hungry children, and sometimes leaving the house vacant, on and off for years, until their sons finally needed a place of their own to live.[2]

By the time we moved back into it, after college, those days of leaving the door unlocked, a rose bush in every front yard, and playing in the street were long over.

In our first few months back home, Andy would sleep on the floor because Yogi Bhajan told him to do it in one of his books. Sometimes he'd wake up to the feeling of something crawling on his face and reach up to brush a roach off his cheek. The cracked window in the bedroom let the sunlight trickle into the back room, and he would do his morning duties in the unfinished bathroom. There were days when it rained so hard outside that it also rained inside because of our leaky roof. We had visitors in the basement that could hear the creatures scurrying across our ceiling. One time a mouse jumped out of one of our cabinets at Ali when he opened the cabinet door.

At the edge of the pavement you could see the old brick road peeking out from under the tarmac. We'd wonder at the history of our neighborhood, and how it might have been in the old days, when those bricks were new. The alley smelled of urine, and the occasional scent of marijuana wafted through the air as you walked to the corner store.

The only trees that we had on our block were there because our block captain who had been living in the neighborhood for years maintained them. Kids would pop wheelies on their bicycles and dirt bike engines whined through the alley along with the sounds of police sirens and helicopter blades. Every so often a fruit cart (known as "arabbers" in the hood) would trot down our road along with the occasional ice cream truck. At night the streetlights glowed blue: a sure sign you were in the hood, since the blue lights were attached to a police camera. As soon as it was dark, the old people retreated indoors and the streets were filled with the sounds of music, people talking, sirens, gun shots, and squealing car tires here and there. Still, the longer we lived there the more our immediate neighbors, who were new to the neighborhood and didn't know us as kids, warmed to us, sometimes smiling and waving when they saw us. We were in it together—at least on our block. We were united by proximity and the necessity of keeping an eye out. We were family.

All of this added up to a realization that the hood wasn't the way we had left it. The connection that had always held places like Smallwood and Turner Station together was gone. The once-well-maintained homes, built solidly out of Baltimore brick, were caving in on themselves. You could buy one for a few thousand dollars if you wished (amazing considering the current housing crisis—these are family-size houses for four figures in a major city, within twenty minutes' drive of a city center and international airport). There was a sadness and anger that was palpable outside of our home. We felt the loss of the unity and family feeling the neighborhood held when we were kids. We spent as much time as possible across the alley at our "other mom" Bow's house, and we had so many older brothers and sisters in our neighborhood. All that was gone, and it felt like individuals trying to survive. Inside, we were feeling the bliss. But we realized that it would be really f**ked up if we just sat in our house and meditated all the time, while all around us people were suffering.

One day, the summer after graduation, we were sitting around reading books on yoga. The TV was on in the background, and Matthew Lesko came on. He said, "Let the government pay for you to start a business." We all looked up and it was like a light bulb turned on. We were going to let the government help pay for us to "save the world." We looked up an EPA grant because of Ali's degree in environmental science and policy. We found a grant for ground-level ozone detection.

Perfect! We would check pollution levels in Baltimore and use the extra money to do programs in the community. Atman had an old printer—one that printed on perforated paper that you had to rip off—that was really slow, so we started to print the grant, then left and went to play basketball. When we got back the paper was in a pile on the floor and the grant still wasn't done printing. When it was finally done we realized we needed to be a nonprofit to get the grant.

So after a bit of a delay, we looked on Ask Jeeves to figure out how to start a nonprofit. We reviewed the checklist and got going.

Meanwhile, we wanted to start doing something for the community. Our friend Antoine Friend gave us access to his modeling studio to teach yoga. We printed up one thousand flyers and advertised a free yoga class. The practice had been given to us, and we wanted to give it to other people in our neighborhood. We arrived at the studio, excited to share our yogic knowledge. Literally no one showed up. For the first few weeks we used it as a place to practice pranayama and kundalini yoga. It was the three of us, Uncle Will, and his two sons, Willie and Oba. People didn't start coming until we started charging for classes—one of our first lessons on the business of yoga. We did an early version of what would become HLF, working wherever we could get space and slowly building up some experience. Meanwhile, the universe waited till we were ready to start our program for real.

A few years into this, we started an entertainment company called For the People to try to fund the HLF. All our friends were either talented rappers or producers, so it made sense to start an entertainment company to work with them.

Meanwhile, our mom, Cassie, was working in the PATH program (Promoting Alternative Thinking Strategies) at a local school, Windsor Hills Elementary. After school we would roll up in that same Corolla and pick her up, since we didn't really have anything going on. One afternoon, the principal of the school approached us about coaching football. Now, we didn't want to do this, so instead we put together a three-page proposal for an after-school yoga program. To our surprise the principal said yes immediately. Turns out she would have said yes to anything because we were going to take on fifteen of her most problematic students.

Living on Smallwood was a challenge. But it helped us grow and be more appreciative of what we had. And as we began to work with kids, we found we were able to connect with them. Living on Smallwood made us legit in their eyes. When we started the first program at the Y, the six-year-olds and seven-year-olds would eye us up warily. They'd seen plenty of well-meaning outsiders come and go. Volunteers who'd drive in from other neighborhoods, full of big ideas, but who would never show up again. Now, in this early version of our first school program, it was the same dynamic. The kids didn't trust us right away. Why would they? So when one of us would try to connect with an angry, hurting kid, that kid would tell us: "You don't know me." We could reply, "True, but I know where you come from, and I know exactly what you're living with. Don't believe me? Let's walk. I'll show you my house. You can meet the pit bull, sit on our stoop, and we'll talk. You'll see, we're no different." Suddenly these three random dudes, who came out of nowhere, felt relatable. We lived on the same terrible turf they did, hearing the gunfire and the midnight fights and the sirens. The kids didn't have to explain anything to us, because we'd lived it all already for ourselves.

One of our first years, we worked with the school to deliver Thanksgiving meals to vulnerable children. A few streets over from Smallwood was a family who was scheduled to get a meal. Atman and Andy rolled up with a cardboard box of food, ready for the oven. As the door opened and they walked in, they saw . . . nothing. There was no furniture in the house beyond a pile of discarded blankets that was being used as a place to sit. The house was so cold. They set the uncooked food down on the counter in the kitchen, said their goodbyes and walked out, got in the car, and looked at each other in disbelief. Even if that family could cook the dinner, what would they eat it off? Was there even power to keep the fridge going and get the oven hot enough to cook the bird? And what was going to happen next week, when those Thanksgiving leftovers were long gone? A few days later we were able to help get them furniture with the help of our friends and our mom's church group.

The Student, the Teacher

When the universe knew we were finally ready, two things happened. First, one of our big brothers from around the corner saw us doing a lot of work in other neighborhoods, and he said, "Y'all are doing work with kids in other places, you need to help kids around here." We had been working in places where people would allow us to work—where we could get space. We had a reason why: The other adults in our area didn't want to help the "bad" kids, and especially didn't want to do anything to encourage them to hang around or loiter on the streets. We didn't think we could start something so impactful without the support of those elders. He straight-up told us that was bullshit, and it got us thinking about what we could do to help the kids we now knew by name. Three of the first kids we helped, Ra'Mon and two kids known as "the two Tays," had made our street corner their de facto headquarters.

Second, while we ruminated about what we could do to help "our" kids, they beat us to it and asked *us* for help. Now, they weren't asking for the esoteric knowledge of the ancient traditions. Instead, Ra'Mon and the two Tays found Ali and Atman after school one day. It turned out they had a basketball team. They had the T-shirts. They had the court, and the ball, and the enthusiasm to want to play. What they didn't have was a coach, and they were getting crushed. Why us? For the simple reason that we were some of the only adults in their lives who weren't telling them to "get the f**k off my steps." We would stop and talk to them like human beings. We weren't antagonistic toward them. We always said hello. And those kids felt the love vibes. So when they had one thing in their life they were excited about—basketball—and no one to help them learn how to play, they knew who to ask.

Here's the crazy thing: We lost every game. The first game we flat-out got destroyed. The second game came down to a last-minute jump shot, which we screwed up. Going home after that second game was bittersweet. We almost had it, against a way better team. All of us were pissed that we lost. But at the same time, there was a bond right there.

Now that we had the relationship, we asked Ra'Mon and the two Tays about joining our after-school program. Whether they wanted to do it or not, we had to get the support and buy-in of these three eleven-year-olds for any *other* kids to sign up. Atman walked out onto the stoop and told them about the program. There'd be snacks, cool computer stuff, swimming, and basketball. We'd help them with their homework. We didn't mention the yoga just yet (though all the kids ended up doing it happily). It would be fun. And because there was a level of trust there, the kids surprised us and said yes.

Kids were one thing; the adults were another. A few weeks after we started the program for "our" kids, the block captain called us over to his front door. There was a petition going around to get us kicked out of the neighborhood for inciting gang activity. For once, Ali was the one to lose his shit. He walked away, cursing out the block captain, telling Atman, "F**k them." It wasn't enough that these kids had done a community cleanup a couple of days ago, or that there was tree-planting coming up? How could our own people be so judgmental of a group of ten- and eleven-year-olds who were dealing with their environment in the exact way you'd expect any tween to do so? Atman, usually the hothead, had to take Ali's regular role of smoothing things over, apologizing to the captain and chasing after Ali to talk things through in a calmer way.

That was the beginning of HLF, and it was a preview of a dynamic that exists to this day. For everything we do to help our kids, there is someone out there who objects to "wasting resources on problem kids." Often it's people removed entirely from our world, sitting on committees or writing opinion pieces in the paper. But every now and then, it's people from our own neighborhood or neighborhoods like it—people we think should know better.

Part of this is a generational conflict that is born from a sense of distrust between the elders and the youth. After the crack epidemic, there was a lack of connection and love. The elders thought that the younger generations had messed up. The younger generations felt judged and shamed in turn.

Years later, when we went to the Mohawk reservation, we saw how older adults were seen as a treasure, and there was less antagonism between the youth and the elders. Nobody was putting the kids down, or trying to make them disappear, or squelching their love for learning. Although we didn't have this firsthand experience of seeing a functional, intergenerational community at the time, we felt the truth of this in our bones. Part of our job, our mission, was to make those ignored kids "reappear" and to give them the tools to do their part to reengage with their community.

The Three Foundations of HLF: Love, Yoga, and the Environment

The three of us started to refine our program as we worked with Ra'Mon and the Tays. We knew that our program would have three foundations.

One was *love*, and we had plenty of that. The kids in our neighborhood were starved for love and attention. They were the kids and grandkids of the generation of "hungry kids" that Cassie and Smit had tried to help. Their parents and grandparents had been under-loved and under-cared for. Now their kids were doubly feeling the pain. They needed to be seen, heard, and recognized. To this day, love is the foundation of everything we do, and it's the core reason why anything we do works. The day the love slips is the day that our system will stop working.

The other essential elements would be things that we knew worked firsthand. By this time, we'd all been regular *yoga* and meditation practitioners for years. At the same time, we knew the kids we were working with were going to be confused at best or openly resistant at worst to these more esoteric concepts.

And finally, the *environment*, both in terms of caring for it and experiencing it—first with small park cleanups and veggie gardens, and later with hiking and camping trips.

First, we had to do as Uncle Will had taught us and meet our kids where they were. So the first step was stuff that any kid wants to do: sports, snacks, and goofing off in a safe environment. We were still in the process of developing the program, and to be honest we just assumed it would be a lot easier than it was. We figured the kids would chill out and we'd do a program. They would leave. We expected them to just listen to us and do the yoga and everything would be totally perfect, but it wasn't even anywhere close to that. It was an ongoing struggle to get them to do anything. It was a struggle to get them to do their homework. It was a struggle to get them to listen. And every single part of it continued to be hard work.

Proof

While we tried to figure out this strange new world of mentoring and teaching children, Cassie was moving forward in her own career. Her new job was working with Dr. Mark Greenberg, who was the founder and director of the Edna Bennett

Pierce Prevention Research Center at Penn State University and a research scientist focused on child psychology. Mark is one of those people who changed our lives with his insights, support, and love. Besides his scientific credentials, he is also a lifelong meditator. When Cassie told him about us, and our work, he wanted to meet. A few days later Mark showed up in our neighborhood and stood on the porch observing the kids hanging out in front of our house and waiting for us to leave for the program. He saw these kids roughhousing, cursing, and disrespecting each other and passersby, and one kid, B-Man, stood out the most because he was extreme. After a bit, we all hopped into Atman's Corolla and our other cars and drove to the Y, where Mark took a seat on a mat among the crowd of kids.

B-Man saw that Mark was new and scooted over to him. "I can show you what to do if you want." Mark, a lifelong yogi and well acquainted with the poses, their names (English and Sanskrit), and correct form, said, "Thank you, that would be very helpful," and for the rest of the class followed the instructions of an earnest seven-year-old, looking to him for guidance and correction.

Together, Mark and B-Man practiced their poses, side by side, and at the end of the session, everyone lay down on their mats for shavasana. Now remember, these are highly active kids! Even with the yoga, and the meditation, and the exercise, they all had energy to burn. When this energy is considered "problematic" (we would dispute that diagnosis in many cases), there is a chronic lack of services for these kids. Most schools have to share a social worker rather than having one dedicated to their students. Added to that, there is a serious distrust of clinicians in the Black community. Parents worry that if their kids go to doctors or clinicians they will be diagnosed with trauma-related behavior problems and be considered disruptive in the classroom—and will be prescribed medication for their behavior, rather than offered meaningful help to get to the root of their trauma.

The room got quiet as the kids settled into final resting pose. The crazy part was that it was really loud. This wasn't a normal yoga studio; it was a recreation center where the noise level was astronomical. Even the adults found it hard to drop into shavasana. Yet the kids got quiet, listening to their own hearts and their own breath. Mark saw that even children who were seen by other adults as highly difficult, and maybe having no sense of an inner life, could, with love and skill, be brought into a state of peace and awareness. And that's a great gift for kids. Eventually we told them to slowly open their eyes, and the class ended.

After the kids were safely home, the three of us and Mark sat down at a vegetarian restaurant called One World Café and talked. The thing that struck us the most was when he said that he talked to the Dalai Lama about us and the Dalai Lama said that he was supposed to help us. I mean, can you believe it? The Dalai Lama actually told someone that he had to specifically help us. You can only imagine the impact that had on three young guys fresh out of college in the beginning of their spiritual journey. It had us zinging with energy. So we are all looking at Mark in awe now because he was and continues to be our connection to the fourteenth reincarnation of the Dalai Lama.

Mark pointed out something that we instinctively knew but had never heard articulated by someone outside of our immediate circle. He pointed out how "yoga helps build children's abilities to have self-awareness and self-regulation. But these kids are also building a sense of connection to others. They're building a sense of community, and because of the way you do things, I think there's a lot of empowerment. These kids are seeing a model of what relationships can be."

Mark asked us what we needed to grow the scope of our program. He'd seen how B-Man could be so extreme in the neighborhood, but then be mindful enough to care to teach a stranger how to do yoga and explain what the benefits are before jumping into his meditation. There was something powerful going on, he told us, and he would do everything in his power to help us grow. We told Mark that every time we tried to secure funding, the foundations would say the same thing—"Where is the empirical evidence that yoga helps kids?"—before rejecting us.

After thinking for a minute, Mark gave us two invaluable pieces of advice. He told us to take every reference to yoga out of our two-hundred-page yoga curriculum. You heard that right. When we said, "We can't do that, every single page of this damn thing is yoga, prana, energy, and chakra," Mark suggested we rename the different components in educational and clinical terms. We'll talk more about language and yoga in a bit, but for now all you need to understand is that there is no school system in the country that is going to welcome a group teaching anything—*anything*—that might possibly be linked to a religion.

Now, we don't consider yoga a religion, but plenty of other people do. School districts were getting sued left and right by shady organizations with unclear motivations, who accused them of teaching kids things like "ninja Buddhism" (which

frankly sounds kind of amazing to us). The Alabama legis-
lature has waged a literal war on the word *namaste*, allowing
yoga poses but banning any reference to anything that sounds
vaguely religious. As frustrating as this can be, we also see the
wisdom in it. We wouldn't want our kids going to a school and
getting indoctrinated into some kind of religious group we
didn't approve of or agree with. (Still: Yoga. Not a religion.)

We did as Mark said and—in one crazy twenty-four-hour
rewrite—swapped out words and names and phrases. We
crowdsourced some of this from our core clientele—eight-
year-olds. Kaki breath became *taco breath*, because your tongue
has to roll up like a taco. Sitali breath became *burrito breath*,
because your tongue had to roll back like a burrito. And of
course, sitkari is the *Bigfoot breath* because of its deep guttural
sound.

It felt wrong: These are ancient techniques; who were we
to rename them? But Mark was adamant, and it was good
advice. (Of course, that didn't change the fact that when we
showed up at a school to do our "stress and relaxation study"
the teacher would get on the PA and say, "Kids, report to the
gym for yoga!" Hey—she said it, not us!)

The next piece of good advice was equally intimidating. "You guys should do a study to prove that your program
works." We all looked at each other like *Huh?* and said, "We
don't need to prove it works. This stuff has been around for
thousands of years. It definitely works." He laughed and explained how important it was for us to accumulate data on our
specific program to show the efficacy. Finally, we were like,
"Cool." If that's what other people need to further our movement, then let's do a study. Especially because we would be

having the names of Penn State and Johns Hopkins backing us now!

If we wanted to take it to the next level and be more than three dudes, one Corolla, and a one-room office in a decaying house on Smallwood, we needed to throw some science at our work. We needed evidence that what we did worked. More importantly, we needed evidence that what we did worked *and* could be replicated in other school districts.

There's risk in doing this. We were pretty sure that our program worked, but there was also a chance that a research study would determine it didn't. If Mark's study revealed that our program had no long-term effect on these kids, it might effectively end everything we were trying to do. After all, who wants to donate to or support a nonprofit that has been proven to be ineffective?

With Mark's help we went to the Bloomberg School of Public Health, where we met Phil Leaf and Tamar Mendelson. Now, Phil and Tamar are two more people we hold close to our hearts, but then they were strangers who had the power to make or break our stress and relaxation study. Together we worked on a series of tests, and the end result was that multiple elements of our program were effective. Finally, we had the evidence we needed to get the kind of attention and grants that would boost our work to the next level.

CHAPTER FIVE

A Man's Man's World

There is a lot of masculine energy in
Baltimore but nowhere to place it.

LAILA, 20

Even as we were beginning to get our program off the ground, another piece of the puzzle was falling into place. A few years into our program, our students were 100 percent boys. To be honest, that felt kind of natural to us. The boys were the ones hanging out on the sidewalk, getting into trouble, and most obviously needing support and guidance. The girls . . . well, the girls seemed—at least to our eyes—to be doing relatively OK. Slowly, however, we realized this was kind of messed up, and that we might have blind spots of our own about the girls' lives and reality.

This realization plays into something that is at the very root of the problems in Baltimore: a lack of balance between the men and the women of the community, and a lack of awareness about how the actions of one group affect the other. A city is like a forest, and in our forest many of the tall trees that hold the community together, and provide shade and safety to the forest dwellers, have been chopped down. Without those trees the small plants burn up in the sun and die. In the next chapter we'll talk more about one of those trees—a missing mentor—and how badly this has affected our youth. But for now, let's talk about how as those trees get chopped down, the trees that remain have to grow even taller and stronger to carry more of the load. In this case the remaining trees are the women of Baltimore, who have to compensate for the missing men of the city. Even as these women work overtime to try to hold the community together, the young men push back, angry and frustrated to be constantly chastised and dressed down by the women who hold authority positions around them. It's a matriarchy, but it's a matriarchy that has lost the strong men who used to support and collaborate with the women. Unlike the Mohawk, the female leaders in Baltimore often lack the buy-in and support of the men. They are sometimes resented rather than revered for their work upholding the community.

It wasn't always this way. We grew up with the strong women of Baltimore: Cassie, Dee Dee (Uncle Will's partner), our godmother Valerie, and dozens of other aunts and big sisters and cousins who shaped and steered the neighborhood. But those strong women were balanced out by strong men: Will and Smit, among others. We always say, "We learned how to be a man from Smit; we learned how to be a gentleman from our mom." That balance was a blessing. One so important we didn't even realize it at the time. For every time Will lectured us on the Panthers, or Smit took us to Rhythm

Skate, or they both talked openly about racism, our mom balanced it out with feminine power. She would tell us about the importance of meeting and engaging with all kinds of people, taking a breath, and thinking things through before we made big decisions. If Smit was about mental toughness, then our mom was about compassion and vulnerability and connection and communication. Even after our parents divorced there was balance between the feminine and the masculine.

Smit always says that a boy has to learn how to be a man from other men. A woman simply can't teach that. So what happens to men when entire generations of fathers, grandfathers, and mentors disappear? Today there is a lack of balance in Baltimore; there is an almost overwhelmingly masculine energy to the streets and corners, but everywhere else it's feminine for the most part: in homes, schools, city government, and business, women have taken leadership roles that men have vacated.

This lack of balance between the masculine and the feminine is something we talk about a lot in the yoga community— but to see it play out in real life, come to Baltimore. With no fathers in the homes or older brothers in the neighborhood to teach them how to be men, boys learn from things they see in music and in the media, and that is no way to learn how to be a real man. At the same time, the boys and young men we work with have spent their whole lives being disciplined by women. Their moms and grandmothers hold it down. Their aunts let them know what's up. The teachers—mostly female—dress them down when they get out of line. All that feminine energy is powerful, but it is no longer balanced by the masculine energy that any boy needs to see modeled in his young life. As he goes through life, chastised by women, he feels their fear for him, and disappointment in him, and he starts to resent them. That resentment turns to anger.

By the time we returned after college something had changed. Our old neighborhood was no longer in balance. And we wanted our program itself to model this balance. We realized that the dynamic between men and women could change. In fact, once we began to work with the Mohawk reservation in the Akwesasne territory, we realized that balancing feminine and masculine power is an ongoing evolution. The Mohawk themselves are still in the process of rebuilding the old matriarchal clan structure—something they have a long tradition of and that goes back to the founding of the Iroquois Confederacy.

The Iroquois people (Mohawk are one of the six nations of the Iroquois) have a founding cultural principle of the Good Mind.[1] The Good Mind is quite literally the practice of being aware of our thoughts and intentions, and letting that awareness shape more kind and loving thoughts. Now, is it just us, or does that sound familiar?

The Good Mind—like our mindfulness practices—came out of a hard place. Back then, the chiefs and the warriors were the absolute authority figures and the tribes were often at war with each other. Many people were dying, but eventually, as peace was established, the tribes stripped the warriors of their complete authority. Rather than command, they would have to persuade. And the leaders would be nominated by women from that day on. The people cast away the memories of war (literally burying the hatchet) and resolved not to fight anymore. When a man and woman married, he moved into her family's longhouse; their children became members of her clan. That system faded away after the Revolutionary War.

There are bits and pieces of it left if you look hard, but they are hidden, unlike the weapons and feathers of the warriors. (The first feminists were inspired by the Seneca women.)

Andy, who grew up in a Puerto Rican household, also lived in a matriarchal family, where his mother and *titis* (aunts) were the decision makers. His family's experience of living on a colonized island helped him to empathize with this Mohawk history and the Good Mind philosophy. As he puts it: "Our history has been splattered with atrocities and colonizers, but our pride and honor is something that they cannot and will not ever take from us."

Today, when Mohawk teachers talk to young people about the Good Mind, they explain, "We talk a lot about grief because grief always turns to anger and hatred; untreated grief leads to war that can last forever." We see that in our home too, where the streets run red with unresolved grief, anger, hatred, and seemingly unsolvable violence, nearly all the result of predominantly male trauma and PTSD.

Once upon a time, Baltimore was a balanced city. Women like Cassie and Dee Dee created a safe container for the masculine energy of the young men. It's debatable whether it's fair or not that containing masculine energy was their job; still, it is a job that their foremothers did for generations. Men like Smit, Peter, and Will guided young men—like us—through their youth and into adulthood, modeling a kind of virtuous strength. We watched them negotiate the world, interact with each other, and deal with the day-to-day realities of raising children and holding a family and a life together.

Today those male elders are for the most part missing. If the father is home, he's most likely only a young man himself, and had minimal male role models growing up. The attitudes and behaviors of the *next* generation—the kids and teenagers—evolve as they watch their father acting in this hypermasculine, controlling way. As this kid grows up, he might see his dad controlling his mother, limiting her movements, and threatening her well-being if she pushes back. If his dad isn't around, he feels his absence sorely.

These two forces warp young peoples' ideas about how men and women respond to each other. A son won't have any kind of love for women coming up. A daughter might think she has to submit to men all her life. As she grows up, she will think she has to attach herself to men—or it will shut her down to loving men and mess up her capability of loving altogether.

Most people in Baltimore are living with trauma and PTSD. They have trust issues because they've seen violent murders, or been physically assaulted themselves, or have ongoing food and housing insecurity. These things can exacerbate the masculine-feminine imbalance. When safety or food and housing are insecure, people throw themselves at the mercy of anyone who can appear to provide safety or the essentials.

Many men—and women—in Baltimore are rigid and unbending. Sometimes the rigidity becomes strength—Smit the Grit was rigid as hell but also strong, pushing us to become our best selves no matter what. But rigidity can also be fragility. Steel seems strong, but stress it too often and it will snap in your hands. In Baltimore we have this way about us where we have to be strong and take matters into our own hands. We don't have help, and we've never been helped. We dealt with situations on our own, since we were kids, because for those of us without Cassies or Smits in our lives, we had to provide for ourselves.

It is hard for most Baltimorians to open up to someone and tell them how they feel. Instead, rigidity in Baltimore is like that steel girder about to fail. People are not going to crack open until the moment they snap, wreaking havoc in their wake.

One of our former students, Laila, explains it like this: "We all share a few things: The majority of us are Black, from imbalanced homes, seeing people on the streets all coked up, our fathers and brothers on the corner selling drugs. That is all that we see. So we take on these kind of internal issues that we all carry with us for a long, long time. It messes us up because we see our peers dying. They pass away due to someone else taking their life and it is traumatizing. Nine out of ten times we feel like we can't trust and talk to somebody. We think they are going to snake us out. Go behind our back and do something that is going to hurt us."

There is nothing inherently wrong or bad about masculine energy. There *is* something dangerous about a world ruled by masculine energy with no space for feminine energy—or vice versa. Feminine energy is being able to connect with the side that is not systematic, and more about your feelings, being in tune with nature, being aware. The act of being. Like Laila says, "The feminine energy is creating life, it's loving, it's warm. Masculine energy is more systematic, problem-solving, working, hands-on. The energy is always moving. Feminine energy is more grounded."

Part of our job is to model what a balance between masculine and feminine energy looks like, and how it can positively affect a community. We always talk about women and their contribution to society. We always model a safe way for women to be around men: being super careful about boundaries and avoiding triggers. We train our staff members to understand that many of our young girls have been hurt by men in the past, and that there are multiple layers of trauma and toxic past experiences. Many young girls in Baltimore (and all over the country) have been sexualized way way too young. Once they "look grown," adult men start to treat them like they are adult women capable of making adult choices.

All of this meant that when it came time to start our non-profit, it was hard at first for us to understand how to approach girls about joining. After all, we were three dudes. A lot of the girls who could benefit from our work had been traumatized by men already. As much as we wanted to jump in and help, it was a struggle to see how to help without risking more harm as well.

Most of the young people we saw in distress were the young boys on the street. At first it seemed obvious that we would focus on them. Eventually, however, the girls approached us: they wanted in on the program, and they were sick of being excluded from something good that the boys got to experience. Which, in retrospect, is completely fitting. The young women got fed up with waiting for men to do the right thing, stepped up, and flat-out demanded we expand the program and include them.

Part of our long-term job is to empower our young women to grow into positions of authority in the community. Another part of our job is to help our young men accept the idea of women in authority—and find ways to step into their power as well. Mindfulness is a huge part of this—the more you can let go of separation and accept our interdependence, the less the idea of surrendering some power will sting.

CHAPTER SIX

The Holistic Brain

Even though there is all this darkness, all of us are still
infinite beings. And we can't let that darkness drag us down.

—UNCLE WILL

P art of the work of any research study is understanding the environment that your subjects live in. We've already discussed this a bit—hopefully you are starting to understand the dynamics of Smallwood and Baltimore for yourself. But we also needed to learn to see our environment with new eyes. Outsiders' eyes. We knew why our kids were struggling, but we also needed to be able to translate their experiences into language the scientific and academic communities could understand and buy into. We started to look at our world with that scientist's eye and evaluate what had gone wrong and why. The first thing we saw was hundreds of human-size absences, and how those not-there people had irrevocably changed our world.

Missing Mentors

When we moved back to Smallwood, we were shocked to realize just how much the family and love of the neighborhood wasn't there like it was when we were kids. When we grew up there, we knew all our neighbors and they were all family. Everyone owned their homes and was a part of the community. We had Black-owned corner stores where you could get the things you needed for your home and not be harassed by store owners who weren't from the community.

We had our parents, but we also had our other mom across the alley: Bow. Her daughter Valerie is Ali's godmother and was the one who taught him to read. Our older brothers in the neighborhood helped raise us: Hump, Darryl, Pot, Damond, Reds, Boobie, China, Ronald, Dexter, Levi, Kirby, Darrius, and others.

Ali and Atman spent every day with and did everything with their friends, Man, Scooter, and Trent. We were always together. Our extended family was huge. And they weren't neighbors; they were legit family. They are just as big a part of us being who we are as our parents. The community-wide family isn't there like it was when we grew up there. It's more individuals surviving, and the population in the community is very transitional because there are a lot of renters.

These people—this long list of names that we still carry in our hearts decades later—were our mentors. Most Black neighborhoods anywhere in America were filled with mentors who were your older sister's friends, the dudes on the block. They were keeping you in line, showing you what to do, what not to do. Showing you how to operate. And then, when crack exploded in 1980, those mentors vanished. As families crumbled, so did communities. When our parents eventually divorced, and we left Smallwood, it was another brick pulled out of a weakening wall. Cassie and Smit were the mentors for a whole bunch of kids and families. Years later, one of our cousins told us how the neighborhood, already rough, started to fall apart for real without them.

The Super Strength of a Weak Tie

These missing mentors mattered. We could feel their absence and how it had affected our community. But it took one of our great supporters, meditator and professor Dr. Phil Leaf, to help explain why. Phil has helped us by conducting studies that prove the value of our work—and has also been an invaluable friend, mentor, and ally as we set up and established our business. He helped us figure out the basics, like how much our time is worth, and all in all taught us to grow our business with pride. He's also helped us understand the scientific principles behind some of the forces that shape our kids' lives. One thing Phil points out is that there's a big difference between your life as a kid, maybe growing up in the '70s, '80s, or '90s, and the life of the kids in our world today. If you had that idealized suburban American childhood or were living in a busy and crowded city environment anytime up to the '90s, you probably had a strong-tie network: your parents, siblings, maybe grandparents and close family friends. But in addition to that, you had a second, equally important network of adults in your life that, like a fishing net or a spiderweb, connected the families in your local community. This might have included neighborhood parents, the school bus driver, a convenience store clerk, or your teachers, all plugged into what's called a "weak-tie network."

The impact of this weak-tie network was twofold: First, you had the security that comes from backup. There were other adults around to keep an eye open and notice if something wasn't right. They might put you straight when you acted out or set an extra place when your mom wasn't going to be home for dinner. Secondly, you were plugged into a network of informal knowledge. As a kid this kind of informal knowledge can be learning social cues, observing healthy relationships, or watching adults set boundaries and hold lines against antisocial behavior. Added all together, this network would have taught you the basics of how to move and live within a society. As you get older, this informal knowledge extends to job opportunities for a teenager, internships for a college student, job openings for an adult, or whispers about the dangers and possibilities inherent in any community.

Here's the thing, though: American children today are spending less time with the adults in their lives than at any time in modern history. (This has fluctuated due to COVID, but the general trends hold true.) Parents across the country are strapped for time, energy, and money like never before. It's bad enough in affluent suburban neighborhoods. There, the modern versions of those Norman Rockwell parents— married or divorced—are both working outside the home, the former-stay-at-home moms trading one type of demanding work for another: no longer raising their kids hands-on but instead working to earn enough money to raise them at all. The dads are feeling the pull to work longer hours in the face of job cuts and COVID insecurity. Neighborhoods like the ones we grew up in suffered even more. There, the jobs evaporated too as businesses left Baltimore City. Suddenly parents were no longer working locally, right at the same time as a whole host of other factors came to disrupt the social network.

Along with mentors, subtract decent-paying jobs, cars, functional infrastructure, and schools that are clean and warm and hygienic from your expectations about society. Throw in systemic racism, food insecurity, domestic violence exacerbated by poverty, and over-incarceration. Those parents and aunties and uncles who used to sit on their front porch and keep an eye out are gone. Those moms who would step in with an extra plate of dinner when necessary are working late too. So how are *these* kids handling the disappearance of adults from their lives?

Today, in Baltimore City, the majority of working parents most likely don't have jobs anywhere near their homes. Most likely they don't have cars either. Baltimore has the second-worst commute in the country (after Los Angeles). These parents are leaving their house at six in the morning and getting home at eight at night. Those jobs that they're taking a couple of buses to get to might not even pay living wages. Snow days mean no-pay days. Sick days mean your paycheck is suddenly a fraction of what you're expecting, even though your landlord still wants the full rent. There's no buffer, no slack, no understanding.

Here's something you need to understand: Baltimore parents love their children as fiercely as any other parents, but they are being pulled ever further from their kids by the demands of a society that makes no allowance for a bad day, a long-ago poor choice, or simple bad luck. Years ago, we heard a story about how an expired license tag led to a Los Angeles teenager dying in jail over a holiday weekend. We all know stories like this.

Today, Ra'Mon works for us. Ra'Mon is a living example of what happens when you have few ties—either weak or strong. He grew up around the neighborhood, untethered and un-moored by family or mentors. His dad—a teenager himself when he had Ra'Mon—had been tortured to death in a hor-rific gangland execution, something that the preteen Ra'Mon was unable to talk about or even acknowledge. His mom and grandma were both alcoholics. All the men in his family had died violently (one grandfather being the only exception—he was a house painter who fell from a ladder and impaled him-self on fence railings). Forget strong ties—Ra'Mon barely had weak ties to hold him and his life together.

When he looks back on those early years, he sees them from the perspective of a child who had no support or backup in the places a kid might usually expect to find them. His dad was dead; his mom was often AWOL. Most of those right-minded mentors—the ones who would have both steered him to make smart decisions and made sure he got a meal every night—were gone. Other "mentors" took their place.

> There were older guys in our group—between the ages of seventeen and nineteen, and they would just say, "Hey, what's up on the block?" They would be teaching us little things . . . so we would be hav-ing gang meetings. It was my environment, and I

had to adapt to my environment. They sent us on a mission. And soon it was an ongoing war. And remember, at this time I'm maybe nine, ten, eleven. I knew I was different, because every time I'd go home I'd pray for forgiveness, I would pray for the people we'd hurt. No one ever tried to stop us, except this one block captain. And I respect him to this day. No one ever put us in our place. And it was right about then that I met Atman. Even then, none of us wanted to be in it anymore. It was just our environment. So one day Atman rolled up in his Toyota Corolla and said, "We're going to the YMCA. It's going to be fun. We'll have snacks, you can do your homework." And from that day everything changed. We got about ten of us in that Corolla. There were kids lying on top of each other. When we pulled up at the Y, they said, "This is what's happening. We're going to play basketball." I'm like, "Cool." "There are some desks and then we'll do homework, and we'll have a snack." "Cool." "And then we'll do yoga." "What?!"

I never thought I was going to be able to control my anger, and I was only a kid at this time. I never thought I was going to be OK with what happened to my dad or the choices my mom was making. I would hide my pain through smiling and stuff, but deep down I'm eating myself alive. I would say right there that yoga and meditation changed my life for the better, because starting that day I began to be able to cope with my anger.

By the time Ra'Mon—or pretty much any of our children—hit double digits, their brains are already stewing in stress hormones and chemicals. Every day these kids—like all of us—use neural pathways in their brains, worn deep by past experience, to predict and prepare for what might happen next. A kid like Ra'Mon is, consciously or otherwise, prepared for things to go bad. His body is in fight or flight before he is even out of bed in the morning.

Jump forward fifteen years and Ra'Mon is still suffering from PTSD from his experiences as a child. Just ask his wife: He regularly wakes up screaming and enraged, shouting, "Oh yeah, that's what'chu want?!" And this is *after* fifteen years of mindfulness practice, the only thing that has ever helped him release the trauma from his body.

All this grinding anxiety, uncertainty, and fear have a physical effect on the body, something psychologists call the *allostatic load*, and it's literally the price your physical self pays for your mental distress. Our brains after all are the key organ of stress: As the regions of our brain are exposed to chronic fear or worry they remodel themselves, changing how they respond to *future* stress and anxiety. As we get older this can manifest as cognitive impairment or chronic depression. Others might get hypertension or turn to eating for comfort, perhaps developing diabetes in the process.

The Child's Brain on Stress

There's a reason why young people like Ra'Mon are suffering. All kids are stressed, but poor kids are stressed to the very limit. Poverty-related stress (a variation of chronic psychosocial stress) is about more than money. It's the accu-mulation of every other fear and anxiety that these kids deal with on a day-to-day basis. It could be a relative who's crash-ing on their couch and who says or does things that feel weird, inappropriate, or seriously traumatizing, while the kid's ac-tual parents are away at work all waking hours. Maybe their parents are out of work or on reduced hours and can't make rent this month. There's no food in the fridge and no one has money to buy more. The guys on the block are harassing them, but so are the police. Or more likely, it's all those things and more, combined.

These kids perceive threats to their well-being but also know they don't have the resources to deal with them. So the brain jumps in with a fight-or-flight response, flooding a kid's body with cortisol, epinephrine, and dopamine. These hormones serve their purpose in the short term: They might give a kid that burst of energy and aggressiveness and the appearance of confidence that he or she needs to rebuff that relative, or walk by those guys on the block, ignoring their comments. Cortisol improves the body's function, allowing it to access more energy to fight or flee. In the long term, however, repeated floods of cortisol suppress the body's im-mune system. Eventually as our kids grow up, they are more susceptible to heart disease, diabetes, and other illnesses. The stress is literally killing them. One study found that kids on the lowest rung of the socioeconomic ladder had ten times the rate of certain diseases as kids at the top of the ladder.[1]

This link between poor health and poverty holds true even in countries with socialized health care: Poor children in countries like England, with its National Health Service, still have vastly higher rates of illness than their well-off equivalents. And it is as true in midwestern farming families as it is on Smallwood. These differences aren't fully explained by lifestyle choices either—as tempting as it is for conservative think tanks to try to pin the blame there. Instead, it all comes back to this constant firing of the brain's fight-or-flight response, and the gradual, grinding breakdown of an overstressed mind and an overtaxed body.

Adolescent Brain Function

The second piece of the puzzle is the relatively slower development of the prefrontal cortex in boys than in girls. The female brain matures by age twenty-one. The male brain isn't fully mature until age twenty-five. Yet a seventeen-year-old can join the army. By eighteen they can legally own a gun or get married in most states. More seriously, in many states teenagers as young as thirteen or fourteen accused of serious crimes can be tried as adults. This is a loaded subject. Teenagers have—in rare cases—murdered, maimed, and traumatized innocent people. Some kids have caused terrible pain. But that pain is nearly always pain that was *passed on* to them. Children absorb their own experiences into their sense of who they are and how they engage with the world. Those experiences are cumulative: perhaps beatings that take place over the years, or the invisible scars of repeated neglect, hunger, or shame. (In the Akwesasne territory we reckon that nearly all the ongoing trauma can be traced back to the residential schools.) Perhaps a parent who is absent either emotionally, due to an undiagnosed mental illness, or physically, due to death or incarceration. In California, teenagers could be given multiple LWOP (life without parole) sentences before they were old enough to apply for learner's permits. Worse—due to things like gang enhancements and aiding and abetting laws—many of these kids were being given LWOP for simply being present while a crime was committed.*

Most of our kids have multiple adverse childhood experiences, or ACEs. ACEs are traumatic events that happen in a child's life and adversely affect their ability to function and develop the way a non-traumatized person does. Research has shown that most people in Baltimore have three or more ACEs.

Eventually these repeated ACEs affect the brain, shrinking the hippocampus (where we process our emotions, consolidate short-term memories into long-term memories, and manage stress). As a result, the brain doesn't develop fully, and the child, already running on fumes from the daily stress of his or her life, is now struggling with self-regulation, fear processing, decision-making, and stress management. These kids are the ones acting out or flat-out not showing up for school. But, as Phil pointed out to us early in our work with him, "the kids who are acting up in class, causing problems, and being confrontational with the teacher are often the kids who want that teacher's attention the most. That teacher might be the one link—either strong or weak—that that kid has in their

---

* Thankfully these laws are changing, and juvenile LWOP is no longer allowed. Young people who were given LWOP sentences are getting the chance of parole and a second shot at life.

life. And they are getting that teacher's attention in the only way they know how."

The Traumatized Brain

Neurologically there is a huge difference between a typical brain and a traumatized brain. The traumatized brain doesn't have access to higher functions. It is pretty much living in survival mode. People who have been traumatized become caught in a state of sympathetic dominance (or fight or flight). Their cortisol levels are really high and lead to problems like weight gain, diabetes, and ulcers. Increased levels of adrenaline lead to increased blood pressure. Executive function (basically the mental skills that we use on a daily basis to go about our lives, like self-control, time management, organization, etc.), located in the prefrontal cortex, is less accessible to people who have been highly traumatized. That means increased impulsivity, loss of emotional control, and decreased self-awareness.

So when you see people—such as our youth—acting out, you need to understand that a lot of those issues you might call bad behavior or anger issues aren't really those kinds of issues. Instead, they are the signs of deep-rooted, multigenerational trauma popping up and taking control of a person's brain.

Trauma also affects the vagus nerve, which is the means of communication between the brain and the body. When people are severely traumatized, their vagus nerve no longer fires properly. They literally lose the ability to interpret the signals their body is trying to send to and receive from the brain.

The severely traumatized also have out-of-whack threat perception: They see everything as a threat, grossly overreacting to small problems, snubs, or angry interactions that non-traumatized people (if they exist) can process and move on from quickly. Studies have shown that ACEs can be passed on through generations, and that children who experience abuse are more likely to abuse when they become parents.

A traumatized brain in Baltimore can look like kids who are fighting over nothing. That is part of that fight-or-flight trauma. An innocent bump is seen as a threat, and that fight or flight kicks in. You can be in a classroom, thinking everything is going well, when suddenly a kid jumps out of his seat and runs. Why? You have no idea. The kid most likely has no idea either.

Trauma can sound underwhelming. We've all experienced bad stuff that messes with our heads. What's different is the intensity and repercussions of trauma in our communities. Nearly everyone who has come up in Baltimore over the last few decades has PTSD from their trauma. They flinch, just like soldiers, at sudden, unexpected noises. They self-medicate: During the Freddie Gray protests, the CVS at Penn and North was ransacked. After that, dealers flooded the streets with drugs like methadone, Percocet, Suboxone, Xanax, tramadol, and other opiates. Suddenly young people were nodding out on this stuff, not just the old people who had legit prescriptions. A few years later the dealers started pushing counterfeit opiates laced with fentanyl, which is fifty to a hundred times more potent than morphine. Ra'Mon has dozens of friends who've died after taking them. Like he says: "It could be people on the corner, or big corporations, but everyone is keeping you messed up on something."

The city had fought hard to get a CVS in the community.[2] It employed thirty people locally (and does again now, since it has been rebuilt). After it burned, all you'd see is people falling out on drugs, nodding out, and the police sitting there in their cars, doing nothing.

Worse, there are almost no resources available to these traumatized people. It would take a state or federal initiative to get mental health care to everyone in Baltimore who needs it, and we all know that ain't coming anytime soon.

Healing the Traumatized Brain

People sometimes think that trauma is irreversible, but with the right tools and support you can heal yourself. Neurogenesis and neuroplasticity give us hope. Our brain isn't a static thing: Neurogenesis refers to the fact that our brains create 750 new neurons every day. By the time you are fifty you have none of the neurons you were born with. There are activities you can do—meditation, exercise, and maintaining a good diet—to increase neurogenesis. Neuroplasticity is the ability to change the brain's structure and function. You can rewire yourself depending on how you are thinking and acting. Given the right tools people can heal themselves from trauma.

Most of the things that people are classifying as attention or anger or behavior problems are more about the fact that kids who have gone through trauma do not have access to that part of their brain—it's not physically possible for them to do the things on the list of executive functions, like self-control and self-monitoring. The way they are behaving has very little to do with anger—it's all trauma issues.

We have learned from working with traumatized children that their body isn't a safe space for them anymore. Practices like yoga and mindfulness can help children relearn that trust by making the body a safe place to be again.

The body receives a constant stream of messages through the skin, the muscles, and the joints and sends them to the brain. For a non- or lightly traumatized person, these messages are benign, even pleasant. But for severely traumatized people, that message their brain is getting is fear and the possibility of danger around every corner.

This is why yoga and mindfulness work for traumatized children: When you do practices like yoga it puts you in the present moment. You feel safe. You're caught up in the moment and that fear is not being registered or sent to your brain. It's crucial to understand potential triggers that can shatter this feeling of safety. For a sexually or physically abused child a physical adjustment can feel like a shocking violation. An instruction to close their eyes can take them straight back to being assaulted. Never assume your experiences are universal—you have no idea what the child or adult sitting in front of you has survived.

After you work with the body, then you can start working with the mind. A lot of teachers want to put people in silent meditation, but the silence allows the trauma to come up. What we do is guided imagery and meditations. You get stillness, but it's a full stillness, where people can start to understand what inner peace can become.

We work with people to develop their inner resources. Help them make their body a safe space, and then help them find inner peace because that's something no one can ever take away from them! If you can help them get to a peaceful place, no matter how chaotic their life is, it is something they will always have, and can turn to in those moments of stress or trauma.

It's important to understand that our brains, like our bodies, respond to exercise. In this case the exercise is an active mindfulness practice. Instead of abs and pecs, our brains remodel and reshape themselves, growing new connections and creating new neurons, thickening the folds of the brain and developing neuroplasticity. It's the saving grace of anyone trying to change old habits or move forward on a more hopeful and positive path. And neuroplasticity is where we come in. In 2008 the Dalai Lama visited DC and spoke at the annual meeting of the Society for Neuroscience. At that meeting—as he had for many years prior, and still does today—he pushed hard for more research into how Tibetan Buddhist monks' brains were changed by decades of consistent meditation. (We'd have invited the attending scientists to check out the classrooms full of kids, putting their theory into practice.)

Maslow's Hierarchy, Upside Down

All of this added up to a fundamental problem. Those "problem kids," hanging out on the stoop, pissing off the neighborhood elders, finding their mentors and support in all the wrong places, weren't meeting even the most basic levels of the classic hierarchy of needs. Forget physiological needs. These kids were sleeping in unheated houses through a Baltimore winter and walking to school with Flamin' Hot Cheetos and Little Hug fruit juice for breakfast. Safety and security? You do the math on that. Sense of belonging and needs? The lucky ones had overworked, overstretched, but still loving parents. Too many didn't have even that. And the missing mentor system meant those crucial weak ties were AWOL too. Esteem needs? If you were a teenager who didn't have access to hot water, food, and basic grooming and hygiene products, how good would *you* feel? Self-actualization? Well, that's kind of where we came in. There was only so much we could do about a lot of these issues, but what we could do was give these kids some tools to center themselves and access their inner light and energy.

In our own HLF way we needed to take that hierarchical pyramid and turn it upside down. We couldn't promise the kids that their home would become safer, or that their diets would become better (at least outside of the veggies and fruit we provided as snacks). We couldn't make absent parents reappear, or creepy and inappropriate relatives disappear. We *could*, however, help with the final two rungs of the five-tier model. We could help the kids find that sense of accomplishment within themselves, and we could help them access more of their own very human potential.

Most of our kids didn't have the bottom rungs of the pyramid filled. They might be in our class, doing breathwork or meditation, but then they had to go out and hustle for their siblings. This conundrum was why we started our workforce development program. Meditation practices are well and good, but they don't put food on the table. They don't put a jacket on your little brother's back. None of that shit is happening because of your pranayama or your downward dog. Here's where we flashed back to what Smit had told us, way back at the very beginning of our work: Don't earn the check, be the check. Whatever work we did wasn't going to mean much if we couldn't bring a whole lot of kids along with us.

Alongside everything else we'd been doing up till this point, we'd also had various kids from the neighborhood in and out of our houses, as they needed support, or simply a place to call home so they wouldn't be sent to juvenile detention facilities for various misdemeanors. J had no real family, was thirteen, and up in front of a judge. When the judge asked him if he had anywhere to live, he pointed to Ali, sitting at the back of the courtroom, and said, "He's my mentor. I'm staying with him." This was news to Ali and even bigger news to his children's mother and their young sons. Ali rushed home, and got the futon in his man-cave sorted out for J, and he ended up staying for six months. Our thirteen-year-old nephew, Ross, had also moved in, and he lived at the house on Smallwood on and off for the next year. Ross will pop up in this story later, but for now he was an added challenge for us. Ross's mom was working full-time, with little support, and there were no male role models in Ross's life. Ross's mom knows how important positive male role models are for young Black boys, so she asked if Ross could spend time with us. He moved in, and he became more like our little brother than our nephew.

These stories matter because they address a fallacy you'll hear a lot—that Black folks don't adopt—and this is untrue.

We adopt, but often we do it informally, taking in neighbor-hood kids who need a place to go. It's our own way of trying to meet the needs on that pyramid and give our kids those foundations that they are desperate for.

Uncle Will was also a huge believer in meeting people where they were. He met us where we were—young men full of am-bition and energy and still looking to enjoy life in its most obvious forms. We would meet these kids where they were: in school, anxious, stressed, with fractured attention spans and defenses calcified over years of hard living.

Uncle Will taught us that you can't elevate yourself out of being able to connect. He'd tell us, "You can't have your head in the clouds while your ass is on the ground." We've used this skill with our kids every day since. And in our own lives too. At one point, as we began to progress along the meditative path, we decided we were going to stop drinking, thinking that was the holistic, meditative choice to make. Will told us, "No, you can't stop drinking. Suppose you were sitting at a bar, next to a fellow. Chances are that person is going through some stuff. That moment, in that bar, is your one shot to con-nect with them."

This advice—to meet people where they are—is some of the most valuable wisdom Will shared with us. To this day we practice it both with the adults we work with, and the kids. Some of our oldest and most committed students started as aggro little ten-year-olds loitering on our stoop, passing time as lookouts for the older dudes. We had to sit down next to them on that stoop—both literally and metaphorically—and start there.

We'll talk more about the program that Uncle Will inspired and helped develop in Part Two of the book, but for now, understand that Uncle Will brought together Eastern philosophy and Black Panther activism into a powerful, righteous mix. Uncle Will passed in 2019, but we still feel him, sitting there, laughing and loving with us. Probably also suggesting we go get more bang, to keep the conversation and the laughter going. We couldn't have done this without you, Uncle Will.

This Little Light of Mine

Involution and You

So there we were.

We had a nonprofit that was slowly reaching more kids, in more schools. The first few years were a constant struggle. We were volunteering more than forty hours a week to support our students, and to grow our organization. This led to us having to get weekend jobs at Sheppard Pratt, a mental illness in-patient facility. We worked a double on Saturdays and a shift on Sundays, which made it feel like our weekends were just one long day, with no time to enjoy life. But we had to do something to keep the lights on and food in the fridge. Even after we got our first bit of funding, we did not pay ourselves as our funders assumed we would. Instead, we hired an administrative assistant, because in our minds, we were the only fools who would work for free, so we had to bring on someone who could help us get more organized and figure out ways to grow. Meanwhile, we tried to figure out the basics: Could we get teachers to just give us a chance and not dismiss our work out of hand? Could we get someone to bankroll the snacks or pay for some kind of transportation?

We were getting little bits of support and press from newspapers and donors. The *Baltimore Sun* wrote about our program in Robert Coleman Elementary School; a few years later it was featured on major networks like CNN and the various nightly news programs. We were jumping on planes, giving talks and lectures. Still. Half the time, when we'd show up at these increasingly prestigious events, some organizer, with clipboard in hand, would come up and mistake us for the band. One time, Atman pointed at the display set up by the conference room door and told Mr. Clipboard, "That's us on the poster!" Eventually we just leaned into it and started telling people we were an aboriginal folk band from Australia. Ali played the bullroarer, Atman played the didgeridoo, and Andy did vocals.

Andy has an MBA, but well-meaning, would-be supporters still give us remedial impromptu lessons on the basics of nonprofit financing. When people would do that, Ali and Atman would look at each other and say, "Like in a bacon, lettuce, and tomato sandwich."* No one knew what we were talking about, but we would laugh. At that point, we probably had as much experience at running a nonprofit—if not more—than anyone else in the room. It was—and is—hard to square this kind of aggravating and even insulting stuff with the work we were doing.

The truth is, Baltimore is a town full of nonprofits. This can be a good thing and it can cause problems. Ask any nonprofit here, and you'll hear stories of the big dollars bypassing Black-owned and -operated groups and being funneled to larger, White-owned operations. Or you'll hear these same out-of-town groups acting as gatekeepers for their dollars, with every nonprofit in town chasing them. There are a lot of well-meaning people who don't always have faith in local people to make good choices. Sometimes people were downright shady, going behind our backs to connect with our funders and having those donations sent to their pockets, not ours. Or trying to have approval over our press—such as being featured in the *Huffington Post*—through their offices even when that press came about through our own contacts. This can get frustrating

---

* It was a reference to the movie *Trading Places*, where the Duke brothers explain what bacon is to Billy Ray Valentine.

to say the least. Some well-intentioned people come in with clear ideas about who they think deserves their help. When they look at the abandominiums, or dudes hanging out with pants sagging, they say no. They don't want to invest in the corner, or address the problems that start and continue there.

Ali often says, "The best solutions are home-grown solutions."* We believe that local people offer the most relevant and most effective solutions to local problems. Yet those are the very people who are often squeezed out of the process by organizations with less experience who have White leadership getting meaningful funding when local, Black-organized groups get scraps. Eventually Black people who do this work end up leaving to go to other cities because they don't get treated fairly or receive the support they need to do nonprofit work here in Baltimore.

Nonetheless, the more word about HLF spread, the more people wanted to get involved. And let's be clear: We were happy to get the offers of help. We were now fielding requests from part-time yogis, retired meditators, and well-meaning people in general who wanted to either be part of what we were doing or replicate it in their own communities. No matter where we go, we get the question from White people: "Hey, I want to help, so what can I do? How do I go into underserved communities and help?"

So, if you're White, and you're wanting to help, these next few pages are for you.

Chances are, if you're reading this book, you care.

You've seen enough, and felt enough, to want to get involved and make a difference.

* Our friend and mentor Charlie Hartwell shared this saying with us.

Still, let's ask a delicate question: Who exactly are you, and what are your motivations for doing this work?

This is part of the challenge for you, the reader. The more self-aware you are, the more honest you need to be with yourself. Where is the need in your community? Where is there a lack of love, and how can you facilitate love to fill that void? If you're looking to help outside of your community, why? Take it from us, there are struggling children in the most exclusive schools in this country. Wealth doesn't protect them from trauma and abuse. So before you come to our neighborhood, get real about your own. Not facing the pain, trauma, and frankly, abuse in your own backyard is a form of spiritual bypassing. It's way easier to look at an impoverished community—far from your own—and swoop in as some kind of half-assed savior than to see with clear eyes how traumatized your own kids are.

So look at yourself in the mirror before you worry about our reflection.

We see a way for Black folks and White folks to work together to build up communities and advocate for children. In fact, White volunteers have a specific value in helping shift the way some of our kids see and understand White people. Most of our kids have limited exposure to White people: the only ones they regularly see are the police locking someone up, or Child Protective Services taking away kids. This is no more helpful than any other kind of racial stereotyping. So when we have volunteers show up to work with the kids—like our friends Galen and Matt from Friends—it helps shift old, stagnant ways of thinking on both sides.

Still, there are some very clear guidelines that any person needs to observe coming into a community that is not their own if they want to help. Step one is understanding your place and your role.

THE EIGHT INSIGHTS OF SUCCESSFUL CONNECTION WITH A TRAUMATIZED CHILD OR COMMUNITY

1. Authenticity. Be yourself, even if you are initially uncomfortable or feel out of place. Galen and Matt didn't change who they were or try to use hip-hop slang to fit in with people. They came from a place of love, and love resonates. If the kids feel that authentic love, if they feel you are being present with them, you'll be able to make that connection.

2. Leave that savior mentality at home. This isn't *Diff'rent Strokes*, and you're not Phillip Drummond, swooping in to save a couple of cute Black kids. The whole point of our program is to empower people to save themselves. So get rid of that savior mentality: that's when you are really ready and able to go in and help people.

3. Get out of the way. We all want to be the hero, but sometimes you need to be the person standing next to the hero, holding her sword and shield while she does the real work. If you're a White person in a room full of Black people who've been living and breathing this shit for generations, ask yourself how likely it is that you really have the most relevant insights into what's going on and how to help.

4. Talk to your kids about White privilege. It is a real thing, and you can use it selfishly or for good. We never blame

people for having White privilege. You didn't ask for it, and it's not your fault you have it. We do criticize people for refusing to see or discuss their privilege. And please don't come at us with that "I don't see color" nonsense— we all see and process the world through a racial lens. It's disingenuous and dishonest to claim otherwise. White people have an opportunity to use their privilege to help those of us who don't have it. So be understanding and empathizing and willing to lift people up.

5. Cultural competency. Work on understanding the nuances of a culture that might be new to you. We have White friends, and one running joke between us is that certain expressions have two meanings: Black people meaning and White people meaning. If one of us says "That song was alright," it's going to have very different meanings depending on if we meant it like Black people mean it, or how White people mean it. You don't need to understand or know all these subtleties, but you do need to acknowledge they exist and do your part to improve communication across the board.

6. Understand that to some extent people need to see people who look like them doing practices. We've learned that over the years: If there are all White yoga teachers the kids would practice and get a benefit from it. But when they go in and see Ali and Atman and Jamar and Ross and Oba and Ra'Mon teaching, they see it as something that's for them.

That's important for Black kids to see. When we were kids, people would laugh if we said "I'm going to be president when I grow up!" Now there's a model for how that might happen—two, in fact, with Vice President Kamala Harris. Accept that you might not be the most impactful role model in the moment.

7. Be consistent. Don't show up once unless you plan to keep on showing up indefinitely in the future. Traumatized kids have been let down a hundred times before. Don't make it a hundred and one. So, don't bite off more than you can chew. Start slow, volunteering as backup for existing programs. It's better to consistently show up once a month than ghost on a weekly commitment.

8. Do the work and give the results to the universe. This means do your best, but practice continual self-care and acceptance if the results aren't what you hoped. Our staff members have to accept their limitations. We do the work we can with the tools we have, and along the way we are able to redirect many kids onto a more hopeful pathway. But for every kid who's able to remake their life, many more can't, usually through no fault of their own. Healthy, loving acceptance and nonattachment are essential for your own sanity and well-being.

Laying the Groundwork for Involution

The second part—at least for the work that HLF does—is to have a developed practice of your own, and to have done your personal work of working through your own triggers, traumas, resentments, and fears. What do we mean by this? Simple:
Traumatized kids can trigger the f**k out of you.

These kids have learned to survive by any means they can. They will promise to do one thing, then promptly do the opposite. They will find your weak spots and vulnerabilities, and push you, right there, repeatedly. They will test you again and again, searching for that sign that you are as unreliable and inconsistent as the other adults in their lives. Deeply traumatized kids will act out in ways that don't make sense to an adult observer—you need to be able to roll with it.

There's no guarantee you'll ever reach the point where that child trusts you. However, there is a daily opportunity to break that burgeoning trust irrevocably. So tread kindly. Tread carefully. And don't get involved if you aren't certain you've done enough inner work to be patient, kind, nonjudgmental, and consistent. (If you need to work on yourself, jump ahead to Chapter Nine now for the mantras and mudras.)

This groundwork is based on having your own practice— whatever that might be. For us, it is obviously going to be poses, pranayama, and meditation based. For you it means that you've done enough personal-growth work to be centered, resilient, and nonreactive. This might mean therapy, or simply that you are physically active in a way that lets you work off your frustrations. Whatever your path, make sure that you:

Actively address any big, unprocessed traumas and emotions. Even if your stuff *seems* small, make sure you've focused on healing yourself before volunteering to help others. Also, make sure you are fully on an inner journey of self-awareness and self-acceptance. This doesn't have to be anything crazy, but you have to face your own inner shit. People are going to ask you questions about it. What will your answer be?

Part of the groundwork is recognizing and honoring that you're not ready to go there just yet. We have a friend who had two of his best friends murdered within one two-week time span, even as he was working for a group called Roca, which helps traumatized sixteen- to twenty-four-year-olds at risk of violence. Ali was supposed to teach him to meditate, and when they met up at the second memorial he said, "Ali, I know I need this, but I'm pushing so much stuff down, and if I start looking at this it's all going to come up, and I don't think I'm ready for it." We are glad he knows that about himself, because too many people don't have that awareness—they aren't ready to have this stuff staring them in the face. So know yourself. Know when you're ready, and accept if you're not.

Here's a secret we don't share too often: Back when we started this work, we didn't think it would be that hard. The kids would show up and we'd do a program. They would leave. We'd go home. Sure, we'd be working with kids during the days, but at night we'd still be living our lives on our own terms.

Joke's on us: The very first day of our very first program, just over half of the fifteen kids we were expecting showed up, and the other half were in detention. We had to *fight* for every one of those kids to be allowed to attend our after-school program.

You could argue the joke's *still on us*. This work is all-engrossing. We are three best friends who work together every day, yet we hardly see each other and communicate even less. It's that consuming.

We started something not knowing where it would go. We didn't know that ten years from when we started that this first cohort of what would grow to be twenty kids would still be actively in our lives. They would all graduate high school. None of them would go to prison for long stints (though sure, a few have bounced in and back out). Many of them would be working with us, passing on the knowledge they'd learned to a new generation. We didn't know any of that. What we did know is that we had fifteen of the toughest cases in a tough school. And their behavior—and indirectly their futures—were our problem. This work is a commitment, so first work on yourself, then decide if you're willing to be involved with working on others.

CHAPTER SEVEN

Bend Yourself into Shape

We've been working on ourselves for decades, and we still get bent out of shape on a regular basis. The situations that cause the bending are the physical and situational stressors that we all face on a daily basis. Those kids in that last chapter? AWOL from an after-school program they had promised to attend. A teacher might look over her classroom on yet another interminable grinding day and think how much she can't stand that douchebag kid who always puts his hat on even though he knows he's not supposed to. All this stuff happens to you, whether you are in the mood to deal with it or not (probably not). Your response is up to you.

If you are aware of your situational stress, you can use your mindfulness and breathing practice to calm down and avert disaster, but if you let those small stressors accumulate, then the physical stressors will kick in. Suddenly you're cutting off the guy in the next lane over, desperate to get out of gridlock. Or you're shouting at that jerk next door. Or going off on that dumb kid, grinning back at you and enjoying your overblown reaction. You may have had the best of intentions when you set out that morning, but those situational stressors have got you bent out of shape. Now you're slipping into that sympathetic side: the stress response. Your brain is in a full-on reactionary response, and it's all downhill from here.

None of this stuff is new. What needs to be new is a doubled-down awareness of how your stress is affecting those around you. You—like all of us—live in a community. You may, if you're reading this book, be living in a community that is already stressed to the edge and breaking at the seams. Or you are thinking about how you can help vulnerable people within your community, or other communities. Seemingly small stressors that should be no big deal can be disastrous when the people being stressed have no slack in their lives, so in all these scenarios your stress can have dangerous or destructive repercussions.

Origami Yourself

The first step of this whole process is acknowledging that we all need to change and grow. We all have the ability to get to a place of self-awareness and say, "I don't like this part of myself, and I want to be better." Uncle Will always told us that when "you point one finger at someone, three fingers point back at you." He was illustrating the foolishness of focusing on behavior you can't control and ignoring behavior you can control—your own. This is a hard, hard lesson to absorb. But the reality is other people's behavior is unpredictable and uncertain. No matter how satisfying it is to blame your crap on someone else, it's ultimately futile. Other people are going to do what they're going to do. All you can do is moderate your own response and not give in to the very human temptation to set a jerk straight.

Whenever Andy feels like someone is getting on his nerves or treating him unjustly, he tries to step back and ask himself, *Hold on, Andy, why are you feeling this way? I'm blaming this person for ruining my day, but did that person do this, or am I reacting to this person, and twisting myself into knots all on my own?*

Asking yourself why you are responding to stress in this way can be painful. After all, the reason you are having a stress response is often that some little wound, deep in your past, is getting triggered. And who wants to go there and think about that kind of stuff? But like we said in the last chapter, any kind of deep, transformative work, be it political, personal, or social, is going to trigger you anyway. So you need to be able to interrogate your own response, ask yourself some tough questions, and take care of your own stuff before you start worrying about anyone else's.

Part one of this is taking a look at your "normal" shape. When you ask yourself questions like *Why am I getting bent out of shape? What's the real object that is causing this bent-out-of-shapeness?* there's an assumption in place that that original shape, the one you are being bent out of, is the shape you are supposed to be. But suppose that's not the case. Suppose you are being bent into something better. Can you get comfortable with letting go of that old shape? It's not easy to be a better person. We all fail and f**k up, so how do you acknowledge that and let it move you into something more useful?

The idea of interrogating your behavior and asking big questions about how you are, and why you are the way you are, is a pretty standard concept in the wellness community, but there is something extremely scary about diving deep into feelings for most of the kids and adults we work with. Most kids—adults even—in Baltimore are instinctively rigid, not showing their emotions or feelings. You're not going to tell your buddies your emotional issues in this city because life here has no slack. Showing vulnerability or fear is a dangerous game in a community where things like gang-initiation killings are a regular occurrence. Admitting weakness feels like creating a vulnerability, even in dumb ways, like acknowledging feelings for another person. Andy's friends always apologize for sharing difficult stuff. "Why?" he replies, "I'm your friend. Talk to me." And if they're feeling comfortable, they will. Most of the time they just need to vocalize their hesitation first.

So, make it a practice, if you don't already, to ask yourself all these questions we've mentioned above: *Why am I getting bent out of shape? What's really going on here? Am I mad at these fools, or is this bringing up something old and deep and painful that I need to deal with?* These are the big questions of life, so cut yourself some slack if you struggle to work through them at first.

Learning to Breathe

The very first thing you need to do to begin to shift how you think, how you feel, and how you process and relate to the world, is re-learn to breathe.

We are all born knowing how to breathe, but as life, and its multitude of stressors, pile on, those deep instinctive belly breaths are forgotten, strangled by anxiety and fear, compressed by anger or resentment. In Chapter Eleven we will share techniques for teaching the young people in your life how to use the belly breath to process through trauma and center themselves. But first you need to breathe yourself.

Think of yourself as a baby, lying on your back, arms in that classic baby cactus pose. You breathed perfectly as a baby: You inhaled through your nose and your belly rose, you exhaled out of your nose and your belly fell. Unless you were born into a deeply and violently traumatized family, you probably felt safe, protected, and content in that moment of sleep. You were at peace, and your deep, full breaths reflected this. At some point as you grew older, two things changed: You began to breathe through your mouth rather than your nose, and that sense of safety and peace faded away. Together these two forces—poor breathing and burgeoning trauma—reshaped the trajectory of your life, constricting your soul and hardening your heart.

The Adult Belly Breath Approach

Your nose is three main things: a filter, a heater, and a humidifier.

Your nose hairs filter out the dust, dander, germs, and microbes floating in the air. When you breathe out of your nose, you push these particles off your nose hairs and out of your body. If you breathe through your mouth, you are just taking all the microbes directly into your being.

The heating system comes from the mucous membranes that line our nasal passage. This warms the air up as we breathe in through our nose. This is important, especially if you live in colder climates. If you are a mouth breather and you breathe inside a heated room and then step outside where the climate is colder, you can seize up your bronchus. (You will be wheezing while you're breathing.) This is why it's important to breathe through your nose in order to warm the air up as it goes into your body.

The glands in your face create the moisture for your tears, creating humidity when you breathe in through your nose.

When you breathe in and out of your mouth, you lose these filtering, heating, and humidifying functions. However, it is also almost impossible to take a full, deep breath through your nose, rather than your mouth—so the next stage is learning how to manipulate the diaphragm to improve the quality of your breathing.

The majority of people breathe backward. Rather than expanding their bellies, they pull the air all the way up to the top of their lungs. We call this the Superman breath: Imagine the caped crusader, hands on hips, with his chest fully expanded. It may look powerful, but all his breath is sitting on the tops of his lungs rather than settling into his diaphragm. Our lungs are shaped like teardrops, with most lung capacity down around our bellies. Superman, for all his apparent strength, is only using 10 percent of his lung capacity. Think how many more runaway trains he could stop if he was operating at 100 percent!

In this exercise, we are gonna focus on manipulating your diaphragm to create a vacuum so that the air comes into your nose and is drawn down to your lower lungs. The inhale is extremely important because it helps with bringing oxygen into your bloodstream: When the blood leaves the heart it is like a pristine mountain stream, clean and rich with oxygen. When it returns to the heart it is like sewage water, because the blood has exchanged oxygen for impurities. So we need to take nice, long, deep breaths in order to reoxygenate our blood appropriately.

The exhale is equally as important. Not only does it remove the stale CO_2 that is in our bodies, but it also helps us remove the ruminating thoughts lingering in our mind. These are the thoughts that are not allowing us to be present, popping up when we're trying to focus on the task at hand: *What am I supposed to do? Will I get there in time? Will I have enough money? What am I gonna eat for dinner?*

Remember: The way most of us breathe is "easy." We breathe shallowly, through our mouths, with no thought or awareness. Breathing consciously and fully, like with the belly breath, is physical. It can get tiring at first, but with practice it will get easier and easier. Accept that you may only be belly-breathing for a few minutes a day at first. But really focus on those minutes. If you journal, write down anything you notice or observe from the practice.

The Belly Breath

Now let's try to practice the exercise, which will focus on using our diaphragms.

I invite you to get into a comfortable seated position with your head, neck, and spine aligned, feet grounded on the floor.

I invite you to close your eyes if you feel like doing so. Take your hand and place it on your belly. Remember, all the breathing will be in and out of your nose. Inhale, and imagine the belly is filling up with air like it's a balloon. Really overemphasize it and push your belly out as far as you can. Now exhale through your nose, pulling your belly away from your hand. Imagine that you're trying to touch your belly button to your spine. You'll notice that there has been a space created between your hand and your belly.

Inhale deep, push your belly back out to the measure of your hand so it is now touching your hand. Exhale and pull your belly away from your hand again, creating space. This is how we learn to manipulate our diaphragm in order to fill our lower lungs.

Inhale deep. Belly out to your hand.

Exhale and pull your belly away from your hand, creating that space.

Inhale deep. Belly out to your hand.

Exhale and pull your belly away from your hand, creating that space.

Inhale.

Exhale.

Repeat.

Last breath. Inhale nice and deep. Hold it. And exhale it all out.

Now take three deep breaths on your own. Here you are being a scientist. You are conducting an internal assessment. Take note of how your mind feels. Is it racing or is it calm? Take note of how your body feels. Is it tense or is it relaxed? Know that if you ever wanna feel this way again, all you have to do is take a few of these breaths. When you finish with the final breath you can slowly, slowly blink your eyes open and come back to your senses.

Dizziness and Panic

Now take three deep breaths on your own. Go through your scientific assessment again. Did you notice anything new?

This new way of breathing may make you dizzy and light-headed, so adjust how you sit. Try lying down on your back if necessary, moving up to a seated position as you get used to the practice. If you are sitting on a lot of trauma, and a lot of rigidity, you may get panicky and anxious as the oxygen floods your body. It's OK. Try to ride it out, accepting the feelings that come up. Don't push yourself to keep practicing the breath if the sensations get out of control. You may feel fear, sadness. Some practitioners find the sensations of focusing on their breath overwhelming and start to panic that if they don't consciously keep breathing they will stop breathing altogether. Accept these feelings if they pop up. Go back to your old way of breathing and relax and recenter yourself. It's OK if you can maintain this breath for only a few minutes at a time—or less. Think of the belly breath practice as a crack in the wall that is keeping you imprisoned in your fears, traumas, or anxieties. Work on increasing that almost imperceptible crack every day, without judgment.

Breathwork is the number one tool to manage your stress and keep you mentally, spiritually, and emotionally strong and resilient to keep showing up, honoring your commitments to yourself and others, and staying present. But it's called breath-*work* for a reason. It can be hard. It can feel unbearable at times. Accept that you are taking small steps on a long path. Thank your body for trying.

In addition to breathwork, you need to understand the forces that are keeping you in shape or bending you out of it. Once you are aware of these forces—or *samskaras*—you can begin to change or adapt them. You can ask yourself those big questions—and handle the answers. This awareness practice—grounded in breathwork—is your key to handling your response to situational stuff. If you are aware of how you are responding, you can use your breath, catch those responses, and bring yourself back to your resting place. First, let's look at the habits that are keeping us locked in place.

Samskaras

Kurt Vonnegut said, "I am a human being, not a human doing." He was onto something with this quote, and though it's lost some of its power by being meme-ified and printed on a million coffee mugs, we still regularly drop it into our teaching. Uncle Will used it to remind us that the most meaningful moments in our lives are often those moments where we are flowing, unaware of our brains making a million little choices, and simply existing as the great wash of life and humanity flows around us. If *human doing* is about hitting accomplishments, and being the person you think you should be, *human being* is what happens when those millions of little choices accumulate over the years, becoming our habits. In Sanskrit we call habits samskaras (*sam*: complete and joined together, plus *kara*: action, cause, or doing). All the little rituals of our lives, be they positive (a morning thank-you to God) or negative (those cigarettes you can't shake), join together to weave the fabric of our lives. Those millions of little unconscious choices might not seem like much, but how we spend our days is how we spend our lives.* Human doings might describe their lives in terms of accomplishments, but human beings are the opposite: They find their meaning and their purpose in the way they live in the everydayness of life.

---

* A quote attributed to another wise writer, Annie Dillard.

Our samskaras create habit patterns that form around us: for good and ill. The more you do the same things the more these habits yoke around your true essence or being. We get used to living a certain way—and frankly, life is often quite a mundane existence. So we get caught up with the whole human doing, not human being, aspect of life.

To *be*, you have to start creating new habit patterns. We use diet, exercise, physical poses, and meditation. That is where you start transforming who you are from the inside out. That's how you make true change in your own life, by really analyzing your habits, seeing what is healthy for you and what isn't. Uncle Will used to say the bad habits fall off like scabs. Once you can change the way your mind thinks about what is important in life, you realize that you are the most important thing in your life. If you are mentally, physically, and emotionally healthy, that is when you can start helping others.

You can only change your habits once you become aware of them. Most of the time they are habits that have become instincts. They automatically happen. So you slowly have to get into the routine of denying them. That's when you can begin to change those negative habits. Think of these habits as lengths of thread. Every time you reach for that glass of wine or that cigarette, or flop down on the couch after work, you are winding another length of thread onto the spool. Underneath all those yards and yards of thread—all those thousands of times you've given in to whatever your habits are—is the spool, your true self, unburdened by these habits. But your habits have completely buried your true self. Every time you wind another drink, fight, self-hating thought, or junk-food dinner onto that spool, you wind that habit tighter. The habit grows stronger. Your true self gets buried deeper.

These habits tie you to the physical plane. No matter how much your soul might long to escape to something more than your worldly existence, those habits keep you locked in place, growing more frustrated, more bitter, more defeated.

The repetition of negative habits slowly moves you further and further away from liberating your true self. The worst part of any bad habit is the awareness that you are better than this. That your potential for joy and purpose in life is being throttled. That you are actively sabotaging yourself. The anger and self-loathing are exponential. Every time you wind that habit tighter it grows stronger.

When you deny those habits, they begin to unravel. Think of pulling that end of thread on that spool: Eventually, if you unwind those habit structures enough, your spool, or your true self, will be revealed.

Atman had a couple of friends involved in the drug scene, and they were spiraling out of control. They knew he was into yoga and meditation. Finally, after years of Atman offering to help, they were able to open up enough to ask him, "Can you help us?" Atman had them come over to his house or office and do yoga with him every morning. It helped them get out of that downward spiral and start changing their life for the better. Every time they did yoga they were weakening those habits rather than winding another length of thread onto their spool. Yoga gave them those small moments of pause. It broke the familiarity and ease of their habits.

We've worked with hundreds of young kids—ten, eleven years old—who have wound the thread of anger so tightly around their true selves that it is the only response they have to anxiety, fear, sadness, or deprivation. When they become aware of this habit, they learn that they can deny it. They can refuse to wind that thread tighter.

Laila, twenty, who you met in Chapter Five, grew up in a stressed family on the west side of Baltimore. Like most of our other kids, she had a lot of anger and fear. Laila uses crystals, meditation, a bubble bath, or a cup of tea to reset herself, and pull herself out of tough times. By making a ritual around her self-care, she is creating a positive habit, one that actively keeps her from winding that habitual, instinctive anger tighter.

Here's another thing: it's possible to deny your habits and partly unwind them, only to succumb to them again. Laila used the practice throughout her teens: "When the practice was in my life, I noticed I was lighter. I could handle things well. I could take situations and turn them around. Once I stopped them I felt like I was at a standstill, stuck. Losing interests, doubting myself. Not wanting to complete something. But once I stepped in and restarted my breathing and meditation . . . it makes you feel better." You may wind and unwind for years, struggling to deny your habits, succumbing to old instincts. If this is the case, first, be easy on yourself. Habits, especially habits that serve the interests of powerful industries like fast food or alcohol, are designed to be almost impossible to break. Second, understand you may have to make bigger changes to truly free yourself from them.

Part of samskara is learning to physically, emotionally, and mentally remove yourself from those actions that no longer work for you. For Atman's friends, this required getting distance from their drug habits *and* their friends and family who were enabling or participating in those habits. Basically, they had to walk away from their entire support system in order to turn their lives around. In order to help these people, we teach them bhakti yoga, or the practice of loving people from a distance. If you can't be around someone physically, that doesn't limit the love you can give them.

Uncle Will taught us the practice of going into your heart center: Get a physical picture of the person you want to love, and see them in your light. You see their physical image fading away. Imagine your light and their light meeting and merging into one light. Stay there for a while and really let yourself feel it. This practice is a way deeper form of love than just being physically around them.

A lot of the pain of love comes from falling in love rather than rising in love. Smit used to say that you've got to rise in love because a fall is a fall is a fall is a fall. Smit was talking about romantic relationships, but this holds true for all kinds of intense emotional bonds. Sometimes you have to separate yourself from your friends, your neighborhood, even your family, just to stay mentally and emotionally well and happy. The love you feel for them drags you down, puts you in danger, and derails whatever progress you've made in your life. It sucks. Because you still love them, and you remember all the times they had your back or supported you in tight spots. But, like Smit said, you have to rise in love, not fall.

Next-Level Breath

Breathing is the first thing we introduce adults to, and frankly we find that most adults use the breathing more than the poses or the mantras. Breathwork is a science, but like Will always said, you are the scientist. So conduct your own experiments. Try different types of breathing, as listed below. Practice breathing lying down or standing up. Play music. Sit outdoors if you normally sit indoors. Remember, the best breathwork practice is the one you do, so try these different techniques to find one that works best for you.

Ujjayi Breath

Ujjayi improves digestion, increases body temperature, and helps with stress reduction, focus, and clearing the mind. It's like pushing the reset button on your mind when your thoughts are racing at a mile a minute. It helps with insomnia because when you retain the breath you lock your chin to your chest. The chin compresses the carotid sinuses on either side of the artery that supplies the brain with blood. This helps slow your heart rate, which induces a state of relaxation. Ujjayi practice can heal trauma: In communities that deal with firsthand trauma, secondary trauma, or even intergenerational trauma, individuals' vagus nerves (the connection of the mind and body, also responsible for threat perception) are not firing properly. Because of this, people from traumatized communities view everyone and everything as a threat. However, the sound of the breath activates the vagus nerve, calming the practitioner and lessening their sense of imminent danger.

There are three parts to the breath: an inhalation, retention, and exhalation. On the inhale and exhale, which are in and out of your nose, make the breath audible. Do this by partially closing your glottis. If you don't know how to do that, we have a tip for you: Hold your hand up to your mouth, and exhale into your hand like you are fogging up a mirror. Keep breathing out of your mouth like you are fogging up a mirror, then after a second, close your lips and continue the breath out of your nose. Finally, inhale the same way. That will make the breath audible. (Remember that both the inhale and exhale are through the nose; we just had you breathe out of your mouth so you can grasp the concept of closing your glottis.) Now that you know how to make the breath audible, we can jump into the practice. Inhale long, slow, deep, and audibly through your nose, then drop your chin to your chest and retain the breath for as long as you comfortably can. Finally, exhale through your nose with a long, slow, deep, audible breath, and repeat.

Alternate Nostril Breath

Until we really started studying with Uncle Will, we had no idea how amazing our nostrils were. Our left nostril was lunar and calming; our right nostril was solar and energizing. And there was such a short period of time during the day when we used them both equally. Most of the time one was dominant: ideally the right nostril during the day and the left nostril at night. Exhale onto your hand and see for yourself. Alternate nostril breathing can be done in three different ways. One boosts your energy, the other calms you down, and the last one brings balance. We are going to focus on the one that brings you balance. The easiest way to practice is by using the thumb and index finger on your right hand. Plug your right nostril with your thumb and inhale deeply though your left nostril. Plug both nostrils and hold for a couple seconds. Release the thumb and exhale through the right nostril. Then inhale back in through the right nostril. Plug both nostrils and hold for a few seconds. Then release the index finger and exhale through the left nostril. That is one complete cycle of alternate nostril breathing. Repeat that at least ten times. It will help balance your energy, focus the mind, and reduce stress and anxiety.

If you want to boost your energy, simply inhale through the left nostril, plug both nostrils, then exhale through the right, and repeat that for at least twelve breaths.

If you want to calm yourself down, it's the opposite, inhaling through the left and exhaling through the right.

When we were in the mountains of North Carolina with Uncle Will, he got us to prove this to ourselves. (Always wanting us to be scientists.) We did five minutes of the breath of fire through our right nostril and we were all up for the entire night, no one slept at all.

When Ali got home and told his son Asuman this story, Asuman said, "Dad, why didn't you all just do breath of fire through your left nostril to balance it out so you could go to sleep?" Children can be our greatest teachers if we listen.

Taco Breath

This breathing exercise has a multitude of benefits for the practitioner. It is great for bringing cool, moist air into the body, which assists with calming down hot-headed individuals, fevers, and decreasing body temperature. It also keeps your skin nice and young, giving it a glow, and helps with arthritis and stomach aches. If you have a stomach problem, when you do the breath, eventually you will have a bitter taste on your tongue; this is the sickness coming out. By the time your tongue goes back to its normal taste, you should feel better.

Curl your tongue and stick it out past your lips. Inhale through your curled tongue like it is a straw. Then swallow the breath like you were drinking it down. Pause for a second or two, and then exhale through your nose. Repeat as needed.

Kapalbhati: Breath of Fire

Atman used to have asthma and he'd have to carry around an inhaler. Eventually Will encouraged him to try to relieve his asthma with the breath of fire. This breath expands lung capacity, keeps bronchial tubes clear, and helps detoxify the blood. Now Atman uses the breath of fire, or *kapalbhati*, as asthmatic maintenance. Even better, regular practice gets him on an alpha rhythm and helps create a protective aura around the body on an energetic level. To practice, sit upright and inhale and exhale in a fast, forceful rhythm at roughly three breaths per second. Exhales and inhales should be the same length. Think of the breath snapping through your body like a force of nature. Practice as long as feels good to you.

Transitional Breathing Exercise

One final breathwork practice that we recommend is the transitional practice. The reality is that we are living lives filled with stress that can overflow from one container ("work," perhaps) to another ("home" or "my kids"). Try this practice to give yourself a brief reset and to keep stress in one part of your life from affecting another.

This practice is hugely beneficial if you are working with traumatized children. You need a buffer between the demands and stressors of your private life and the life you are living with the children in your care. Use this transitional breathing exercise to add a sense of ritual and mindfulness as you move between these different worlds.

Twice a day, while sitting in your car, or on the bus, or in any place of transition between home and work, do fifteen uj-jayi, or stress, breaths. These will help you take whatever you've accumulated at home and leave it in the car and be present for your coworkers. And then the same thing when you go back home. When you get into the driveway, or on the bus, or before you walk through the door, take fifteen stress breaths so you can be present when you get home.

Every morning, before you leave your room or get your kids up, do five sun salutations; if you're not familiar with this sequence, you can watch YouTube videos to follow along online. These will make sure your whole body is awake and your circulation is flowing and your energy level gets up.

The stress breath is for your mind; the sun salutation is for your body. If you do nothing else, do these.

CHAPTER EIGHT

Meditation

Our personal meditation practices look nothing like what we teach in school; in fact, there is a profound disparity between how we teach yoga and how we practice it. At home, we use mantras (sounds and vibrations) and mudras (hand positions and gestures) all the time. Uncle Will described mantras as formulas. We picture them as individual letters and vibrations brought together to create words/ phrases that invoke power. As for mudras, think of them as seals that connect circuits of energy. The energy that flows out through your hands can be coupled like electricity to elicit certain things (knowledge, communication, health, etc.) in oneself. These ideas are the heart of our practice: at home or with adults outside of the school system, we talk about deities, energies, and the nature of the universe. We have to leave these ideas behind once we enter school. In the classroom, we don't talk about meditation, or mantras, or chakras. Instead, we guide kids through short periods of silent reflection, bending and stretching for relaxation and physical health, and breathwork for relaxation and de-escalation of angry thoughts and actions.

Even when we know that some of our older kids have familiarity with ideas like energy, or have heard Sanskrit terms, we keep it out of the classroom. We don't share our knowledge about energy or the universe. This isn't our choice, but it's the rules of the game when you're working in the school system. And hey, we aren't really complaining. So long as the school system applies this logic uniformly—and keeps religious or fundamentalist dogma out of our kids' schools—we're OK with it, even as the limitations on language frustrate us. But this is our book, and no one except us gets a say. In this chapter we are going to go deep with the secrets of mantras, and everything Uncle Will shared with us. We'll soon tell you about how those mantras have literally saved our lives (no metaphor when you are living in the neighborhood during gang initiation season). But first, let's meditate.

Mindfulness Practices for Adults and Children

We use a variety of meditations and mindfulness practices, for ourselves, for other adults, and for children. Here's the thing about meditation and mindfulness: There's no right way to do it. Neither is there a "wrong" way. Meditation, like any other form of mental, physical, or emotional practice, works if it works for you. A relaxation practice that puts an adult into a blissed-out state might actively panic or upset a traumatized child. So, as Uncle Will always told us, "Be a scientist." Try different practices, and see what shines a light in your soul, or the soul of your child or children in your care.

Remember: We don't tell people what position to meditate in. Let your meditators get comfortable in any way that suits them. You can lie down or sit in the chair or even pace.

Meditation is always guided, not just empty space. *Empty, quiet space gives room for trauma to pop up.* Some kids will be actively re-traumatized by sitting with their own thoughts for ten minutes. (Remember, many people go to great lengths to avoid being with their own thoughts for very legitimate reasons. Don't assume that silent meditation is better than guided meditation just because that's what you learned early on. Help your meditators access the practice in the safest and most positive way for them.) *Let your meditators know that things that are coming up are coming up to be released, because they created space for it. Those feelings aren't coming up to attack them.*

Remember too that these kids live in environments where focus is literally impossible: There are multiple people crowded in a few small rooms. The TV is always on. It's never quiet. They may never have had a chance to focus or draw a peaceful breath. Mindfulness is going to feel strange at best, frightening and potentially dangerous at worst. So start slow, undersell the process (no Sanskrit words; keep language simple and centered around relaxation), and understand if your child is struggling with sitting still.

Remember that all forms of yoga are a personal practice. You can keep it as simple as guiding someone to focus on their breath and feel their stomach rising and falling. A simple mindfulness script will include variations on this: *Listen to your breath, pay attention to the inhale and the exhale because they make two different sounds. Feel the rise and fall of your belly. Feel the breath expanding your belly like a balloon.*

And finally, remember that love is everything. If the kids feel your love, your kindness, your humor, and your empathy, they will respond. If you're not in a loving frame of mind, if you're actively pissed off or having a bad day, make sure you center and reboot yourself before you jump in with the kids. Do the transitional breathing exercise. Go for a fast walk around the block. Do whatever can knock that annoyance out of you and shift your frame of mind. Try giving yourself some compassion and acceptance. Ideally you have a partner in this and can take turns leading the kids. If not, sit in a room for a few minutes, and use the variation of the loving kindness mantra to help get you back to a more neutral or positive place.

Guided Meditation Scripts

Breath Meditation

Get into whatever position or pose is most comfortable for you.

Begin by breathing deeply at a comfortable, relaxed rate. Something you can get going and forget about, putting no extra effort into.

First, we are going to focus on how our breath feels. Pull your sense of feeling away from your body and take notice of how the breath feels going in and out of your nose and the rising and falling of your belly. You no longer feel the weight of the clothes on your skin or your body on the chair or your feet on the ground. All you feel is the breath going in and out.

If you happen to get distracted by a thought, sound, or sensation, don't worry about it. Recognize the distraction, let it pass, and return your attention back to the breath and how it feels.

Next, we are going to focus on how our breath sounds. Pull your sense of hearing to the breath. Start to ignore any outside noises, and only hear the breath. Again, if you happen to get distracted by a thought, sound, or sensation, don't worry about it. Recognize the distraction, let it pass, and return your attention back to the breath and how it sounds.

The last part is centering your mind on the breath. Every time a thought pops into your head, recognize it, let it pass, then bring your mind back to the breath. Repeat this process until your mind is calm and relaxed as well.

Keep practicing this for five minutes or so, longer if you are feeling it. The goal is to completely fall into the meditation, but don't stress if the kids are squirming or unsettled. Remind your child (or yourself) that relaxation is a work in progress.

Variation of Loving Kindness Practice

In this human experience, it's just human nature to love other people before you love yourself, and to take care of other people before you take care of yourself, and that leads to burnout, jealousy, resentment, and a lot of other negative emotions. This practice is all about starting with your inner foundation full of self-love, and taking care of yourself, which makes it easier to love and to take care of others going forward, without burning yourself out. Try reading this aloud as a guided meditation or simply practicing it yourself. Either way it is a powerful tool to rewire the way you or your students think and feel about themselves and others.

If you are sitting in a chair, make sure your feet are flat on the ground; back, neck, and head are aligned. (If you are lying down, make sure your back, neck, and head are aligned, ankles are uncrossed, and arms are by your side, palms facing the ceiling.) If you feel comfortable enough, you can close your eyes. If you don't feel comfortable enough, you can soften your gaze, closing your eyes most of the way, or you can leave your eyes open and just focus on a point. If you feel comfortable enough, we suggest you close your eyes because this limits distractions.

Start off by taking three long, slow, deep breaths, in and out through your nose. Then after the third deep breath, just begin to breathe naturally, don't put any effort into it, just make sure you are breathing in and out through your nose. Now begin to use your imagination: with every inhale feel and see yourself pulling in all the positivity that the earth has to offer you into your body with the breath, whatever that looks and feels like to you. Feel and see that as you inhale. With every exhale feel and see yourself pushing out all the negativity: all the stress and anger, resentment and jealousy, sicknesses and ailments. See them leave your body with the outbreath; once again, whatever that looks and feels like to you, feel and see that with every outbreath.

Continue this for a couple of minutes. Distractions can arise when you try to meditate, or do a silent reflection, or a variation of a loving kindness practice, just like in life. If you do get distracted, have empathy toward yourself, understanding that this is the nature of the human mind. Just acknowledge the distraction, whether it is a thought, sound, or sensation, don't fight with it, let it pass naturally, then anchor yourself back with the breath, and with every inhale pulling in the positivity from the earth, with every exhale pushing out the negativity from within.

Next, we will again use our imaginations, and with every inhale we will pull in the healing oxygen from the trees, plants, and bodies of water and see and feel it energize and replenish our internal muscles, bones, and organs. With every exhale, push out all the stale carbon dioxide, feeding the trees and plants that gave us oxygen. Whatever that looks and feels like to you, just feel and see that as you breathe. There is no right or wrong with this practice, there just is. Continue for a couple of minutes. This practice is all about extending the time or breaths that you can remain focused. If you do lose focus after three breaths, once again have empathy toward yourself, understanding that this is the nature of the human mind. Acknowledge the distractions, let them pass, then try to get four breaths, then five breaths. Once again it's all about extending the amount of time or number of breaths that you can remain focused, and it's less of a battle with yourself than it is a play, but definitely try to extend the time or breaths that you remain focused.

Now you are focused on, with every inhale, bringing in the healing oxygen with every breath energizing your muscles, bones, and organs, and with every exhale pushing out the stale carbon dioxide, feeding the trees and plants that gave us oxygen. Next, focus on all those people you love, whether it's family or friends, no matter how far away they live, no matter if they are living or not—love knows no boundaries—so with your breath, send your loved ones love with your breath, whatever that looks and feels like to you, feel and see that as you breathe.

Continue for a couple of minutes. Next, focus on those people who stress you out or make you angry, whether it's family, friends, coworkers or clients (if you're working with students, you can say "teachers or classmates" instead of "coworkers or clients"), people in your community, or politicians, we are going to send them love too. Even though they stress you out or make you angry, they probably need love more than anyone, and we know that whatever you put out there, it comes back tenfold, so always lead with love.

So once again, with your breath send love to those people who stress you out or make you angry, love with your breath. This is a great way to evict people from renting space in your mind, or in other words, a release.

Continue this for a couple of minutes. You have now sent love to people who you love, and to people who stress you out. Now it's time to send love to the most important person in your life, and that's yourself.

Once again, if you start with your inner foundation full of self-love, and taking care of yourself, it makes it that much easier to love and take care of others going forward without burning yourself out. So with your breath, send yourself love with the breath, whatever that looks and feels like to you, feel and see that as you breathe. Continue for a few minutes. You are going to use your imagination again, and this time with your breath, you are going to send love to Mother Earth and all that resides within—animals, plants, humans, inanimate objects—anything at all that resides within Mother Earth, and Mother Earth herself, we are sending love with our breath, whatever that looks and feels like to you, feel and see that as you breathe. Continue for a couple of minutes.

Then slowly bring yourself out of the practice. If your eyes are closed, keep them closed, and start wiggling your fingers and toes, then roll your ankles and wrists, then do a neck roll both ways. Next, slowly, slowly blink your eyes open and come back to your senses.

The beauty of this practice is not only do you fill yourself up with love of self, but it actively allows your brain to re-wire itself, a process called neuroplasticity, in real time. We have had the pleasure to share space with renowned neuroscientists like Richie Davidson, Dan Siegel, and Bessel van der Kolk, and they talk about the fact that the brain can rewire itself with healthy habits and other contemplative practices.

Our students prove this. We have students who do not know how to peacefully resolve conflicts, so they resolve them with their fists, but when they practice sending love to the people who are stressing them out or making them angry, this anger transforms. Instead of being easily triggered by others, our students adapt to sending those people love and evicting them from that rented space in their minds. It doesn't happen overnight, but it does happen, and it's so empowering to these people after they make that transformation because it helps them respond, instead of react, to adverse situations.

Next Thought Meditation

After growing up meditating as children, Ali and Atman's meditation practice stopped after their parents' divorce. Uncle Will knew he was pretty much starting from scratch with their practice. The first meditation he showed them was the next thought meditation. Most people fight with their minds during their meditation practice and try to block out thoughts; this has the opposite effect and actually makes more thoughts come. The mind has natural stillness there; you just have to know where to find it. Sit in a meditative posture with your back, neck, and head aligned.

Begin by doing deep rhythmic breathing.

With each breath feel yourself becoming more and more relaxed.

Now that you are relaxed, allow your breathing to slow to a nice, easy, natural rate, one that is effortless and just goes on its own.

Now bring your focus to your mind. You are going to start by watching the thoughts that are flowing through your mind. Watch them like you were watching a movie or TV show. Don't judge them or take ownership of them, just be the witness and watch them. Do this for a couple of minutes.

After doing this for a couple of minutes, whatever thought is in your mind, allow it to reach completion, then watch for the next thought to form. If another thought pops up, see that one, without ownership or judgment, let it pass, and then watch for the next thought to form. Just keep repeating that process. A thought arises, you see it without ownership or judgment, let it pass, and watch for the next thought. Just keep watching for the next thought.

Do this for a few minutes, then gradually bring yourself out of the practice.

The first time Ali did this practice, he walked over to Uncle Will with a confused look on his face and said, "Uncle Will, I think I broke the meditation."

Uncle Will said, "What?"

Ali repeated, "I think I broke the meditation, Uncle Will."

Uncle Will started laughing and said, "How the hell can you break a meditation?"

Ali said, "Well, I was watching my thoughts and then when it came to an end there was nothing there, it was an empty space. So I put a thought there because there should have been a thought in my mind. Then I watched that one to the end, and when I watched for the next thought there was a blank space again."

Uncle Will, still laughing, said, "That's what was supposed to happen. There is space between your thoughts; most people just don't know it's there. When you watch your mind, your mind is like, 'Oh shit, he's paying attention' and freezes up and gets still."

Ali smiled and said, "Ooooooooh!"

When most people do this practice, that's what happens. They disrupt their own mental stillness by inserting thoughts into that stillness because they are used to thoughts being there. So embrace the stillness when you find it. Once you find it, you can cultivate it, and the stillness will get longer and longer.

Mindful Walking

Sitting or lying still can be almost impossible for some traumatized people. What feels relaxing to you can feel threatening and stressful to them. So another mindfulness practice that might work better is mindful walking. Since the practitioner is active, they feel less vulnerable: their fight-or-flight response isn't kicking in automatically, and they have a better chance of dropping in and finding some peace and relaxation.

Mindful walking is exactly like it sounds: being mindful while you are walking. Staying present, not letting your mind wander, and paying attention to your breath and senses as you take each step.

Start by taking a few deep breaths to center yourself. Now begin walking at a pace that is comfortable for you, and with each step notice each of your senses. Notice what you feel, what you see, what you smell, what you hear, and even what you taste. Give yourself time to connect with each of your senses as you are walking. Then take notice of which senses you are most connected to and which senses you are least connected to.

Take a few deep breaths to close the process. If you are working with a group, bring them back together to share about their experiences.

This practice is ideal for outdoor spaces: If you are outside with your group, tell them to space themselves out so that they are not too close to anyone. If indoors is all you got, it can still work.

If you are working with an indoor space, instruct the students to line up around the perimeter of the room, all facing the same direction, with about five feet of free space in front of and behind them. Less than that if the room you are in is not that big. If the room is not large enough for this, have the students line up across the room with at least an arm's length of space on either side of them, and their mindful walking can be done straight across, then they can turn and walk back, going back and forth across the room.

You can also challenge your students to see how many steps they can take while being connected to all five of their senses.

CHAPTER NINE

Mantras and Mudras

Talking to God

Uncle Will used to tell us how prayer and meditation are two parts of the same conversation. He'd remind us of the classic meditation saying:

Prayer is asking for something.

Meditation is listening to the god or the universe within you answer back.

Achariya Peter added to this idea. He used to tell us that you should never go into your prayer begging for anything. Abundance is your birthright because you are one with God/the universe. When yogis pray, we are demanding because we know abundance is what we are and what we deserve.

We may have grown up steeped in spirituality, but we were surrounded by friends and family who had a more traditional background at Methodist churches. Prayer was part of our community life, even if we ourselves never prayed in the way traditional churchgoers did. Smitty remembered the church of his childhood being lovingly conservative, discouraging questions, repeating parables and platitudes like *God moves in mysterious ways*. This didn't sit right with him or Will. They wondered how this omniscient, omnipotent, and omnipresent arthropod in the sky could be so oblivious and uncaring to the struggles of our community. They longed for communion with a deity who was connected to them in a more honest, human, and personal way, and they began to find it with the study of yoga. Still, there was good stuff in the Bible, and they began to unearth ideas and elements from it that pointed toward a more all-encompassing and nonjudgmental spirituality.

Later, Andy experienced something similar in the Catholic Church. He remembers asking his CCD (Confraternity of Christian Doctrine, Catholic religious education) teacher, "If God made everything, who made God?" His teacher told him that he wasn't supposed to ask those types of questions. From that day on, Andy was always skeptical of the church. Eventually he and his siblings stopped attending. Even though part of them longed for that sense of connection with the unknown, there was no room for inquisitive minds within the walls of Catholicism.

Even though conventional Christianity or Catholicism wasn't Smit's or Will's or Andy's (or any of our) bag, there is still wisdom and clues within it:

> To the angel of the church in Laodicea write: These are the words of the Amen, the faithful and true witness, the ruler of God's creation. (Revelation 3:14)

In the beginning was the Word, and the Word was with God, and the Word was God. He was with God in the beginning. Through him all things were made; without him nothing was made that has been made. In him was life, and that life was the light of all mankind. The light shines in the darkness, and the darkness has not overcome it. (John 1:1–5)

Later, Will and Smit (and eventually the three of us) read the Sama Veda:

The essence of all beings is the earth; the essence of the earth is water; the essence of water is plants; the essence of plants, man; the essence of man, speech; the essence of speech, the Rig-veda; the essence of the Rig-veda, the Sama-veda; the essence of the Sama-veda, the Udgitha (which is Om).

As we learned with our spiritual mentors, we started to realize that whether you say *Amen*, *Shalom*, *Om Amun-Ra*, or *As-salamu alaikum*, you are tapping into something that all major religions understand: the power of a specific vibration, om.

Om represents the creator, the sustainer, and the destroyer. It's all-inclusive. And it works. There is an asshole born every minute of the day: om is your protective shield, keeping that person's shit off you and dissipating it throughout the universe rather than bouncing it back on the offenders. We've omed our way through the most frustrating, infuriating, dangerous, and dispiriting moments of our lives. Even now, we'll be dealing with assholes throughout the day and muttering to ourselves, "This m****rf****r." (Let's be real, some of the time that full *m****rf****r* is out of our mouths before we catch it.) But more often our brain reroutes to *om*. We surround ourselves with the meditation, and that funky *f**k 'em* thought evaporates. This is powerful when you're dealing with simple stressors. It's vastly more powerful when you are trying to avoid the kind of stressors you're dealing with in West Baltimore. You'll read more about that in a moment.

You can incorporate that om vibration into other words: *amen* or *shalom*, for instance. (Part of the reason why some Christians' fear of yoga makes no sense: Rebrand it however you want, just work that om sound in somewhere. You say it at the end of every prayer anyway!) You can even find some personal tweak on the sound that works for you. These simple om-based sounds work because they are rocket ships to your higher self, pulling you out of the mundane, f**ked-up shit. Instead of cursing people out, you can catch that thought before it can fully construct, and jump into om instead.

This is some deep stuff. It's one thing to ask God to be present in your life; it's another to be able to hear God and literally converse with her. For us, the key to communicating with God is mantras. Om is the big one, the Jedi Knight of mantras. It recognizes the ultimate reality, the oneness of the universe. It's the cosmic sound of the Big Bang giving birth to the universe, the essence of everything. It's the sound of a scared kid centering herself while her parents fight. It's the primordial everything. It's three dudes jamming at 4:00 a.m. in Baltimore. Om is what ties it all together.

Om is what makes up and creates all. But we make sure to go beyond its creative power and mention its ability of sustentation and destruction. We've always imagined it as being like a cord on an instrument. Before the universe was formed, this cord was completely still and all was completely one. Then the cord was strummed and that vibration created everything. Om always gets props for creating but doesn't get enough credit for sustaining and destroying, which are equally important. When we think of om we think of God. We think of the soul. The infinite. All of which are me. My real self. Uncle Will would describe om as a rocket ship that could quickly take your consciousness deeper into the light. It is the universal vibration that everything in the universe gives off, so it connects with and to everything.

You've probably chanted om at yoga class or in your own practice. Perhaps you built on that and learned Transcendental or Vedic meditation (maybe being given a mantra that you were told to never share with another person or say out loud). Maybe you've logged into an app and been guided through a quick meditation built around om or another simple sound. Either way, we are guessing you found a singular mantra that you use all the time, or a small group of mantras that you occasionally vary for different situations. This makes us wonder: *How do you have a discussion with God if you only have one or two things to say?*

Uncle Will was in a constant conversation with his own personal deity. He saw his God everywhere. They jammed together, even during the prosaic moments of his life. He felt the experience of knowing God, and being loved by God, so deeply, that he wanted everyone else to have the same profound and intimate knowledge. Few things made Will happier than seeing other people have that moment of connection. Uncle

Will *loved* TV. One day we walked in and he was watching *Live! With Regis and Kathie Lee*. He was ecstatic: They'd just run a segment on meditation, and Regis, playing the fool as always, had chanted a few quick oms. Uncle Will was beside himself with excitement. "Regis was talking about mantras and he was saying 'om, om, om, om' over and over again. After a minute he had to close his eyes and catch himself. You could see something happened, even though he was only doing it for laughs. See, the mantras work!" And this was core to his belief system. Mantras are formulas, the same as anything you might learn in a physics or chemistry class. It doesn't matter if you fully believe in them; if you practice them they are going to work.

Uncle Will also taught us that meditation isn't hard work. Early in his practice, Ali read a book called *Man's Eternal Quest*. This book said that once a week you were supposed to meditate for six hours a day. One day Ali tried it and was physically exhausted when he was done. The next day he went to talk to Uncle Will about it, and Will chuckled and said, "Man, if you don't come out of your meditation feeling refreshed and rested, you aren't doing it right. The Light recharges you. Stop spending so much time trying to go inward the whole time and experience the levels of bliss where you are, then go a little deeper and feel that, then a little deeper and feel that. The bliss is unlimited; you will never run out or hit the end of it. And when you feel the bliss, don't grab onto it too tight, you will lose the vibe. Lightly connect to it, that's the key." That one conversation changed Ali's meditation practice and the way he would teach it for the rest of his life.

What Are Mantras and Mudras?

There are a lot of misconceptions about mantras—people often think that anytime you repeat a phrase over and over again it's a mantra. But a mantra and an affirmation are two totally different things. You can tell yourself *My mantra for the week is going to be self-love or to be more loving to others.* Now, that's cool to believe, and cool to have in your mind, but that is not a mantra. Instead, think of a mantra as a combination of syllables and sounds that lead to spiritual liberation. The word *mantra* comes from *man* and *tra*, or "mind"/consciousness and freedom/protection. So you are literally freeing your mind and protecting your concentration from all those worldly things. Most people think they are just sounds you repeat, but they are more than that.

Mudras are ways to harness the energy that is constantly flowing within you and through you. By closing circuits with your hands or your tongue in certain ways you can use that energy to help you along your path, bring certain things into your life, and heal you on many levels.

The first mantra Ali and Atman were introduced to was om mantra—Smit would make us meditate in the morning or at Sunday school. We didn't even realize it was a meditation, it was just something our dad made us do before we could go out and play with the other kids. When we started studying with Uncle Will it was more physical, like kriyas, kundalini, and breathing practices. But it eventually became more subtle. Will taught us the mantra to remove all obstacles and the mantra to help all suffering souls. After hours of breathing and chanting we'd be itching to get to the real stuff. We'd ask him, "Yo, are we going to hit the mat?" And he'd tell us, "Nah, we are doing yoga right now."

All the while, Will was having his ongoing conversations with his own internal deity. We kind of assumed he had it all down, but no, he would constantly throw more mantras at us. He was a scientist: keen to experiment with different sounds and vibrations and see how they affected us and the world around us. As he shared his discoveries, we adopted them, using them in our everyday lives and reporting back our experiences. For years we continued like this: Uncle Will deepening his knowledge, and us trying it out in the real world.

Every few days we'd head over to Will's to download some vibes and catch up with him. We'd squeeze around the kitchen table and Uncle Will would tell us about the new mantras his God had shared with him. Then he'd teach those mantras to us. As the evening wore on, it would transform into mantra jam sessions. Uncle Will had always wanted to be a jazz singer. He loved music and he loved singing, so late at night, when he was sharing some new language down-loaded straight from his own personal inner God, and he was tapping out a staccato jazz rhythm on a handheld drum, it was a jam.

To this day, when we hear the mantras we hear them the way Uncle Will would say them, and we still hear his voice laughing and loving us into a fuller understanding of the practice. When we first started chanting om we'd do it really long: "Oooooooooooommmmmmmm." He said, "Y'all don't have to make it so long. You can do it short." And he'd grab that drum and start to bop it out in double time: "Om! Om!

Om! Om! Om! Om! Come on, everyone up!" Suddenly all four of us, no doubt buzzing a little to begin with on Crown and Heineken, would be colliding into each other as we danced around the table. That was Will: In the midst of true spiritual teachings he'd have you doing the Aunt Viv along with the lion breath.

Mantras

The older sciences say that you have to say or hear mantras at the correct vibration, but we think that is out of date. Will's mantras sounded like he was singing jazz music: It wasn't the way they were written. We purposefully don't share our mantras in the written form unless we really, really have to (and we will, in a few pages, since this is a book!). Mantras come alive when they are used. Simply reading one on the page doesn't convey the magic contained within it. Whether you say it out loud, sing it, or recite it internally is up to you. Andy can rap for days, but his singing voice leaves something to be desired, so you'll never hear him say them out loud. That works for him. Ali mentally vibrates the mantras, Atman chants out loud. That works for them.

And frankly, we don't love the way a lot of mantras are played to that kind of drippy spa instrumental music. We are hip-hop fans. We want to hear mantras set to hip-hop instrumentals. Ali has a Pandora station he's been working on for years: J Dilla the Greatest Radio—it's equally good for some soulful mantras or a Saturday night pregaming jam (back when he used to go out more than once every few weeks and had the energy to pregame, that is).

Ali has tried many types of music from all over the world, but hip-hop speaks to his soul. He's tried to chant over his favorite hip-hop artists' songs (Nas, Biggie, Mobb Deep, A Tribe Called Quest, De La Soul), but he gets caught up in the artistry of their lyrics and the mantras slip away.

A few years back we were at 13.5% Wine Bar in Hamden having some beers. One of the bartenders was playing this station in the bar and Ali asked her what it was because the combination of instrumentals was amazing. When he listened to it a couple of days later, it just spoke to his soul as mantra music. So he spent like a month perfecting it with thumbs-ups and thumbs-downs and had his own personal perfect mantra station.

So long as you are coming from a place of love and happiness and your light, you are going to get the effect of the mantra. Be a scientist and investigate what works for you. You might not like hip-hop instrumentals, but we love them. You might like Taylor Swift instrumentals. Whatever! Just try something out. We're not precious about intonation either.

The Payoff

All meditators are slowly walking toward an experience called *samadhi*. Samadhi is the moment when a yogi is able to see their soul as spirit and fully feel the divine ecstasy of being completely at one with cosmic consciousness. It is the closest you come to stepping outside of your body while still residing within it. Great yogis can reach samadhi in the meditative state. There, they are united with all the universal energy, wisdom, and knowledge within them. While they are in this state, they receive mantras and bring them back to help humanity. Samadhi is regarded as the final stage, at which union with the divine is reached (before or at death). Meditators can also receive mantras in a state called *turiya*. That's like the superconscious state beyond deep sleep.

It makes sense to us, because we don't think that the human mind can come up with those combinations of sounds that have these effects on spiritual life and physical life and manifesting things in your life.

There's something more to mantras than the human mind just throwing things together, and there is plenty of neurological science behind why you should practice these. The recitation in the left hemisphere of your brain creates positive emotions. The intonation—changing the sound of the mantras as you sing it—affects the right hemisphere, decreasing negativity.

Research has shown that chanting a mantra can quiet the default mode network (the part of the brain that is active when we are not focused on outward activities or thoughts, creating the sense of being distracted or unfocused).[1] When the default mode is quieted, it allows for a sense of calm and centeredness. We (and most meditators) say, well, yes, of course. But we built upon these scientific discoveries. For us, the energy and vibration behind the mantra are what affects the physical body, depending on the mantra you use. Whereas most research says that the mantra itself doesn't matter, we disagree (and we would love to see further research on the powers of individual mantras). After all, our teacher, Uncle Will, believed that understanding mantras would allow you to have a true conversation with God.

Ganesha: The Protective Shield

Once we'd all settled down from dancing and chanting, Will would reinforce the need to *be a scientist. Find out what works for you.* A mantra that changes one person's life might be meaningless to another. Find the mantras that grab hold of you and don't let go. Make them sing. Uncle Will would tell us, "You've got to funk up the mantra." We'd be in there with our friend Max beatboxing and our friend Tron or Uncle Will's son Oba breaking out some random instrument. Before we'd know it the sun was coming up, and it would be time to go to work, but we were still flying high on an astral plane light-years away from our jobs and regular lives. For years we focused on learning more and more mantras and incorporating them into our lives.

Here's the thing. While we were having monster all-night mantra jams in Uncle Will's kitchen, sitting around the table, Uncle Will funking the mantras up, the real world was still out there. We were living in one of the most violent blocks in America. Outside we'd hear gunshots and sirens and shouts. The adults slammed front doors shut while the kids took off running through the alley as they retreated from the BPD or other gangs. The walls of the kitchen would light up with red and blue as the cops rounded up suspects, even while we were deep into a mantra vibe. There was nothing peaceful about it. So when we say meditation and mantras were lifesaving, we don't mean in some #blessed way.

We mean they were *literally* lifesaving.

Atman had a music studio in his house. He had to be careful about who he let in to use it. The local gangs had a strict initiation process. You want to join, you have to kill someone or get jumped in.

Atman didn't want to let the local gangs in his studio because one: that's where he lived, and two: they were murdering a lot of people, so there were a lot of people who wanted to get revenge on them. He didn't want any of the retaliation happening on his doorstep, let alone his block, which already had its own problems to deal with. Even though he made this a policy, one of the producers let a small group of gang members in when he thought Atman was supposed to be at his local after-school program. Their program ended early, and as Atman walked down his alley to get to his front door, he heard some music coming from the studio. He walked into his house, and as he walked up his stairs, he heard the people who were in the recording booth talking about representing their gang, and talking about the people they had killed and the dope they sold.

His instinct was to curse everyone out who was in there and tell them to "get the hell out of his house," but then he thought about it and decided to try to uplift them instead of causing friction. He told them, "You gotta be more diverse in your lyrics. It can't all be about killing people, flipping bricks, and all that other stuff. Y'all might be able to sell to more people." Instead of inspiring them, this really pissed the young men off. By trying to teach them about marketing and diversifying their lyrics, he had inadvertently made things much, much worse. He noticed they were in a funk when they left his house, but he didn't think about it again because he thought he had done the right thing.

For a little while, all was OK. We figured that maybe things had calmed down, or perhaps the situation wasn't as bad as it had seemed at that moment. At the time we had two houses on the same block. Late one night, Atman was walking a friend to his car from the first house. Out of the corner of his eye he noticed a group of twelve to thirteen kids standing on the corner across the street from the second house. As Atman and his friend walked down the steps and their feet hit the sidewalk, he saw the group of kids cross the street and stand right in front the second house. The kids were dressed all in black, so Atman knew what time it was. If he didn't think fast, he was going to be a statistic.

The kids were quiet, not looking at him, but clearly focused on him. The gang initiations were in full swing and people were getting murdered around the city every day. Playing it cool so his friend wouldn't panic and make things worse, Atman pretended he had left his phone at Ali and Andy's house. When Atman and his friend were inside, he called down to the studio to see what the group of youths were doing. Their plans had been foiled, so they just took off running down the alley to regroup.

The friend was by now shitting bricks. Atman got him to his car, and he peeled off, no doubt blowing through red lights all the way home, or at least until he was out of the blue light district. (In the hood, we call our neighborhood and most of North Avenue the blue light district because there are surveillance cameras on every corner, and they have a flashing blue light on them, like police lights.) Atman walked to his house, got his car keys, and drove to Uncle Will's.

Uncle Will, besides being a spiritual person, was a gangster too. Atman told Uncle Will, "Yo, I need some protection at my house. I'm going to be proactive, and I know where these dudes are, and I'm going to check them, but I need something more." And that is when Uncle Will first gave him the Ganesha mantra. He told Atman that the mantra would work like a protective shield around him. Atman was expecting some more real-world, ex-Panther kind of advice. And, to be blunt, he was looking for a firearm to handle the situation. But when Will insisted the mantra was where it was at, Atman lost it. "These kids are straight-up planning to kill me. Mantras are cool and all, but I need firepower! This shit isn't going to work!" Uncle Will shot back, "What have I told you about being a scientist and doing the work?"

Atman started using the mantra, even as his eyes started twitching with stress because the energy was so crazy around the neighborhood. He chanted it over and over in his head as he slowly checked out the alleys and evaluated safe paths home, or to wherever he was going.

He didn't only say the mantras, he saw the mantras. As Atman walked through the streets, he visualized Ganesha striding beside him, holding his gifts in one set of his hands and the weapons in the other set of hands. He felt the power of Ganesha, remover of obstacles, elephant-headed god of wisdom, running through the neighborhood beside him. He felt the thunder as Ganesha's feet slammed against the ground. He felt the air shift around the massive form of the god. Atman no longer felt alone in his troubles: Instead, he quite literally had an invisible deity running alongside him. One way or another, everyone else felt it too. Very quickly the main person who was trying to put the hit out on Atman left and never came back to the neighborhood.

Damn, Uncle Will knew what he was talking about.

The Rocket Ship, the Shitsville Express, and the Cheat Codes

Soon we'll get into the mantras and how you can use them for yourself. But first you need to understand the three reasons why they will help you, even if your obstacles are not as bad as gang initiates looking to level up by taking you out. Uncle Will had three phrases that he used to explain the importance of mantras.

The Rocket Ship

Will used to tell us that "mantras are your rocket ship." What he meant was that if you are floundering at surface level in a meditation, a mantra can take you deeper in your meditation almost instantly. Don't fight with your mind in meditation; all you are going to be doing is fighting, rather than getting deeper in your practice. Hop on a mantra, ride that vibe, and it will shoot you deeper almost instantly.

Shitsville

Uncle Will would say your "mind always ends up in Shitsville." Let's illustrate this with another *Star Wars* reference. Remember when Luke is lining up his X-wing starfighter down the little pit in the Death Star and he hears Obi-Wan telling him to *use the force*? Well, Uncle Will may have transitioned, but there are certain phrases of his that we still hear in our heads on a daily basis, just like Luke in that moment. One of them is our personal Obi-Wan telling us, "The mind goes to Shitsville." What he meant is that if you let your mind go, it's just going to spiral downward and downward to the darkness, or what he liked to call Shitsville. The second you feel your mind heading to that place, remember that your ticket out is your mantra.

Sometimes it can feel like you are going to live your whole life in Shitsville. Ali's old dog was called Grady, after Grady from *Sanford and Son* and the singer Grady Tate. He was a pain in the ass. He ate up everything in the house, including Atman's prized breakfast specialty of four waffles and four veggie sausages, and was generally the worst. Ali finally took him to the SPCA (Society for the Prevention of Cruelty to Animals), yet even when Grady was gone Ali would swear that he heard him howling and barking through the walls. Ali—of course—went back and got him, and kept him for fifteen years till he eventually died. When HLF was really struggling, and people who should have been helping us were screwing us over, Ali would spend hours just walking Grady, getting angrier and angrier with every step. Ali was basically in Shitsville, a lot, so to calm his mind he would take Grady out and start walking. The long walks would slowly burn off a little of the anger, but the pissed-off side of his brain was still sending out negative vibes: *Those m****rf****rs think they can steal our ideas.* Ali's higher side was telling him, *Man, these bad vibes are going to come straight back to you.* The back-and-forth and back-and-forth would get overwhelming and he would jump to a mantra and it would clear that stuff out. Remember, anything bad you send out is going to come back even stronger. Who really wants that?

Cheat Codes

Cheat codes—remember them from your childhood? Ali still knows the way to get to Mike Tyson is 0073735963.

Don't even have to think about it. That old shortcut is locked into his brain forever. He still knows that if he's playing *Super Mario Bros.*, he can take the Warp to 3-1, and jump up and down on the second turtle, and get as many lives as he wants. And he knows for a fact that if he's playing *Contra* and he goes up, up, down, down, left, right, left, right, B, A, and Start (select START for two players), he'll get thirty lives.

These cheat codes stick with you. They're designed to be hard to find, but once you find them they become instinctive: lightning-fast reactions that you can use whenever you need them. When Ali started explaining mantras to his oldest son, Asuman, he said, "So, Dad, these are like cheat codes for life. If real life is a video game and you have cheat codes, you can make all these things happen."

A few years later Asuman and his friend Billy were opening up the Mindfulness in Education Conference at Omega Institute. Ali saw them doing mudras and mantras in the corner to get themselves together before going onstage. This is the proudest dad moment of Ali's entire life! We hadn't told them to do this; in fact, we were socializing and meeting people and all the while they were over there in the corner getting ready with Ganesha mantra and mudra. They were using their cheat codes, psyching themselves up to do something that felt overwhelming and scary in the moment.

There's no escaping Shitsville. We're all going to spend parts of our lives there, no matter what. Your Shitsville might be relationship worries, or anxiety about your life. Are you a success? A failure? Or perhaps you're worried about more flesh-and-blood things: keeping safe on streets that are out to get you. Avoiding cops who grab guns instead of Tasers "by mistake" and suffer no repercussions from their actions. Wherever your Shitsville is, you can blast your way out of it with those cheat codes. You need to energize yourself? We got a code for that! You need to slow your breathing, stay calm, and avoid confrontation? We got a mantra for that too.

If there are certain things that you really want to happen in your life, then use the cheat codes that will get you there. These are formulas to help you get what you want. Using a mantra will force something to happen in your life. Our friend and mentor Sat Bir Singh Khalsa would always say, "One of the coolest things about yoga is that you can be a total skeptic, but if you do it, it is going to work."

That was the stuff that Uncle Will really wanted us to get out there—he was super happy we were teaching about breath and centering and awareness, but there was a huge chunk of knowledge we couldn't share. Uncle Will realized that the science of yoga does not depend on belief. Those kids who cat-cow their way to some kind of peace in class don't know the ins and outs of mantras or how meditation affects the pre-frontal cortex. They're just kids, burning through a few hours at an after-school program. They can't even start to work with mantras till they graduate. Still: it works.

Somewhere Uncle Will is sitting out there like Obi-Wan, looking at us very, very happy. He told us to share the practices, and he wanted us to use technology. COVID has forced us to use technology more, and it's allowing us to share mantra yoga widely. He would want the healing ones out there. He would want all the ones that raised consciousness out there because of all the turmoil in the world. And definitely the one for all the suffering souls in the universe because of all the people suffering on so many levels.

The Core Mantras and Why to Use Them

Mantra yoga was the perfect form of yoga for Uncle Will. It could be practiced any and all the time, and he loved to sing. It was natural that he would make sure he passed on as many mantras as possible to Ali, Atman, and Andy. All three of us are terrible singers and can't "funk up the mantra" like Uncle Will, but we definitely use the practice a lot.

Uncle Will would sing the maha mantra ("Hare Krishna, Hare Krishna, Krishna Krishna, Hare Hare, Hare Rama, Hare Rama, Rama Rama, Hare Hare") all the time. Ali and Atman had been introduced to it by their dad and at Sunday school but had never delved deeply into what Will referred to as the "formulas."

The first two formulas that Uncle Will gave us were the mantra for all the suffering souls in the universe and the mantra to remove all obstacles and ensure success. Uncle Will knew that one of the main reasons we started the Holistic Life Foundation was to alleviate suffering, so he wanted to give us a tool that could help people around the globe we couldn't physically reach and even those aliens that might be suffering. It quickly became one of Ali's and Atman's go-to mantras, and still is to this day.

Mantra for All the Suffering Souls in the Universe

Devae Prat Penardee
Hare Praceeda
Praceeda Maha Jagato Akalesha
Praceeda Wish Wesh Schwahay
Pahee Wish Wum
Tramesh Schwahay Devi
Chara Chareshya

Knowing that life throws many challenges at you, particularly when you are doing the universe's work, Uncle Will also gave us the mantra to remove all obstacles and ensure success. When he was teaching it to us, Ali and Atman's older brother, Darryl, and his business partner Eric were there. Darryl, a lawyer, has said he used the mantra every time before he went into court and was undefeated when he did, even for some cases he probably should have lost.

Mantra to Remove All Obstacles and Ensure Success

Aum Vacratunda
Mahakaya Kudusurya
Samaprba Neviknam Kudumae
Devasava Kareshu Sel Veda

One time our nephew Ross lost his cell phone and was pissed and didn't have the money to replace it. He walked over to Ali in the office and said, "Uncle Ali, I need my phone back, you gotta do the mantra for me." Ali got up from his desk, went into the conference room, and went into the light and did the mantra for about five minutes. He came back out and told Ross he was good. Ross called his phone, and a homeless person walking past our office window answered it. (Ross had tried to call a bunch of times before and no one answered.) Ross told the person it was his phone and waved at them through the window. The person laid it on the window-sill and walked away. Ross ran out and got his phone and was happy as hell. And that's just one example of how that mantra has worked magic in our lives.

Uncle Will taught us close to a hundred mantras, but another one that stands out is the mantra to purify the mind. Energetic influences can come from all over to affect your thoughts, and sometimes it can be hard to get them back to a higher vibration. When Ali was in Shitsville, this is the mantra he would practice. When Ali felt like he was trapped in a scenario that seemed like he was in a Tom and Jerry cartoon—with the devil on one shoulder telling him to be pissed at someone for whatever reason and send them negative energy, and an angel on the other shoulder telling him to send them love and not to put out negative vibes because they would come back to him—he would practice this mantra to elevate his vibration and look at the situation from a higher place. Because that angel on his shoulder didn't win all those arguments.

Mantra to Purify the Mind

Chandra Yahee Namah

Mudras

We were introduced to mudras formally by Uncle Will with the gyan mudra, which is for wisdom. *Mudra* means "seal." And they are associated with the hands, but other parts of the body can be used for mudras as well. Uncle Will would have us use one when we meditated or whenever we had a free hand that wasn't doing anything. Mudras are shapes that you form by moving your fingers and palm, sometimes hands apart, sometimes hands together. Think of your fingers, and the different areas of your palm, representing different facets of yourself and your life. When you manipulate your fingers against each other, or your palm, they work in a kind of spiritual acupressure, stimulating the energy fields within your body, and triggering sensations and feelings that can invigorate, relax, or clarify your body and thoughts. We generally don't teach mudras in class since there is no easy way to "de-yoga" them for the school system. However, we use mudras constantly in our own lives.

Energy is constantly flowing in and around us; mudras are a way to harness that energy and get it to flow through to achieve many different things: healing, manifestation, elevating consciousness, self-confidence, and more.

Three of our favorite mudras are:

Hridaya

Used to open up the spiritual heart so that you can tap into your true self. It is also used to heal and strengthen the physical heart.

Kubera

Used for wealth (material, knowledge, and spiritual). Also used to manifest your goals.

Khechari

This is a mudra that doesn't involve the hands. With this mudra, you place your tongue on the roof of your mouth, on the soft palate, and press up.

This mudra keeps you young and recycles the energy in your body so that it isn't lost. It also keeps your energy high. The yogic theory behind this is that *amrita** drips down from your soma chakra and usually drips down and burns up in your gastric fire. When you use *kechari mudra*, that amrita rises back up to higher chakras.

Again, be a scientist. Exploring mudras would require a book of its own, so check out our Instagram pages to see more detailed information on how and why to do this.

Hong Sau

This is the first meditation Ali and Atman learned outside of their home. They learned it at Sunday school at the Divine Life Church and have started practicing it again as adults.

It is great because it is a combination of a breath meditation and mantra meditation, helping you get closer to your true self.

Amrita is the ancient yogic elixir of immortality.

Get into a comfortable meditative position and take a few centering breaths. Then allow your breath to become relaxed. As you inhale, mentally vibrate *hong* and as you exhale mentally vibrate *sau* (pronounced *saw*).

Keep your awareness centered on your third eye—the spiritual eye, located between and above the eyebrows, that perceives things beyond the visible world—the entire time. Mentally vibrate *hong sau* until you feel mental stillness, then let the mantra go and notice the energy you feel. Once your mind starts to stir, bring the mantra back until you feel stillness again, then let it go again. Keep flowing between the mantra, stillness, and the mind stirring. One thing you will notice is that every time you bring the mantra back, you will flow deeper and deeper into that stillness and the vibration will be stronger and higher, never reaching an end.

CHAPTER TEN

The Child's World

It's one thing to bring mantras and breathwork into your own—adult—life. It's another to share the practice with children. Especially traumatized children. When we first got HLF going, we were regular meditators and practitioners. We quickly realized that there were only three of us, and uncountable thousands of deeply traumatized children who needed our help. We also learned the hard way that, for the most part, Baltimore kids weren't going to respond to someone who doesn't empathize or understand where they are coming from or what they have experienced. For our program to succeed, we needed to turn our students into paid, credited teachers. From the early days, we mentored kids who were serious about their personal practice, and worked with them to prepare them to teach.

Our nephew Ross was one of our first students-turned-teacher. At thirteen, Ross needed a place to live, so he moved into the Smallwood house with us, until eventually his mom was in a position to take him back. All the while he did some of the practices with us, half-assedly, only occasionally, and giving us plenty of shit about it.

Ross graduated high school and college. He got a sales job. Then he made a few dumb mistakes, it got back to his job, and he got fired. One day, Atman caught up with Ross at Uncle Will's house. It didn't take much spidey sense to tell that Ross was putting his feet back on a less-than-positive path. Atman asked him, "What are you doing?" And Ross replied, "I'm out here surviving." Atman told him if he agreed to stop what he was doing and clean up his act, he had a job with HLF, and he could start (and start getting paid) today. Ross was nonchalant—"Sure, I'll try it out"—and after a quick course in teacher training, he was on deck at Robert Coleman, with his first cohort of students.

Here's where yoga has a divine sense of humor—or the ability to strip you down and show you a truth about yourself, or your life choices, that you might not have ever been able to see on your own.

The first summer Ross started working with us, he had a student called James. Now, we were very familiar with James. He was a character—only five years old and with an attention span you could measure in nanoseconds, and an Allstate Insurance voice that was deeper than any of ours. James was always in the center of any commotion: You would think he was bullying the other kids, but he was actually standing up for other kids who were getting bullied.

James was Ross's instant karma, and we figured that working together was the perfect test for our newest yoga teacher. James would do everything that Ross would do as a kid. That first day, James walked up to Ross and told him, "Mr. Ross,

I'm not doing no yoga, but I'll do football." OK, rule number one is never force a kid to do anything they don't want to do. That's cool. James was up for the belly breaths and the mindfulness even if the poses seemed dumb to him. Frankly, he was absorbing plenty of yogic energy just being around the kids who *were* doing it.

A few days later we were at the movie theater with a big group of kids. Just as the trailers rolled, James jumped out of his seat and ran out of the movie theater, Ross in hot pursuit. The two of them pretty much collided with Atman at the concession stand. Ross was fuming mad. Atman asked him, "Why are you so mad? You used to do the same thing. If he needs to run, let him run. Maybe you have to take him outside, let him run some more." After the movie, we got on the bus, James stuck his middle finger up at cars, and then he turned around and chomped on Ross's hand till it bled. Ross thought, *I'm going to be on WJZ, cuz I'm going to hurt this kid.*

The other instructor shared the story with James's mom at pickup, because Ross was too mad to talk. But the next day James walked in and said, "Mr. Ross, I'm so sorry." His mom had laid it out that James might get cut from the program if he drew blood again. From that day on he was open to the yoga and the other practices. We still didn't force him, of course— but he wanted to be part of the group, and eventually he threw himself fully into the yoga as well as the movies and snacks.

Here's the thing about trauma: It pops up in ways that don't make sense to adults (or to the kids either). None of us can unpack what exactly set James off in that particular moment at the movie theater. All we could do was communicate clearly with him, listen with empathy, and meet him where he was.

The only way James could process whatever was kicking off inside of him was to run. Forcing him to be where he was "supposed" to be—in his seat—would have backfired into disaster. We had to trust that in some way he knew what he needed in that moment, and roll with it.

Seeing this, and understanding this, gave Ross a little insight into himself as well. Some of that crazy shit Ross had done as a child or teenager—those moments where his family was under intense stress and he'd done something dumb that added to that stress—was a reaction to trauma, and that trauma manifested the only way it could in that particular moment. Once, when Ross was thirteen, he tried to pimp-smack Andy with a handful of talcum powder. (This was inspired by the *Jackass* movie that had just been released.)

Now, Ross and Andy love each other, they trust each other, so while another adult might have seen this as a sign of disrespect, Andy guessed there was more to the story. Part of childhood trauma is understanding that when it does manifest in seemingly nonsensical ways, there is a logic to it. Andy was one of the few people in Ross's life who could absorb this kind of shit, process it, and talk it out without knocking Ross upside the head or straight-up kicking him out. Consciously or unconsciously Ross picked one of the few adults who was willing to give him the space he needed to work through his complicated feelings in a safe setting.

By Andy giving Ross space to work through his stuff, he got closer to being able to forgive himself, a critical step in processing and dealing with any kind of trauma.

Likewise, Ross in turn built a rapport with James based on not judging him, just accepting him. Eventually he started doing better in class. His teachers told Ross, "We don't know what you are doing, but he talks about you all day." As James started to embrace more and more of the program, he continued to mature, and to take ownership of his own behavior. He ended up being one of the leaders in the class, leading yoga from the front of the room, even as he had been the kid who insisted, "I don't want to do nothing, but the meditation part is cool with me."

Yogic practices take you out of the reality you think you are in, and show you the world from a slightly different perspective. Ross needed to see and recognize himself in James to heal his own wounds—to forgive himself for his own wildness and youthful choices. He needed that lesson in compassion, not just compassion for a difficult kid acting out in seemingly irrational ways but also compassion toward himself.

Of course, Ross still had to go out and earn that compassion and forgiveness from the people he'd pissed off (or seriously infuriated and hurt) along the way. One day we sent him to take part in a presentation at his old high school. We wanted to introduce our practices there and figured he was the perfect ambassador. On the way in, Ross ran into one of his former teachers as she took her seat. She gave him the *I know you from somewhere* look. Then it dawned on her: The last time they had interacted they were cussing each other out over Ross's wild behavior. Ross was no joke—he'd been expelled for starting a fight with a teacher. She had good reason to feel extremely triggered by seeing him again.

So when the principal introduced Ross, she audibly swore, "You m****rf****r!" Ross joked, "Oh, so you want to keep this going?" You could see that Ross's presence was taking her back to the worst days in her classroom. Yet, as he finished his presentation about yoga and mindfulness, she ran down and grabbed the mike from Ross—still shooting him the dirtiest of dirty looks—and said, "If this worked with *him*, we got to put this program in the school. Do whatever it takes."

The Breakthrough

If you are lucky, you've had a moment in a meditation or yoga class where something slips away. For a moment you feel all the possibility of a life without separation, where you are literally *at one* with . . . well, everything. Some of us get this moment once in our lives. Some, like Uncle Will, seem to bathe in it, feeling that connection and community so intensely that the outside world loses its luster in comparison to the inward journey of your own soul.

In a way, the nature of your experience matters less than the fact you got to experience it at all. We have one friend who had one moment, while she held her knee like a baby and circled her lower leg. In that moment she had clarity, and a sense of mirroring, or time slip, back to when her own mom held her, in just the same way. That moment of equanimity and peaceful acceptance helped her heal from her own complicated relationship with her parents. That moment might have lasted five seconds in Earth time. It may have been her only moment, but in the great karmic shuffle it is still happening now, and it is enough to confirm the bigger picture of unity and oneness.

Part of that sense of oneness is self-forgiveness. At some point in our lives, we've all had the same acting-out reaction to stressful stimuli as James and Ross experienced. If you were lucky to grow up in a more resource-rich household, maybe your parents sent you to a therapist who was able to talk you through your behavior. If you were a teenager or adult, perhaps you self-medicated with drugs or alcohol, or mishandled your anxiety and anger until they became an eating disorder or outlet for self-harm.

For most of our kids, therapy isn't an option. Even if their parents were in a position to be able to pay for it, there simply aren't enough therapeutic resources in the hood to reach all the people who need them.

Yoga Changed Our Lives

There has been a ton of research on the benefits of yoga for stressed adults and kids. The scientists and researchers we work with talk about the efficacy of yoga for reducing stress and improving mood and overall sense of well-being. They point out that yoga improves mental and physical well-being, and is particularly valuable when it comes to developing a sense of mind-body awareness, self-regulation, and physical fitness. We'd like to add another observation. Most of our schools are almost solely focused on academic achievement and getting as many kids past the graduation line as possible. This works when it works. Every school has students who are so clear in their motivation, and so determined or talented, that they are able to succeed. But this isn't all kids. It's not even most kids. And in an area like Baltimore, this is exacerbated by the poverty and limited resources in the school system.

In an ideal world, schools would focus on the holistic wellness of the whole child. Education would be a huge part of it, but helping the student develop the social-emotional learning (SEL) tools he or she needs would be equally important.

Because this is the crazy part: Yoga is a practice and process for developing a deeper contemplative state. Anyone who's had a transformative moment of oneness through yoga, breathwork, and/or meditation is changed. For good. This is a radical, powerful force. If you've ever experienced it, you know a little of how it feels. In one moment the clouded screens that block the true nature of existence seem to shift, opening up a clear and unimpeded view of something bigger than you could have ever imagined. You open your eyes and the world is still the same. Your living room wall at the end of your yoga mat, the crack in the paint, the slightly askew painting hanging on the wall, remain as they were. Yet you are different in a way that can never be undone. You can observe those external aspects of your life with equanimity. They are not you.

My Word Is My Word

Now imagine entire generations of people who are desperate for the space and opportunity to feel that change and that expansiveness and that hope. They're not getting the help from outside the community, and certainly not from the government. They are often living in circumstances wholly outside of their control, and often miserable. Their physical, tangible world is unchanging, and seems to offer no immediate hope of change or improvement, so why not at least give them the skills and ability to open up and change their inner world?

Here's where our yogic philosophies tie into Uncle Will and Smit's observations about growing up in Baltimore. When people are hopeless, angry, hungry, cold, and struggling to survive, they are controllable. When there is too little employment, poor food, decaying infrastructure, and inadequate schooling, people are too focused on surviving to think about a bigger picture. When families living on one block blame families living on the next block over for their troubles, well, they're not pointing the finger at the people who actually have the power to improve their circumstances but choose not to.

We think it's in the interests of many powerful forces to keep people's hearts closed off and hopeless. Look at just about any policy that's been enacted by White politicians against Black communities. There's a constriction, a tightening. When people protest in Florida, the state enacts RICO "anti-mob" laws—then only use them against BLM protestors, even when the Proud Boys, spitting in their faces, are doing worse. (Ron DeSantis seems to have dedicated his life to this kind of stuff.)

During those months that thirteen-year-old Ross lived with us, he'd occasionally come home with a detention or some other problem. It was nearly always because of a fight that seemed so pointless, so futile, that most people would struggle to understand what had caused it. "What happened, man?" And the answer was always the same: "My word is my word." Ross didn't have much. No fresh clothes. No money. Not a whole lot of stability. The one thing he did have was his word, and if he told you that your actions would have repercussions, he meant it.

We get it. And this is why we believe that helping people like Ross develop a yogic sensibility, and foster feelings of self-love and self-respect, is a powerful political act. In the next chapter we'll expand on this idea and talk about how meditation, breathwork, and yoga can help keep young Black and minority men and women safe in interactions with authorities. But for now, let's say that yoga is a radical force both of peace and equanimity and righteous, justified anger. Meditation can cure many things, but it can't cure systemic racism and structural inequality. It can, however, give practitioners the inner resources to fight back against forces that would hold them down.

CHAPTER ELEVEN

Shedding Trauma, Finding Self-Love

Don't focus on the past, because that brings up anger,
don't focus on the future, because that brings up anxiety,
focus on the present, because that's all that is.

Everything the HLF does starts with self-love. No matter if we're working with teachers, kids, or adults in a corporate setting, the first task is to guide people toward a place where they can feel that acceptance of themselves. There is a self-love crisis in America right now—and globally too. We aren't at peace with ourselves, we don't fully know ourselves, and as a result we don't feel comfortable or safe. Sometimes this lack of self-love reflects our psychological underpinnings, but often it's a reaction to stuff fully out of our control. And when people don't fully know or understand themselves, they lash out, punishing either themselves or the outside world for something they can't fully explain or describe.

Let's be real about something. Life is easier when you don't care so much. Life doesn't hurt quite so bad if you just don't care what happens to you or the people around you. If you're scared about how you're going to feed your kids, it's easier to watch them go hungry if you harden your heart and shut off the flow of love between you and them. If you're failing out of school and can see no future for yourself, it's easier to get through the day if you tell yourself, *F**k it. I don't care.*

Learning to let yourself care, to accept the pain that comes with seeing the people you love suffer, and to be OK with suffering yourself, is the first—maybe the biggest—lesson we all have to learn in life. Distilled down to its essence, this impulse to love is *self-love.*

This isn't easy for adults. It's even harder with kids. When we sit in a circle and tell a group of eight- or nine-year-olds, "Be kind to yourself. Have patience with yourself," we might as well be telling them to fly to the moon. Normally, we hold off on using the term *self-love* because . . . well, they're kids. Telling them to love themselves is going to equal some confused looks and some giggles. But you? The Adult in the Room? There's no excuse. So in this chapter the challenge is simple. You got to figure some stuff out, make peace with that unkind voice deep in your head—let go of the anger, or the fear, or the resentment—and learn to love yourself.

Uncle Will used to sing "This Little Light of Mine." It was his jam, day in, day out. Uncle Will had seen his fair share— more than fair—of pain and despair. You don't join the Panthers because you think, *Things are just fine the way they are.* He knew what it was to hurt. And he embraced that hurt. He understood that pain was as much part of him as the happy Will, or the Will charming the ladies into buying that extra insurance policy. Will had to literally will himself into a place of self-love. He had to power through hearing the N-word, and feeling the disrespect from White folks. He had to turn off the stuff telling him he was less than or not good enough. By the time he became our spiritual mentor, he knew that the secret to self-love was rooted in turning away from those outside voices—and turning in to that voice that lived in his heart through yogic practices. He helped us through our traumas with these techniques, and eventually we passed on his teachings to our kids too.

Trauma and Self-Love

Here's one thing to understand before you move forward with helping and understanding the kids in your world to find that self-love. Our kids are living in trauma—and that trauma is the single biggest obstacle between them and self-love. Most of them have been steeped in trauma their whole lives, both overt (physical, mental, sexual abuse) and less easy to see (food insecurity, hygiene shame, and painful interactions with authority figures).

Our kids deal with more subtle traumas too: a deep disconnection with the natural world, for one. Pollution from incinerators—always located in the poorer areas—that until recently belched a toxic cloud over South Baltimore. A degraded environment that leads to chronic rates of asthma. As Farmer Nell, a Baltimore local who leads farming workshops for South Baltimore kids, put it: "You ask any of those families of the victims or the families of the perpetrators—when was the last time their bare feet touched dirt or snow?" Study after study backs up the need for access to wild spaces and nature for mental health.

Our kids are literally breathing in different air. Not just the pollution, but the weight of death and despair, the drugs, and the grinding hopelessness of worlds where many haven't left a five-block radius of their home their whole lives.

Irrationally Crazy Love

Urie Bronfenbrenner was a famous child psychologist. He had many good things to say, but none more so than this: "Every child needs at least one adult who is irrationally crazy about him or her." This lack of committed, no-conditions love—just like the broken weak ties and absent mentors—can cripple a child. Think of the adults who loved you irrationally as a kid—who laughed at your goofy jokes, were reliably delighted to see you, comforted you when your parents were enraged by your behavior, maybe provided a safe haven when your family was falling apart. What would you have done without them? Now, imagine a world where they were never there to begin with.

Trauma, compounded with adults who are spread too thin to offer that irrationally crazy love, adds up to an undeniable feeling that you are not loved and not valued, full stop. This trauma compounds itself again when parents and grandparents have decades of unheard stories and unprocessed feelings. They may love their kids desperately, but they are not equipped to help those children work through the trauma of their lives. Their children in turn grow up in an environment that says that no one gives a damn about them.

Sometimes kids do feel loved, but it is such a toxic, dysfunctional love that it makes their lives exponentially worse. We've had grandparents *give their grandchildren knives to handle street fights*. Now, those grandparents love those kids, and they are doing the best they know how for them. But their best is inappropriate as hell.

It's a little different for kids who are living in wealthier, more privileged communities. Their basic needs are met, often in abundance. No food or hygiene insecurity for them. And yet they are also deeply distressed: How are they supposed to love themselves when their parents are AWOL on their smartphones or Zoom 24/7? Perhaps their parents compensate for absences with expensive gifts, teaching the child an empty, transactional kind of love. Or can't hide their disappointment at their child's academic failures. The reality is that many, many kids today are traumatized. *These crisscrossing realities of trauma on top of trauma affect every facet of their lives.* Trauma closes their hearts. Self-love practices can open them.

It's impossible to overstate how important this recognition of the omnipresence of trauma is when you are working with *all* children. Just because you don't see or recognize something as a traumatic response doesn't change the fact that it is one. Part of our job—and now your job—is to be attuned to young minds trying to make sense of stuff that is literally inexplicable to them. Kids often don't have words to put to their distress, so you need to help them get to a place where they feel comfortable trying to find them.

Added to this is the reality that a child who is receptive to being helped has already made themselves vulnerable.

Simply showing up might be a huge step for him or her to reclaim ownership over themselves and to start to deal with that traumatic experience (or more likely, experiences).

Not all bad experiences become trauma. Sometimes it's less about what happened, than what happened *right after* the traumatic episode. If you were nurtured and allowed to tell your story and felt safe, it might not create trauma that lasts forever. But if people denied it, ignored it, then that awful moment becomes trauma. In wartime, people often become very connected. The lucky ones hold on to that connection throughout their lives, sharing a common story that they may retell over and over again, with their combat buddies, until the last of them dies. These people may feel pain and despair, but being able to talk about their experiences defangs them, so the experiences of fighting do not necessarily cause unsurvivable trauma.* But if you go through terrible situations in isolation, without having the space and the witnesses to share your story—or worse, having people mock or deny it—a bad experience becomes traumatic.

In the aftermath of the Capitol Hill insurrection, @AOC livestreamed about her experiences with the trauma of surviving the attack, and her own history of sexual assault. As she put it: "Telling our stories is key to healing." We couldn't agree more, and that's why it is key to recognize that anytime a child is somewhat receptive to a new meditative or therapeutic practice—even if they aren't fully engaged, or "drift off" during the teaching sessions—they are taking that first difficult step to dealing with their trauma.

---

* *Tribe*, by Sebastian Junger, is a great book about this phenomenon.

Inner and Outer Worlds

Another way to understand how trauma affects kids is to see it as related to two different ways of existing in the world: *interoceptive* and *exteroceptive*. Interoception is the state of being aware of and focused on sensation coming from within the body. Think of a moment when you were aware of your heartbeat or heard your bones creak. The interoceptive system uses nerve receptors to send messages to our brain and alert us to how we feel. In a balanced individual, this system will contribute to regulating energy expenditure, alerting us to our needs (hunger, thirst, the need to urinate, etc.).

Of course, our bodies do not exist in isolation from our minds. As our emotions ebb and flow over the day, our body mirrors these changes. An angry conversation with your spouse might cause your neck to tense and your skin to turn red. Here's the key part: *Our ability to interpret these physical markers of our internal state is a good indicator of how well we can read other people's emotional and physical signs.*

Exteroceptive individuals are the opposite. They live in a world of heightened sensitivity to external stimuli. They are the kids who are going from standing still to full speed, oblivious to everything around them, including their own feelings and emotions in the moment.

We call these kids high flyers, and they need a little more attention and focus. These kids are aware of everything around them. Hypervigilant, always thinking a block farther on their walk, clued in to the dudes walking ahead of them, the look on the face of the dude they just passed. They're the kids who don't even notice that their teeth are grinding or their fists are balled up. Every nerve ending and neuron is on high alert, waiting to see *what's gonna happen next*. These kids may be surviving on Little Hugs fruit punch and Chee-tos. As a result, their GI tracts—where 95 percent of mood-regulating serotonin is generated—are shot.[1] Their brains are simply unable to regulate and process the emotional inputs their minds are getting, even without the fresh stresses of the day.

Our students are nearly all exteroceptive due to accumulated trauma and their need to be fully aware of their external surroundings in our community. Mindfulness can interrupt this pattern. We may not be able to change their outside world, but we can change how they deal with it. At least in our programs, they can turn off these exteroceptive edges, and instead drop in and become more aware of what's happening on the inside.

Self-Love Practices

The core of our self-love practices lie in developing an inner spaciousness. Think of our exteroceptive kid, fully living in the external moment. His external world is in bold color, full of loud sounds and stimuli. His brain is processing a salty look or a side-eye, even as it absorbs movements in his peripheral vision, and the sounds of traffic coming up behind him. Meanwhile, his internal world is like an unwatered garden, dying from lack of attention and love. So our first step is drawing that kid back inside, to his internal world, and the very best way to do that, for anyone of any age, is with breathwork.

Breathwork for Kids

A few chapters back we covered breathing for adults. Hopefully you've tried a deep belly breath or stress breath yourself at this point. These next few pages will give you a framework for sharing this practice with children.

Breathing is the foundation of everything we teach. It's the reset to that exteroceptive overdrive. It's a way of regaining a sense of control over a situation that is entirely outside of your control.

This is important; hopelessness can crush a kid's—or an adult's—spirit in no time. And we work with kids who have almost nothing to feel hopeful about. That hopelessness might come from poverty, social isolation, fear of disappointing their parents, or a hundred other reasons. Where there is no hope, there is no love, and certainly no self-love. Without self-love, every other hope of change fades away.

Breathing disrupts this well-grooved track that tells a child or adult *You are not loved, you do not deserve love, you are bad*, which we all have in our brains, based on our past experiences and expectations about "what happens next." Instead of —literally—taking a breath, stepping back, assessing a situation, and responding in a detached way, a kid who is back on that familiar path of panic and fear is unable to regulate their feelings.

Instead, that emotional reaction floods their nervous system with chemicals telling him or her, *This is bad, you need to react*. That kid follows that well-worn neural pathway and does something ill-advised—mouthing off, starting a fight, or refusing to communicate with a teacher.

Breathwork disrupts this.

Breathwork connects a disconnected child to their body. For a minute they drop out of that sensory overload. The room gets a little quieter, and they are less aware of the hubbub around them.

After a minute they start to tap into the subtler level of connection that comes from inner self-regulation.

Even that kid who's always starting something, always pushing buttons and seemingly itching for conflict, is starting to find more quiet inside. As they sit with themselves in these brief lulls of quiet, they get a glimpse of a thought or tune in to a feeling.

The Belly Breath

The belly breath is like a circuit breaker for a brain that is careening out of control and taking the kid (or adult) along for the ride. Belly breath can be a peaceful practice: getting you centered and your head straight for a day at work. Or it can be a lifesaving practice: overriding adolescent instincts that can take a kid from a bad situation to a terrible one.

Either way, you need the belly breath in your practice, and so does your kid. The adult breathwork practice is too complex for a child, so try this simpler practice together.

The very first thing we will have this kid—or any kid—do is to bust out in the gym or the playground. Figure out a way to release that restless energy that every kid has. Maybe some ball or some other game. Whatever it is, we want that kid to burn up as much of that wild child or teenager energy as they can. Then, when you've reached a point where your kid is a little more relaxed, and more receptive, sit them down on a mat in a quiet spot.

In a perfect world you'll have a little ambiance going. Maybe a salt lamp or lava lamp for some mellow lighting, and a white-noise machine or a fan if there's a ton of traffic noise. A comfortable cushion and some blankets to bolster the kids and help them get comfortable. All these elements have an important role: You're taking a familiar space and, by making a few small adjustments, adding an element of ritual.

Take a minute to visualize how releasing trauma and embracing self-love might feel: self-regulation, empowerment, beginnings of self-acceptance, even if you can't get to self-love. Just starting to accept yourself.

As you begin to talk through the belly breath with your kid, remember that the biggest win on this first day of practice is simply having your kid willing to show up and sit down. Don't worry if their breathing looks off or they can only hold the practice for a few seconds. Simply agreeing to try is a victory for both of you.

INSTRUCTIONS

Place your right palm on your belly. As you inhale through your nose to fill your lower lungs, use your diaphragm to expand your belly like a balloon. Expand your belly slowly and as much as possible. Pause for a brief second. Now exhale, leaving your hand in the same position, pulling your belly button to your spine, creating a space between your hand and belly. Inhale again, expanding your belly until it touches your hand. And repeat.

Inhale deeply though your nose, using the diaphragm and expanding your stomach to fill your lower lungs. Then fill your middle lungs by pushing out your rib cage, breastbone, and chest. Then fill your upper lungs by poking out your chest to lift it and completely fill your upper lungs. Pause on the breath. Exhale slowly, relaxing and lowering your chest, breastbone, and upper rib cage. After your upper and middle lungs are emptied, slowly contract your stomach using the diaphragm to empty the lower lungs.

ADDITIONAL NOTES

Remember to have your kids pause for a second after the inhale and for another second after the exhale. This will help keep the breath natural and help reduce the chances of difficulty breathing. The breath should also be very smooth with no jerking motions.

We take 21,600 breaths per day, so make each one count.

When Trauma Pops Up

Every time you practice your belly breaths—or yoga poses and meditation—you're opening a door to an expanded consciousness. As adults, we can generally handle what's on the other side of that door. For kids, it's more difficult. Anytime you do these practices with a young person, you have to be prepared for trauma to pop up. Remember what we said a few chapters ago: *Things that are coming up are coming up to be released, because you created space for it. Those feelings aren't coming up to attack you.*

Granted, this is a complicated idea to explain to a kid. But the key takeaway here is to help a young person understand that they are working toward a place where those scary memories and emotions lose their power. And this happens when they learn (through meditation and mindfulness) to be more strongly rooted in the present moment. They learn that they have the tools to return to a place of acceptance and peace when their awareness drifts back into an unhappy memory. They learn through their mindfulness practices that those memories are from the past, and are a part of them, but don't have to rule them. The memories are something that must be faced and released, not suppressed and hidden from. As a result, their inner life becomes a space of peace and not a place of fear.

In order to get there, you have to have a huge amount of reciprocal trust. A great way to build that trust is to honor a young person's boundaries and always be aware of how other people in that person's life might have broken those boundaries. We *never* physically touch a child who we don't have a deep and connected relationship with already, and if we do, we still ask for permission prior to making an adjustment. We are three big guys, and we have to be aware of how other guys may have hurt these kids.

So, boundary number one is to always emphasize the child's or teen's bodily autonomy. They are in control of what they do with their body, and who is allowed to touch or hug them. Because of this, we never instruct anyone to "close your eyes." We invite them to "close your eyes if it feels good for you." Your kid may be a sexual or physical abuse survivor, and closing their eyes will take them straight back to that moment of being vulnerable and afraid.

Boundary number two: We never talk a kid into doing something that doesn't feel right to them. We have had cases with kids who have experienced so much trauma they can't even deal with doing the physical yoga some days. They do other physical activities like push-ups or pull-ups, which start to calm them down, and by the end they are able to participate in the meditation. *It is crucial to ask if students want to participate. Accept that they might not, and just ask them to not be a distraction to the other participants.*

Boundary number three: Language is also important. Be careful with what words you use because they can be triggering. An example would be the word *relax*. It may seem like an innocent word, but understand that your child may well have been sexually or physically assaulted in their life. Their attacker might well have told them to *relax, calm down*. So we avoid any language like that which instructs a child to lessen their emotional reaction to a situation. (This is more important when you are doing one-on-one work. If you are in a large room of students, and kids are acting up, it's OK to tell a group to chill out or calm down. As much as possible you want to avoid singling out a young person with this kind of language and demands.)

Remember not leaving empty space in meditations. We use guided meditations so the kids can be introduced to stillness and inner peace, but it is a safe, guided stillness.

It can be helpful to acknowledge your own pain and vulnerabilities. Andy remembers sharing with a student about how his uncle had died. By sharing his pain, he was able to give the student the confidence to open up and share about his own experience.

Finally, it's important to always remember that anger and outbursts are often a cover for pain. These aren't behavior issues; it's trauma acting out. These moments can be exceptionally triggering for you. Give yourself a moment to acknowledge and accept your own reactions: anger, exasperation, frustration. Your feelings are most likely legitimate! Acknowledge and honor them. Then release that feeling and meet the child where they are, if necessary getting down to their level to simply hear and acknowledge what they are saying. Even privileged children are unheard most of the time. Traumatized children are often openly ignored. Give them the gift of your attention, even if you don't necessarily agree with or understand what they are describing.

The Long, Long Road to Self-Love

Learning to love yourself is the work of a lifetime. Ideally you start young, but we have plenty of friends and loved ones who are only now starting to work on the idea of accepting and embracing themselves. We all have layers upon layers of trauma, accrued over the course of our lives, that can keep us mired in anger at ourselves, and stewing over incidents from our lives that may have happened decades ago. Part of the point of starting these exercises with your kids is to get them into a self-love mindset now, and give them the tools to handle trauma and process the experiences of their lives without adding unnecessary shame or embarrassment.

Your single greatest approach is to use empathy and find a way to connect with your kids—where they are.

Andy has a trick that he uses to make a point about self-love. When one of our kids is crying because of being bullied, or feeling alone or scared, or for whatever reason feeling that suck of misery that comes from feeling worthless and unwanted, he'll sit down next to them and say, "Do you think I'm kind of a cool guy?" Andy *is* a cool guy, and since the kids trust him enough to get real, they'll say, "Yes." So then Andy says, "You think people bully me or treat me bad?" Kid: "No." Andy: "Well, I didn't always have it this good." And then he'll pull out his fifth-grade school portrait. The picture is Andy at eleven or twelve. He has buckteeth that are several sizes too big for his face, and glasses so big they must have been hand-me-downs from a 1970s *tía*. His hair doesn't lie flat, and he's got that faraway look in his eyes of a hopeless nerd. No matter how bad our HLF kid feels in that moment, they instantly know that Andy had it rough too. Because the reality is no kid gets to walk through the world looking that awkward, that self-conscious, and that vulnerable, without suffering for it.

More importantly, the picture makes them laugh like crazy. The humor and laughter are key. It's so powerful because it immediately transforms them from this state of sadness to having a smile and giggling, still with the tears in their eyes from the recent traumatic event. Andy always reminds them about the way they are feeling now compared to how they were feeling a few seconds ago. *This one simple observation really makes an impact in terms of them understanding that they can control their emotions.*

We come from a place of love. Part of this means that you don't really hold anyone at fault. You hold empathy for everyone, even the parents who can't love their kids the way they need to, or the teachers who are too burned out to educate as well as they should. We believe that when you see a system that is unfair, you use your momentum and resources to try to attack it the best way you can, with love and wisdom. We try to fix the chaos that is going on without blaming people for it.

Ra'Mon grew up knowing "My dad was killed, and they found him in a trunk." His family was going through tough times his whole youth. But he stayed "strong," hustling when he had to as a youngster, then throwing himself into working with us. As part of that work, he joined our annual retreat at the Omega Institute. One evening we did a circle meditation session with our close staff. Each of us took a turn to go in the middle of the circle. The idea is simple: the people sitting in the circle focus all their loving energy to the person sitting in the center of it. Ra'Mon took his turn, and we all closed our eyes and focused all our love on him.

Our eyes were shut, but we could hear Ra'Mon start to cry. Eventually, when he came out, he said, "This is the first time that I finally came to grips with my dad's death." It took Ra'Mon till he was twenty-four to finally let himself feel and process the trauma of what happened. It's not that the pain and the trauma went away, but that Ra'Mon was able to integrate it into his sense of himself and his life story. He was finally able to mourn his dad, acknowledge the pain, and move on.

When you are starting to get into contemplative practices, like meditation, do whatever you can to be present. When your mind is still, those things come up. You are opening yourself up and it is natural that now you have to deal with things that you've been hiding. And it can be overwhelming. So cut yourself some slack. You bottled it up for a reason, mainly because you didn't want to deal with it, or maybe it was too much to deal with at the time.

When you're explaining this to children, try this metaphor. Explain that when uncomfortable thoughts come up, because they will come up, it can be as explosive as a shaken-up soda can. It can really rock your world. But quickly the soda subsides, and goes back to normal. It's the same with that big, uncomfortable feeling. Once you finally come to grips with it, or finally get over it, or finally face those demons that will inevitably reveal themselves during your practice, it is so incredibly liberating. The silence that you create during your meditation eventually ends up speaking volumes!

CHAPTER TWELVE

Mindful Moment

Mindfulness and breathwork are tools that a kid can use to regulate themselves and give them a better shot at safely navigating an often unfriendly world. With less reactivity comes better odds of real connection and communication. However, for this to happen, everyone—kids, teachers, adults, and parents—has to learn to listen. This—as we all know—can be harder than it should be.

Years ago at Robert Coleman, we worked with a kid named Daron. He'd wanted to be in our program for a really long time, but our budget at the time meant we couldn't offer him services. We could tell that he had a lot of emotional stuff going on inside of him, because he was the biggest, toughest kid at the school but at the same time he would cry a lot. You could see there was a lot of pain inside of him. Eventually we were able to get him in our program.

One day we walked in to see the principal and the assistant principal before the afternoon program started. They looked at us and said, "Your boy Daron, he's a little off today, like he's in there tripping." We walked in, and right as we got through the door, Daron grabbed a kid named Tyrone—probably one of his best friends there—by his collar, picked him up, and threw him onto the floor. Ali pulled Daron out into the hall and the bravado and anger melted away. Instead, Daron was huffing and puffing and crying. Ali looked him in the eyes and said, "Daron, what's going on, man, stop! Slow down and tell me what's going on." And Daron finally got his breathing together and said, "Look at my pants, look at my pants." There was a big hole in his pants. "They were making fun of me all day, and I don't have another pair of pants to wear." So Ali said, "Alright, Daron, go get your coat." While Ali collected his car keys, Daron asked Atman and Andy not to pull him out of the program—he couldn't see any other reason for Ali to drive him anywhere other than back to his home, and out of the program for good.

Ali and Daron got in the car and started driving. Ali always has a lot of stuff to handle. As they drove, he made a few calls, and completely failed to see that Daron was nervous the whole time. Once he did realize that Daron was silently freaking out, Ali couldn't figure out why. He pulled into Target, and Daron said, "What are we doing here?" Ali said, "It's cool, we'll get you some new pants." So they went into Target, got him two new pairs of school pants, paid, and were about to walk out. But Daron was slowing down. Ali asked, "What's wrong?" He said, "Can I put a pair of pants on?" Ali was like, "Yeah, go ahead, put 'em on." Daron went into the dressing room, put a pair of pants on, and there was a big smile on his face. He threw the ripped-up ones in the trash can and walked out with the other pair under his arm and the proudest and most triumphant look on his face. He was all happy. When we went into the school the next day the principal and vice principal pulled Ali to one side and said, "Whatever you all did with Daron it was magic, I can't believe you all, whatever you all did was the most amazing thing ever."

What had actually happened? We just listened to him and asked him what was wrong. That was all we did. And he told us what was wrong. We helped him fix it. And then he was able to go about his day without shame or embarrassment.

Stop Talking, Start Listening

If you do one thing for your child or children you are helping—or for yourself—learn to listen. We work with kids from every corner of the country, and the one thing they are united by is distress. Our kids are anxious. They're scared. They feel utterly alone. And often, frankly, they're correct in feeling that way. What they need—more than just about anything else—is to be listened to.

There are multiple ways to listen. The first is obvious: Sit down and engage your child in conversation. The second way is more nuanced and more likely necessary for teenagers: Pay attention to them, set aside your preconceived notions of who they are and what's going on in their life, and try to experience their reality from their perspective. Daron had the ability and the openness to share what was really bothering him. Many kids don't. Your job is to understand where they're coming from without putting your own preconceived notions (or personal recollections of your own teenage years) on top of their experience.

Why? Because when a kid isn't listened to, there is no place for that emotion to go, except either inward, into self-harm, or outward, into explosions of anger or negative behavior. This is harmful enough for kids who have support systems and safety nets. But it is exponentially worse when they have neither of those things.

If you don't know this already, you need to understand that Black kids aren't allowed to be scared, or distressed, or angry. There are very few safe environments for a Black child or teenager to feel big emotions and to express confusing and conflicting feelings out loud. There are even fewer opportunities for them to do this in front of a nonjudgmental witness, who can hear them and hold space for them without reacting or punishing them.

There's a simple reason for this: Black emotion has been pathologized, mocked, and criminalized. (The school-to-prison pipeline is no joke.) A White eleven-year-old having an emotional outburst is most likely going to be talked off the ledge. A Black eleven-year old—perhaps one like the late Honestie Hodges—may well be put in handcuffs, or body-slammed to the floor by a cop or school security officer who wouldn't dream of doing that to a back-talking White student. Look at Simone Biles and Naomi Osaka—two ultra-high-achieving young Black women who were mercilessly demonized for putting their mental and physical health ahead of press conferences or yet another gold medal.

White kids and teens might not have to worry so much about how the police are going to respond to an outburst, but they still need to be heard, listened to, and understood. Doubly so, since online radicalization is a growing issue for young White men and women. Kids who feel socially isolated are vulnerable to these kinds of predators. According to research by the Southern Poverty Law Center, teenagers who join (or aspire to join) groups like the Proud Boys, or any kind of White supremacist or neo-Nazi group, are driven by a combination of trauma, disruption, uncertainty, and loss. Most feel unwanted or unheard and long to be accepted and to feel a sense of belonging. (A much smaller percentage are simply supporters of these belief systems.) If a child is living in a household with a radicalized parent, the desire to be loved by that parent is a strong driver to begin adopting those beliefs (something that is also applicable to kids whose parents are using or dealing drugs, or involved in any kind of criminal or gang life).

They are *feeling* the same things that Black kids are experiencing, but they are reacting to them in very different ways. An angry White child is more likely to act out—perhaps hurting or threatening others. An angry Black child is more likely to withdraw, acting in ways that primarily harm themselves. Put this into visuals: Most mass shooters fall into a very predictable demographic of White, male, and middle class.

We struggle to have empathy for kids or young adults who take this route to mass-casualty violence, but the truth is that most of these people would have benefited from active listening and intervention from empathetic, concerned, and consistent adults.

Either way, the best kind of intervention for these kids is to create places where they can be seen, heard, and empathized with, without judgment or reflexive punishment.

The Unheard Child

There is a catastrophic lack of listening within our schools. We're not here to put blame on anyone. Life is complicated and full of nuance. Teachers and parents are stretched to their breaking point. But we have to learn to hear our children, even when their voices are barely whispers above news, social media, and the intense stress of trying to survive in contemporary America.

This was especially important in our community, where Black and Brown kids from underserved communities are punished in school at vastly higher rates than their equally mischievous, distracted, depressed, isolated, unhappy, or traumatized White classmates. One middle school in Minneapolis suspended Black students at 338 percent higher rates than their White classmates. For this particular school district, "Black students were 41 percent of the overall student population, but made up 76 percent of the suspensions."

For White children, their parents' biggest fear might be that their child's grades slip. Perhaps he or she will not get into their first-choice college, or struggle to get a letter of recommendation from a highly regarded teacher.

For Black children, the stakes are higher. These early encounters with angry authority figures create additional layers of trauma, stigma, shame, and depression on top of what is already going on in that child's life. Think of Daron. *Every interaction in school was a source of pain and shame because his clothes were old and dirty and ripped.* He was riding a knife's edge of anger, despair, and embarrassment that flared up in constant small social collisions—even with his friends.

Those collisions ended with trips to the principal's office, and often punishment or detention. All it took was a new pair of pants to ease some of that shame and hair-trigger response. Now, those pants didn't fix the bigger problems in Daron's life. But they did lower the odds that he would end up in detention—or some kind of altercation with authority—on any particular day. For simple financial reasons, we can't buy new, fresh pants for every kid who needs them, but at this point we had a small group of students we were working with, and Atman, Andy, and Ali were doing everything. We weren't working with an entire school. It was more of a family than a program—so buying pants was still realistic at that point. Now, since our group has grown so large, it isn't.

This matters for one big reason: Every time a Black child—especially one who has been labeled as troubled, or from a "bad" neighborhood or underserved community—ends up in detention, or suspension, or having their very understandable trauma in some way criminalized, it normalizes a punitive relationship of unempathetic, authoritarian punishment with no allowances or compassion for a child's origins or reality. One former student, fresh out of jail, told us, "All that detention got me ready for was incarceration."

This becomes fully apparent when you look at our "justice system," where 44 percent of children held in detention centers, or incarcerated in other locations, are Black.[1] The racial disparity is getting worse, increasing by 22 percent since 2001.[2] This stuff has deep roots. More disturbingly, recent research has shown that racist and aggressive policing depresses civic engagement. Black people who have repeated negative interactions with the police become deeply skeptical that anything good can come from the state. Instead of engaging with politics or advocating for themselves, they withdraw, hoping to avoid the attention of law enforcement.[3] They don't vote—not seeing any point in it—and as a result these deeply racist policies stay firmly in place.

In 2017, *Mother Jones* magazine reported that "In an era of racial segregation, especially residential segregation, Black youths' lives are surrounded by police officers, and their teenaged mistakes are more likely to land in the juvenile justice system. White youths' mistakes are not."[4]

In January 2021, the Rochester Police Department was forced to release body camera footage of multiple officers pepper-spraying a nine-year-old Black girl who was experiencing a family disturbance and was clearly in extreme mental and emotional distress. A White female officer negotiates with the girl as she sits half-in, half-out, of the police cruiser. While the child begs for her father, the officer tells her she will get pepper-sprayed in her eyes unless she complies. Eventually a White male officer authorizes the female to spray her. The girl begs for help to wipe the spray from her eyes as the officers close the door on the child and step away from the cruiser. The male officer says "Unbelievable" as he leaves the child to deal with her fear, pain, and trauma on her own.

Frankly, we'd love to sit down with those officers and have a conversation about just what the f**k any of them were thinking at that moment.

Unbelievable is that multiple adults couldn't figure out a way to help this child—who is clearly in a difficult home situation—with compassion, understanding, and tolerance.

Unbelievable is that after having traumatized her, they left her alone, crying hysterically, in considerable pain, without any awareness or acceptance of the fact that she was literally a child, scared, desperate for her dad, and utterly alone.

Yoga as Self-Protection

All these different issues were a big part of our desire to develop practices that could spread out to other schools and facilities across the country. Our after-school programs were keeping kids safe and happy, and encouraging them to develop the techniques that would help them navigate the adult world with more equanimity and peace. However, we knew we needed to offer some kind of emergency care: a buffer between a kid processing trauma and the authority figures who would slap her or him in handcuffs rather than try to help them.

We are slowly starting to work with adults in various positions of power and authority (including the Baltimore PD). However, our most powerful and impactful work was—and is—with children, helping them to develop the inner reserves of resilience, equanimity, and self-control to survive and thrive in a world that views these officers' brutal, callous, and incomprehensible behavior (and that of all the other officers, teachers, and authority figures) as acceptable.

If authority figures won't learn how to understand, respect, and love vulnerable children, then these vulnerable children need to learn how to regulate themselves in two ways:

- One is the standard meditation practice that you may practice yourself: breathwork for balancing, yoga for strengthening, meditation for harmony.

- Two is a defensive practice: something that will keep you safe when you are a child, teenager, or young adult, surrounded by multiple angry, compassion-free police or authority figures, judging you like you're twice your age.

We already had many of these techniques in action. Our kids were learning breathwork, stress management, and stretching. It was helping. But we needed something more—an active, in-the-moment intervention that would keep kids out of detention and away from school security officers (often retired or moonlighting police officers, and often woefully under-skilled at handling childhood trauma).

We needed a place where a child could *be heard* and process intense trauma in a safe space with very little fear of repercussions. Where he or she could let off the steam that comes from having an untreated learning disorder, or eating nothing but processed junk for breakfast, or being mercilessly teased for a sloppy fade or unwashed and smelly clothes. This safety valve became the Mindful Moment room.

The Mindful Moment Room

The Mindful Moment room started at Patterson High School. Shout-out to Principal Vance Benton, who had the vision and enthusiasm to OK the program. In the first meeting Ali had with him, Vance quoted Yoda: "Do or do not, there is no try," and we knew he was the right man and we were in the right place. He cared so much about the students there and wanted to bring in interventions that not only would help them succeed in school but also help them survive growing up in Baltimore.

The Mindful Moment room is an emergency reset for a kid in distress. In the room, you are putting together breath and body awareness and teaching kids how to name a feeling. They may be feeling undiagnosed trauma especially intensely, or be in a heightened emotional state, or just having a bad day. We decorate the Mindful Moment room with Himalayan salt crystals, fountains, oil diffusers, and inspirational posters that read: *You Can Do This! Believe in Yourself!* There are cushions to sit on. In high school the kids can self-refer; in elementary school or middle school the teacher refers them. Each referral equals twenty minutes in the room, usually with the focused attention of our staff members.

We do not counsel the kids; we actively listen and mirror, which empowers the youth and lets their voice be heard. Then we help them analyze their stressors, how they play out in their bodies (clenching their jaw, balling up their fists, playing with their hair), then we do breathing techniques that can ground them to respond and not react. With time they come to know their triggers and how they play out in their body, and they can "graduate" to grounding themselves so they don't need our staff in the room, and in their lives.

The Mindful Moment room (or detention to meditation program) has changed how schools in Baltimore handle children who are having a difficult day. Instead of disciplining the kids, the staff redirects them to a safe space of listening and loving presence. The kid will open up to our staff and share a little—or sometimes a lot—of what is going on in their life. Often it turns out that they have not eaten that morning. They may have been physically abused that morning. This stuff manifests as acting out in class, but that's not the real problem.

The Mindful Moment Protocol

The first thing a kid hears when they walk in is "Let me know when you feel ready to talk." Both student and staff member sit in a peaceful silence until the student feels drawn toward wanting to talk. (The silence is key. Our staff are taught to let the child initiate conversation unless there is clearly something very wrong going on.)

Why is it so important to give children the power to start a conversation? Because every "troubled" kid is dealing with constant demands from adults to *talk, explain yourself,* or *tell me what happened.* Yet many kids don't have the language or insight to fully answer those questions. By giving students more than what they are used to having—power—it changes the whole vibe of the room. In the classroom setting, you only do what you are told. We try to give them more mental empowerment. Even as adults we tend to lack that control.

Setting Up Your Mindful Moment Room

The key to the Mindful Moment room is creating a container where the participants feel comfortable and safe. You want to create an oasis in the school where it doesn't feel like you are in the school building. We do this by adding the oil diffusers, Himalayan salt crystals, zafus, yoga mats, inspirational posters, fountains, tapestries, tea machine, rugs, etc.

Once the oasis is created, then you need to work with the staff and the administration of the school to make clear the purpose of the room and to share the techniques and practices so that they understand firsthand what the benefits are with these types of practices. This is essential because if the staff and admin don't buy into the program, then there is no way that it is going to be successful.

Next you introduce the practices to the students. This can be done over a few weeks where staff goes into every individual classroom and explains the practices, their benefits, and when they should be used. Once the practices have been introduced to both staff and students, along with the rules of how and when to use the Mindful Moment room, then the room can begin to operate on a daily basis.

- Our staff aren't there to enforce good behavior. Instead, they are there to be active listeners.

- Our staff actively listen and mirror back the child's words and movements to empower them, let them know they've been heard, and allow them to have a voice.

- Once the kids have shared what's bothering them, we do some breathing exercises or sit quietly together in silent reflection.

- The staff member asks them where in their body they feel stress. Maybe their stomach hurts, or their hands are balled up in fists.

- Once they identify where the stress plays out in their body, we guide them through thinking of that physical sign of stress as an indicator that they need to practice their deep breathing or to use their silent reflection time to prevent another negative interaction.

- Then we do some breathing and meditation.

- After the session is finished, participants return to their classrooms. We try to keep sessions to fifteen minutes.

- All visits are logged and recorded.

Eventually our staff can reach out to individual classrooms to see if they are interested in receiving mat-based classes and/or other sessions to assist with behavior and classroom management.

Another key aspect to this program is creating Mindful Ambassadors. Our staff will eventually identify students who have really taken to the practice. We will give them some extra in-depth training to allow them to begin facilitating practices throughout the day in the classrooms. This means that the ambassadors start to do outreach, recommending the program to their peers and learning the techniques outlined above (though they are generally supervised by a staff member). The idea is to empower these ambassadors to see they can have a positive effect on fellow students. They can notice a struggling classmate and stage quick interventions in the moment, for instance, advising their classmate on breathing exercises when they are getting heated.

An important element of this program is to not force it. Let it flow naturally and soon the entire culture/climate of the school will change. It will become normal to either breathe or meditate when one faces adversity. It is very important to stress to the staff that this room is not to be used as a form of punishment or to just get a "high flyer" out of their classroom. We want to make sure that teachers are not abusing the room by just trying to get rid of students so that they don't have to deal with them.

To that end, it's critical that the room is not seen as someplace for bad kids to be sent, but as a resource for all students, where they can learn skills that will help them be less stressed. Even the "smart kids" at school have achievement anxiety and other types of stress. Equally important, make sure the room is used for the practice only and not as a place to hang out.

One goal is to get the staff and administration to actually use the room instead of simply punishing kids for their behavior with detention or suspension. Within the room, we try to take the situation from punitive to empowering. Kids are used to getting into trouble for certain things, but the room gives them an opportunity to figure out what's wrong, recenter themselves, and then go back to class in a better place.

The Mindful Moment program works because it reflects what traumatized and distressed children actually need and want in these moments. When was the last time you responded well to being told to *calm down*? Yet that is generally what kids hear from the adults charged with talking them down from a fight.

Worse, parents and teachers practice *separation-based discipline*, ignoring their kids when they are behaving badly, or telling them to *go to your room* or *leave me alone*. Kids can be infuriating. We get that. They can drive you to the edge of reason and sanity. Yup. That's true. But when a child is at that point of pushing you to your breaking point, it's often the moment that kid needs you to show up for them the most. Think about what you are saying when you punish your kids by sending them away from you—*if you mess up, behave badly, or f**k up, you will be separated from the people you love and need the most.*

Remember Phil Leaf's insight that badly behaved kids are often the kids who most desperately want and need your attention, and that often that beleaguered teacher, dealing incessantly with that one disruptive kid, is the *only* adult who pays that kid any attention, ever? How is yet more rejection going to affect that kid, right when he or she is desperate for connection?

The Mindful Moment room gives students who are in distress that space to be connected to another caring adult, without judgment or punishment. It gives the teacher—on the edge of losing it with that kid—a break. Both adult and child can reset and try again.

Our staff members don't have all the answers, but they are willing to listen (in fact, we aren't there to provide solutions, simply an ear and empathy). And this is another core part of the Mindful Moment program—traumatized people need to tell their stories in order to process what has happened to them and begin to heal. Every child who is willing to share a little of what has hurt them is a step closer to one day recovering from it.

Simple, right? Well, it works. At Robert Coleman, in the epicenter of where the Freddie Gray uprising happened, there hasn't been one suspension in six years. At Fort Worthington, suspensions have gone from 179 in our first year, 80 the second year we were there, to only 8 suspensions the third year we were there.

So this is one of the coolest programs we have, because it is changing the whole outdated education system in three profound ways:

- Offering an alternative (if only for twenty minutes) to the authoritarian, brick-wall, *do this because I said so* approach.

- Giving the child an opportunity to practice holding healthy boundaries about what is appropriate and what is not within the Mindful Moment room.

- Empowering the child to understand that they are not dependent on the staff member in the room but on the techniques and the breath itself. During the course of the year, the referral numbers go down because the kids begin to understand their stressors and use the techniques we've taught them to relieve that stress and achieve homeostasis. Nothing makes us happier than a child who no longer needs to use the Mindful Moment room.

The Mindful Moment room has given kids the skills and tools to deal with their anger, trauma, and lack of focus. In addition, it's given kids the chance to learn self-regulation and methods to get back to center. Every year follows a similar pattern: The Mindful Moment rooms are used more at the beginning and less at the end. In the beginning of fall semester the kids need to go to the room to center themselves, but then later in the year, it's used less because the kids are familiar with the practices and can do them without any guidance or even a dedicated space. The practice becomes innate, and a kid who's kind of freaking out in the back of the room in class can catch themselves: *Wait a minute. Alright, I caught myself. I'm going to bring myself back with my breath.*

Vance has been a big booster for us, implementing all the programs throughout his meticulously neat and organized school. He tells the story of how he really didn't notice how peaceful the school was until he went to another Baltimore school and saw how chaotic the hallways were and how stressed out the students, the staff, and the administration were. When he went back to his school, he felt that peace just going over him.

One day, just before COVID, he saw a student pulling at the locked door of the Mindful Moment room. The student was having an intense feeling of crisis. He needed that moment in the room, to recalibrate himself, but there were no staff in the room and the door was locked. As Vance watched, the student sat down in front of the door, on one of the most heavily trafficked areas in that school, and did his practice, by himself. Once he felt better, he got up and walked back to class. When Vance told us the story, he emphasized, "You have no idea how much the culture has changed in the school. A couple of years ago, before the program was in place here, somebody might have just kicked them or punched them in the face when he was down there like that, and for the fact that it's just part of our school culture and that's normal is a beautiful thing."

Making the Most of Your Mindful Moment Room

We use the Mindful Moment room for kids, but frankly it's a helpful tool to have for any cohort of people, young or old. When you set up your room, use what you have to create an ambiance. You want that sense of ritual, or of a space outside of the normal work- or school-life paradigm. It doesn't need to be fancy, and if your budget doesn't swing to salt lamps and sound machines, well, OK. So long as you can make it somewhat comfortable and relaxing. Perhaps swap out overhead fluorescents for plug-in lamps, and molded plastic chairs for a few cushions on the floor.

As you move forward, always remember that you are working with traumatized people whose trauma can pop up in unexpected and unpredictable ways. It's on you to be aware and mindful, and to minimize triggers.

Ross was in the Mindful Moment room at Patterson High School one day. A young girl walked in, clearly agitated. She slammed the door, threw down her book bag, and slumped to the floor. She wrapped her arms around her knees and stared down, ignoring Ross's greeting.

Ross was still pretty new. He'd been mentored during his earlier shifts in the room, but this was his first time on his own. Because of his inexperience, he made a simple but significant mistake. He went up to the girl and asked, "You got a hall pass?" When she didn't look up, or respond, he got up in her face and said, "Hello, hello, hello?"

Worse, when that didn't work, Ross touched her shoulder with a tap to get her attention. Instantly—as if he'd touched her with an electric wire—the girl exploded. Cussing, shouting, telling him to "leave me the eff alone, what the f**k is wrong with you, man." Ross's first thought was *I want to toss her out of the room*, but instead he centered himself, went over to the desk, took a couple of deep breaths, and got himself together. He realized, *I've got to give her ten minutes and then* *we'll start from the beginning.* Instead, she sat for a few more minutes, then got up and walked out of the room.

Next day, the girl came back and said, "Hi, Mr. Ross, how are you doing today?" Ross was like, "You cussed me out yesterday! What happened? What was going on with you yesterday?" She looked Ross in the eyes and said, "I didn't cuss you out yesterday!" And the thing is—she really didn't remember cussing out Ross yesterday. That intense, emotional reaction had burned across her brain so fast, and so instinctively, that the analytical side of her brain had shut down. That exchange hadn't even registered with her, and she was being honest when she said she didn't remember it.

So, you need to remember what Ross learned from this episode: We never really understand what anyone else is going through, or how they are going to respond to situations that feel very bland and unexciting to us. This is why it is crucial not to trigger kids and instead—as much as is appropriate and safe—let them set the terms of how they engage with you.

This student had a difficult home situation, with no real support from her parents, and limited and unpredictable access to clean clothes, food, hygiene products (imagine being a teenage girl with no way to get pads or tampons), or any other essentials. She was considered a habitual truant. Rather than try to help her with some of the factors that were going into her truancy, the school instead had an aide who followed her from classroom to classroom to make sure she didn't skip school. No wonder she was on edge.

Here's another important lesson that Ross learned from his time working in the Mindful Moment room. A few weeks later, Ross worked with a kid who was upset that he didn't have a book bag and was carrying around his things in a plastic shopping bag. This seemed like an easy fix for Ross, so he went to Target and bought the kid a bag. The next day he had a line of kids, asking, "Mr. Ross, where's my book bag?"

Just as it's important to honor and respect your students' boundaries, so is it important to honor and respect yours. Ross can't buy twenty book bags, as much as he might want to. So it's important for him—and for you—to come to this work with a personal practice to stay strong and grounded, and to keep showing up from a place of love. Remember that a personal practice is like an invisible force field that will help you integrate your own life experiences and reality (*Damn, I'm going to be late with rent, and why is my boyfriend being such an idiot?*) with the stressors of the kids you're working with. So as you tell your kids or other loved ones to *breathe*, make sure you are remembering to do it yourself.

CHAPTER THIRTEEN

Meditative Movement

Yoga is something you are, not something you do.

So, right about now you're probably wondering where the yoga is in this book. After all, that's primarily what we are known for, right? You may well have googled around at this point and seen videos of our Robert Coleman kids cat-cowing on mats. So how come we haven't mentioned an asana yet, or prescribed a single pose? Well, there's a couple of reasons for that. First off, if you're interested enough to read a book on yogic practices, you've probably spent years on the mat yourself. You've heard the science, and experienced the benefits that come with a regular practice. Chances are, you don't need us walking you through a downward dog.

Secondly, the bending and stretching that we generally associate with yoga is in many ways the less important element of yogic practices. Now, don't get us wrong, physical practice can be incredibly powerful: Smit cured himself of a serious health condition with a prescription of poses. But too many people stop at the physical stuff, thinking that they are practicing yoga, without moving on to the deeper practices. The sun salutations and asanas are as popular and all-pervasive as they are because they are the most understandable form of yoga. We can all wrap our heads around feeling calmer and physically better after a session on the mat. But the truly deep work is less about the body and more about the mind, and the magic way we can affect our well-being by regulating our thoughts and feelings through breath, mantras, and mudras.

One of Andy's pet peeves is getting up in front of a crowd and saying, "We're going to do some yoga, meditation, and breathing." Why? Because *all* of this stuff is yoga, and suggesting that meditation or breathwork *isn't* yoga misses the point of what yoga is: an all-encompassing practice that engages mind, body, and spirit. Now, we've used this *yoga, meditation, and breathing* framework ourselves, over the course of the book, and in all our teachings. It's not accurate, but it reflects how people understand these elements to be discrete and optional, in a Choose Your Own Adventure kind of way. We've found over the years that simply calling it all "yoga" can get in the way, confusing people at the very beginning of their yoga practice, and potentially putting them off pursuing it.

So here's an idea for you to think about. All this stuff—the breathing, the meditation, the postures—is yoga. It is very tempting to focus on the physical-movement aspects of yoga. We live in a culture that rewards momentum, action, and tangible achievements. #yogabody is a lot easier to throw up on your socials than #meditationmind. But simple physical movements alone are not going to get you where you need to go. We've all walked out of a yoga class feeling that serene buzz of sudden peace. And we've all had that sudden peace go up in flames the first time some jerk cut us off at a light. Only meditation can turn that sense of peace from a fleeting to a fixed state of mind. We have a friend who had out-of-control road rage. She religiously went to yoga classes but was still furiously f-bombing anyone who got too close to her lane on the drive home. We prescribed meditation, and the next time we hung out she told us, "My husband said he hasn't heard me lose my shit in months. I'm not stressing when people cut me off or I miss a light. It doesn't even register as stressful!" Physical practice alone can't get you to that place.

So, when we think of the postures and asanas, we see them very much in the traditional yogic way: They are part of an overall approach to yoga, rather than the beating heart of it. And frankly, yoga doesn't need to be overly complicated. There are a lot of places to find some pretty questionable yoga, either online or in in-person classes. A lot of the online streaming options offer a version of yoga that has very little to do with traditional postures, skewing more toward a sweaty workout rather than a divine practice. Now, we still think this is good, because it introduces people to the practice and some people go deeper and do more research on their own. But then there are people who see it only as a workout (the same as Pilates or going to the gym) and never understand the depth of the practice and its real meaning, getting into how it informs the way you live your life, the breathing practices, and the meditation.

All these reasons are why we are keeping the physical postures simple. Poses like cat-cow, the sun salutation sequence, tree pose, and child's pose are both a healthy physical practice for keeping your body limber and a way to quickly de-stress. We're not going to illustrate these poses here, since they are available everywhere from fitness magazines to YouTube tutorials. We recommend taking ten to fifteen minutes every morning to run through them at least once. Add in some forward and backward bends and neck and shoulder rolls.

If you are feeling especially antsy, add frog pose to your practice. Since this pose is less well known, we'll explain it here.

The Frog

We love our amphibians. When we were kids, playing in the streams with our Friends cohort, we looked for frogs. Seeing one was like catching sight of an otherworldly messenger, because let's be real, frogs can be kind of weird looking. Frogs are also powerful AF. There is a huge amount of potential strength in those back legs. This exercise works to strengthen and tone the muscles in the thighs, calves, and butt. It also helps release and open up the hips and strengthen the joints and ligaments of the legs. The frog is great for amped-up kids with energy to burn, who are struggling to center themselves.

Humans store a ton of emotion in the hips. It's not unusual to see a student in tears during a deep stretch that hits the hips. Practicing the frog and slowly working out that tightness in the hips will give you a good place to start releasing that emotion and trauma.

INSTRUCTIONS

Stand with heels together, toes pointed outward, and heels off the floor.

Squat down to the floor, keeping your back straight and your heels off the floor.

Place your fingertips on the floor, keeping your elbows inside your knees.

While inhaling, extend and straighten your legs, keeping your fingertips on the floor and your heels off the floor, and bring your chin to your chest.

Hold.

While exhaling, come back down to the original position, and bring your head back up.

Repeat.

TIPS

Keep checking in to make sure your heels are together and off the ground, remembering to keep your elbows inside your knees. Keep your fingertips on the ground and be mindful of your knees—if the pose starts to hurt, pull back the range of movement.

Straighten your legs as much as possible, without pushing yourself into pain or discomfort. With practice, you will be able to straighten them completely.

As you become more experienced, bring your fingers closer to your body to make the stretch more intense.

PRECAUTIONS

Remember that this pose is very strenuous, so start slowly, then increase gradually.

Kundalini Spinal Twist

Another less-well-known pose that will build some heat and fire is the kundalini spinal twist.

INSTRUCTIONS

Stand in mountain pose.

Hands are in front of your heart in the bear grip (palms facing each other, fingers clasped, forearms parallel to the ground, and your fists are about an inch or two away from your body).

Inhale while twisting to the left.

Exhale while twisting to the right.

Repeat.

On the last breath, inhale and come to the center, holding your breath and pulling your arms in opposite directions for as long as possible.

Exhale, and relax.

BENEFITS

Increases flexibility in the back

Strengthens and tones the arms and shoulders

Strengthens the heart

TIPS

There should be tension in your arms at all times.

Make sure to keep your hands in the center of your chest at all times.

Be sure that the twisting is in your spine and not in your shoulders.

PRECAUTIONS

Have students start twisting slowly, then increase speed, to decrease the chance for injury.

Keep your base wide enough to maintain balance.

Only hold the breath for as long as comfortably possible; the exhale should be relaxed.

Don't over-twist, as it can put extra strain on your lower back.

All of these poses are suitable for children or adults and will give you a good grounding in yogic movement. Experiment with a posture sequence such as: cat-cow, sun salutation, tree, frog, spinal twist, cat-cow, and corpse pose. Do as many as feels good to you, and keep it brief if you are practicing with kids. As you practice, try to let your mind get into the zone, letting go of thoughts as much as possible and really experiencing the sensation of movement.

One thing that is very important is remembering the breath. A lot of people think yoga is all about bending and stretching, but the bending and stretching only complement the breath, so when doing poses, be mindful of your breath.

Finally, let your kids giggle and goof if they need to—accepting that even if they don't seem to be taking the movements seriously, they are being affected by them. Remember that practicing the postures isn't about striving for perfection. In many ways it is the opposite: giving your body the freedom to move to its own abilities and on its own time. Enjoy the pleasant sensations, and observe the moments of strain or effort without judgment.

If you don't already have your practice locked in, use the five rites here to get started. If you're working with kids, these poses are the perfect introduction. For adults, they can be modified and enhanced to reflect your needs in the moment. Be a scientist. Figure out what works for you. Make it personal. Atman has sped up the sun salutation to the point where it becomes a serious cardio workout. Conversely, Ali sometimes slows it way down, losing himself in the meditation element and calming his mind for the evening.

What can you learn about where your heart, mind, and body are in this moment? Remember that simply giving your body your permission to exist, to feel, to be, can be incredibly cathartic. Our society is a ruthless, capitalist system where one's body is a commodity to be sold until it is too broken down to be worth buying. We push our physical selves to the edge of survival in order to make wages that don't cover the cost of living, and when our bodies fail it is our fault, not the fault of the billionaires who've killed small family-owned businesses to centralize wealth in their pockets. Our politicians benefit by keeping us angry and at odds with each other, and with ourselves. Magazines and pop culture and social media apps are filled with images and stories about the unacceptable nature of our bodies. Our bodies absorb this anger, fear, and unhappiness on a somatic level—of course your back hurts, your stomach is in knots, and your knees ache.

We've seen in Baltimore that systems aren't built to support people they don't really care about. Sometimes they're actively set up to break people down, break down their economy, and break down their education opportunities. Society punishes people who make the powerful uncomfortable, and kids in prison, struggling families, and decaying cities make the powerful very uncomfortable indeed. Audre Lorde memorably said, "Caring for myself is not self-indulgence, it is self-preservation, and that is an act of political warfare." Being OK with yourself or, even better, actively loving yourself, when whole social structures rely on you to *not* love yourself, is a radical act.

For the time it takes to practice the Five Tibetan Rites, imagine what it would be like to reject everything society tells you to think about yourself and your accomplishments. Instead, imagine accepting and loving yourself, and accepting and loving your body. Keep imagining until you actually do.

The Five Rites Practices Introduction

The Five Tibetan Rites are two-thousand-plus-year-old yoga asanas, first developed by a wandering group of Tibetan monks, and later adopted by British officers during the colonial era in India. They were first introduced to the West in a book called *The Eye of Revelation*, which claimed that ill health was caused by the slowing of seven psychic vortexes (or chakras) in the body. These poses reignited those vortexes, and presto: good health. They are simple moves, repeated twenty-one times each day. Some of them are familiar to the average yogi—one is a move between upward and downward dog, called the two dogs. Another is a deep backbend called camel posture. Another is a simple standing rotation with arms outstretched. None of them are overly difficult; what they do is pull us firmly back into our bodies (often with giggles, as kids briefly lose their balance) and give us a little bit of a workout. Anyone who does this regularly will feel that pleasant sensation of muscles that have been used and are slightly sore. This, as much as anything else, calls one's attention to their body, and the sensations that come from living in it.

1. *Helicopter*
INSTRUCTIONS

Stand on your mat with your arms parallel to the floor.

Spin around in a circle clockwise (look at your right hand, then follow it around in a circle).

Inhale deeply for half the turn, and then exhale deeply for the other half of the turn.

Pick a spot on the wall and count that as one rotation every time you pass it.

Try to stay in the same spot on your mat.

BENEFITS

Strengthens the arms

Strengthens the shoulders

Improves balance

TIPS

Remind students to keep their arms parallel to the floor.

If you are dizzy when you finish, stand with your arms by your sides, close your eyes, bring your focus to the point in between and above your eyebrows, and then take three deep breaths. This will help you get your balance back.

Remind the students that they need to stay under control and stay in the same spot on their mat as they spin.

Stagger the students on their mats so there is no slapping.

PRECAUTIONS

Students may get extremely dizzy, so remind them to go slowly.

Watch out for students intentionally trying to bump into and slap each other.

2. *Leg Lift*
INSTRUCTIONS

Lie flat on your back with your arms by your sides, your legs together and extended.

Hands should be palms down by your sides.

As you inhale, bring your legs up, perpendicular to the floor, and bring your chin to your chest.

Hold at the top, tightening your stomach muscles.

As you exhale, slowly lower your feet and head to the floor, so your head and heels touch the ground at the same time.

BENEFITS

Strengthens the muscles of the stomach and thighs

TIPS

Say "Inhale and up, exhale and down."

Beginner students can place their hands under the small of their back for more support.

As much lifting as possible should be done with the stomach muscles.

Keeping the legs straight is more important than bringing the legs up high.

Students tend to ignore lifting their head and only lift their legs. Remind them to bring their chin to their chest.

Do not let your legs bend when bringing them up.

Bring only your chin to your chest; do not let your shoulders leave the floor.

Remind your students to let their feet touch the ground silently.

PRECAUTIONS

This puts a lot of strain on the stomach muscles, so allow students to take a break if needed.

3. Back Bend

INSTRUCTIONS

Start on your knees.

Your hands can be down at your sides or on your lower back for more support.

Inhale and bend at your lower back, going back as far as possible.

Point your chin up and back toward the ceiling, letting your head fall back.

Hold this position briefly.

Exhale, and come back forward until your body is straight, bringing your chin all the way to your chest.

BENEFITS

Opens the front of the body

Relieves muscle tension and stretches muscles that shorten as we age

Lengthens and tones the spine

TIPS

Say "Inhale and back, exhale and forward."

You should not be sitting on your heels; your body should be straight above your knees.

If students need to, have them get into child's pose after finishing.

If there is too much pressure on the students' knees, they can fold their mat over a few times for extra cushioning.

PRECAUTIONS

The back is very sensitive and fragile, so stress being careful and listening to your body.

4. *Table*

INSTRUCTIONS

Sit down on your mat with your legs extended and touching in front of you.

Palms should be on the ground next to your hips with your fingertips facing your toes.

Inhale, flatten your feet to the floor, push your hips up until your torso is parallel to the floor, and bring your body up into a table position, letting your head fall back.

Hold this position.

Exhale, and slowly come back down into the starting position, with your legs flat and your hips between your hands.

BENEFITS

Provides stability and balance

Strengthens the arms, wrists, shoulders, and lower body

TIPS

Say "Inhale and up, exhale and down."

Instruct students not to slide their feet up to get into the table position, but to keep their heels in the same spot on the floor the entire time (heels move in a hinge motion).

Make sure hands aren't too far back; this places strain on the shoulders.

If students need to take some pressure off their wrists when starting, tell them to turn their hands out to the sides.

When students finish, have them roll their wrists and shake out their arms.

PRECAUTIONS

This pose puts a lot of pressure on the wrists.

Remind students to let their head hang in the upward position so they don't strain their neck.

5. *Hanging Cobra to Downward Dog*

INSTRUCTIONS

Lie on your stomach with your palms touching the floor by your armpits, keeping your legs extended and your toes curled under, touching the floor.

Extend your arms until they are straight, pushing yourself up off the floor, and keep them straight the entire time.

Only your palms and toes, not your knees, should be touching the floor, your head looking forward.

Inhale, bring your hips up into the air, your chin to your chest, and try to get your heels to touch the ground. (Your body should form a triangle shape.)

Hold this position.

Exhale, and slowly come back down to the starting position.

BENEFITS

Builds bone density

Eliminates back stiffness

Boosts circulation

Strengthens almost every muscle in the body

TIPS

If students need to rest on their knees when in the starting position, that is alright, but have them build up to not needing it.

PRECAUTIONS

This pose puts a lot of pressure on the wrists.

As you practice, experiment with adding more and more postures. Try moving through a sequence with music. How does it affect your experience if you turn the lights down? Make the poses your own, and do what affects you most powerfully. Atman's favorite poses are the sun salutation, five rites, stomach retraction, sat kriya, frog, and stretch pose. They are his favorites because they are intense, and when he does physical poses, he wants to get a physical workout while also getting the esoteric benefits. Uncle Will would always say if you do the big three—five rites, sat kriya, and the stretch pose—every day, you will be good. So, try to do those, then add a couple of your favorites on to his big three.

Here's a final thought. After years and years of practice, Andy no longer spends much time practicing physical yoga. If he does hit the mat, it will usually be a combination of the sun salutation, five rites, stretch pose, and sat kriya. While he loves all these poses and sequences of poses for a variety of reasons, whether it be the mental, physical, and spiritual benefits or just the memories of practicing them with Uncle Will and the fellas, Andy wouldn't choose any of them as his favorite.

Instead, Andy's favorite pose is the corpse pose. It is extremely basic, but it is the pose that he meditates in, so it has had the most impact on his life. He loves how it makes him feel grounded and connected not only to the planet but to the universe. "I am so grateful for its ease and its gift of transition that it gives me between my waking and sleep states. I always remember how great it made me feel as a little kid when I would lay down in the grass, or the sand at the beach, and look up at the sky and the clouds. Sometimes it's the simplest things that end up being the most powerful. So many people say they can't 'do' yoga, and yet they each are probably in my favorite pose once a day."

Andy hits on something important here. Poses aren't the end result. They are a step along the path toward something bigger than our physical selves. The poses that get you to that state of connection and communion are the poses that matter. Remember what Sat Bir said earlier in the book, about how, once you have that transformational moment, you can never undo it? The physical poses in yoga are a conduit to get you to that place, rather than an end in themselves. If—like Andy—you find a posture or sequence that takes you to a place of joy, epiphany, or connection, then that's the physical practice for you.

CHAPTER FOURTEEN

Off-the-Mat Practices

As we said in the last chapter: Most yoga happens off the mat. Once you have an established practice, that yoga sensibility will be your constant companion through life. You may find yourself fully in the yogic moment at the DMV, hanging out with your kids, or, like our friend in the last chapter, in those precious moments where your road-ragey self stays chill during yet another aggravating commute. The point of all this practice isn't to "be good at" yoga while you're in a class, or on a retreat, or sitting comfortably on a meditation pillow. The point is it embodies these concepts day in and out, naturally and without effort, and allows the resilience and peace that comes from yoga to sustain and fortify you as you go about your life.

For our students, be they kids, young adults, or adults, being able to access that yoga mindset during moments of stress and fear is doubly important. For all the emotions and energy that are going into the social justice movement, Black and Brown children and young adults are still being harmed and killed by the police (and by each other) on a daily basis. If they are being chased down an alley by the Chicago Police Department (like thirteen-year-old Adam Toledo) or having a mental health crisis at a foster home (like sixteen-year-old Ma'khia Bryant), being able to stay centered and nonreactive might save their lives.

So, as you move throughout your days, consider these three powerful components of yoga, and make sure you are incorporating them into the way you live your life, and modeling them for your children and peers.

Jnana Yoga: The Yoga of Wisdom

Jnana yoga is called the Yoga of Knowledge, and it is considered the most demanding of all forms of yoga. When you practice jnana yoga, you are using your mind to look deeply into both yourself as an individual, and yourself as part of the universal collective of humanity. After many, many years of practice, the jnana yoga practitioner will begin to shed their most self-limiting practices, letting them fall to the floor like a discarded coat, as they walk away to a more enlightened future.

Jnana yoga invites us to step back, look at our thought patterns, and ask questions about what we are feeling and why. This self-questioning is *hard*! We all want to believe that we have the moral high ground in an argument. Our instincts insist that we are right, and that our thoughts are the objective truth in any particular situation. It feels pretty fantastic to swat away the concerns of our spouses and children and say, "My way or the highway." Well, it feels fantastic in the moment. The next moment, when you are looking at the hurt and fearful faces of the people you love most, it feels pretty terrible.

This is hard AF. More than our bodies, more than our families, more than our shared collective history, we identify with our thoughts. Most people never fully understand that there is a difference between their true self and the thoughts that their brain generates in a constant, never-ending flow. Instead, they identify with their thoughts and become slaves to them. Those thoughts run the show, altering their moods and affecting the way they engage with the world. The more you let your thoughts dominate how you live, the more you begin to identify with them. We use the idea of *manas* (mind) and *buddhi* (awareness) to explain this: When your consciousness is in a manas state, you are identifying with your thoughts, ego, and lower vibrational things. Many of the practices we teach are designed to get your consciousness into buddhi: focused on your light, observing your thoughts rather than identifying with them, and other higher vibrational activities. But it's hard, and it's a constant struggle no matter how long you have been into the practice.

Many of the young people we work with are essentially trapped in that manas state, forced to make constant fight-or-flight choices, with no time to think through the ramifications of their actions. Their lives can quite literally be an ongoing choice to kill or get killed. It could be a dangerous choice to be the first person to step back, break that reactive cycle, and question one's own thoughts.

When you practice jnana yoga, you witness your thoughts, rather than identify with them. You recognize that your mind is making thoughts—the way it was designed to do—but that these thoughts are not an objective truth. We've all experienced that downward spiral of dark, negative thoughts. They pull us away from everything positive in our life, downplaying the good and happy things in our world, and swirling us into a simmering rage and resentment that usually has nothing to do with the reality of our life. Jnana yoga uses the six virtues—*shama* (tranquility, calmness); *dama* (restraint, control); *uparati* (withdrawal, monasticism); *titiksha* (fortitude in the face of adversity); *shradda* (belief and trust); and *samadhana* (focus and non-distraction)—to train the consciousness into being a witness to, rather than an active participant in, our thoughts.

Whole books can and have been written about jnana yoga. The most important thing to understand is that you are not your thoughts, and your thoughts are not you. In many ways, your brain works like a social media app, bombarding you with stimulation until you respond. As you move through your life, get into the practice of interrogating those thoughts and unwinding their origins. Are you mad at your partner, or is your brain nudging an old emotional trigger related to your parents? If you're losing your temper at your kids, look deeper. What need are they expressing that you don't feel capable of meeting? If you're sitting in traffic, fuming, why? You have no clue who's driving that Honda Civic, so why are you cursing them out? Ask yourself, *Why am I hurting? What's really going on?* Eventually you will begin to get answers.

Jnana yoga is not about denying these thoughts. They are there for a reason. The point is to learn to look at them again, and not accept them at face value. Do the yogic work to heal the pain and trauma. Eventually you will find those low vibration thoughts evolve into something higher vibrational.

Karma Yoga: The Path of Unselfish Action

Karma may be the most abused word in the English language, so let's definitively say that no, karma is *not* a bitch. Nor is karma really luck, or payback, or some kind of cosmic reward for doing a good deed. The simplest definition is that karma is the act of doing a positive thing for the right reason, without the expectation of a reward. Think of karma yoga as a kind of outward meditation. If mantra meditation engages your mind in a kind of focused flow, then karma yoga does a similar thing by likewise focusing you on one point in the present as you do an act of service. Part of the "service" is that concentration. Taking out the trash for your neighbor, even as you're cursing and moaning about it, isn't karma yoga. Taking out the trash and fully focusing on the task, taking care to do it to the best of your abilities, without resentment or annoyance, is.

Karma yoga helps you to learn from your world. A lot of times as a yogi, people think you are supposed to retreat from the world and disappear into a cave to meditate—well maybe—but a lot of really learning about yourself, and identifying your shortcomings, comes from interacting with the world. You start to see what you are drawn to, and what you are repelled by. Understanding this is a huge part of karma yoga, because it allows you to know more about yourself so that you can grow and overcome these things.

Karma yoga is inherently selfless. Doing a small good deed and then posting it on your socials isn't going to cut it.

Likewise, celebrities who drag their families (and a photographer) to a homeless shelter on Thanksgiving are missing the point. Sure, these acts might temporarily benefit others, but there is no benefit to yourself and your own ongoing growth as an individual. To fully experience karma yoga is to be a conduit for good works. The works flow through you without interference from the ego. The work belongs to the universe, not to you.

We've all experienced a world that feels fully out of our control. It could be politics, pandemic, or police. Authority figures shape our world, making policies that punish or kill the most vulnerable, and seem to be unmoved by the toll their decisions take on the poor and unprotected. Many local politicians became unreachable over the course of the pandemic, no longer staffing offices or holding town halls. If you are a concerned citizen who pays attention to policies that affect people in your community, this is infuriating. Frankly, we feel angry a lot of the time these days with how many people seem to be abdicating their responsibilities to everyday people.

Karma yoga can counter all this. Think of karma yoga as your chance to push back against the forces of injustice in the world. By doing some small act of service or kindness, you are creating change, and doing your own part, however small it may seem to be, to push the world toward a kinder and more enlightened place. Think of those good works, flowing through you, without ego, without "ownership," as tiny points of light. Enough tiny points of light, added together, can illuminate the world.

Karma yoga can also put you in the position to help people you wouldn't normally want to deal with. And this can be incredibly powerful. Helping a person who expects to hate you is true karma yoga, even if you do the good work and walk away without any expectation of reward or acknowledgment. Again, these tiny actions add up, turning the world a micron closer to enlightenment.

Bhakti Yoga: Love for Love's Sake

Bhakti yoga is about deepening and intensifying your relationship with God or the divine. For some old-school practitioners, this means singling out Hindi deities like Shiva, Krishna, Kali, and Vishnu, and focusing your practice on them. Others don't identify with a specific named figure, preferring to seek a connection to the universe or to an unnamed spiritual presence.

For us, it's simpler: Bhakti is about how we are all connected at the soul level. Bhakti yoga is all about seeing the light in you and seeing the light in that other person or that other thing. Uncle Will always taught us that the most important part of bhakti yoga is to see the light in yourself before you can see it in anyone else. This isn't easy. We live in a hierarchical culture. We are all unconsciously evaluating our status, all the time. Setting that aside and simply seeing yourself as a human, full of light, feels deeply unnatural.

Seeing that light reminds you that you and everyone around you are souls, you all have that universal spirit or that God within you. You are the same. Uncle Will would always say it's the hardest and the easiest form of yoga to practice because there's no physical practice, it's just loving something else. But it's hard to love the people who have hurt you or the people who piss you off or the people who make you sad. It's hard to love when you are in a situation that you might not want to be in, and it's *really hard* to love things that might repel you.

So, Uncle Will would always tell us to look again. And how looking again was quite literally a way of respecting both yourself and the other person involved. When you keep looking, you will eventually see that light, and it becomes impossible to really hate another person.

Part Three

I'm Going to Let It Shine

Uncle Will always told us, "Do the work and don't look for the results." By this he meant our job was to be a vessel for love, light, and service to flow through. Our ego is what gets tied to the results. You don't know if the results will come instantly, in a week, in a year, or in your next incarnation. When you get tied to results, you start to question yourself as a teacher if you don't see them—but your job is to come from a place of love and be present while you do the work.

He taught us that twenty minutes of meditation helps you burn off all that shit and negativity. Uncle Will would always say, "Burn that shit off in the light" or "You can't have darkness in the light." So when you do feel that darkness, negativity, and shit weighing on you, go deep into your light and burn it all off and then come back out into the world.

He would never call himself a guru or teacher. He was a reminder, helping us tap into the universal knowledge within us that we have forgotten. That's the same thing we are doing, reminding people of that knowledge and their inherent greatness.

Even though Uncle Will didn't stay in his physical body long enough to see 2020 and 2021, he must have seen forward enough to anticipate the wisdom of this advice. The truth is that, as the old-timey evangelical Charles Swindoll said, "Life is 10 percent what happens to me and 90 percent how I react to it." You—as someone who is most likely infused with yogic principles—probably understand this. You have a bad day at work, you take a minute or twenty to meditate. That meditation slows down your reactivity, helps you get a bit of perspective on the day's frustrations, and helps you reset. As you've read over the past few chapters, this skill is the cornerstone of our work.

When we started, we were crazy enough to think we were going to save the world. We're really into comics and *Star Wars* and Jedis, so we thought we were kinda like superheroes. But that truly was our mission. Early into it, we saw that three people can't save the planet or change the world. We started to realize that we weren't here to save anyone; we were here to give people the skills to help save themselves.

When Ali's son Asuman was young, he asked, "Daddy, what do you do at work? You seem to love it so much." Ali said, "I teach people to help themselves!" This is a huge part of our philosophy. We won't always be there, and our students will one day need to manage their own practices. So a big part of our work is our reciprocal teaching methods; we turn everyone we teach into a teacher. Everyone who comes through our program leaves it with the ability to share what they've learned: meditation, breathwork, being centered and connected to themselves. We turn them all into teachers—from a four-year-old pre-K student to a forty-year-old in a drug treatment center—so they can share the practices with as many people as they know. We teach them to know how to use them, why to use them, why they're practical, and then they go home and share them with others.

There was the little kid at elementary school whose parents would come home stressed: He would be cursed out, and instead of just taking it, the kid said, "Come on, sit down with me, let's breathe together and meditate." Or the lady who we taught at a drug treatment center, whose son was suffering from asthma, and she was able to teach him a few breathing exercises to relax and not tense up during an attack.

We always say love is the most powerful force in the universe. We're creating love zombies; we want to infect people with love and have them go around spreading it—minus all the eating people and stuff. We think, in particular now, with what's going on in the state of our nation, there are a lot of people who are scared, worried. People ask, "What's it like in Baltimore? What's the impact there?" Well, it's the same— it's not that different from eight years ago—there are still a lot of underserved people in the neighborhoods. But we can't get frustrated; we have to love more. And we have to *provide* more. This work only works if the opportunities and resources to survive and thrive are put in place too.

The ones who are suffering, the ones who make you most angry, or have the most frustration, they're the ones who need the love *most*. We really need to go out there and spread love. So making a change, making people teachers, empowering them with the practices, is what you do to make a bigger change.

Part One of this book was our story: who we are and where we came from. Part Two was the basics: breathwork, postures, and meditation, and the deeper work of helping people dealing with long-term trauma. Part Three is the holistic vision of spreading this work outward. All our kids are given the chance to lead a class. There are multiple reasons for this. Sometimes our instructors are stretched thin, and they need another pair of eyes to jump in and help the newbies. Sometimes we get the most disruptive child to lead so that they can get the attention they need and so that they may feel what it's like to try to lead something and not have people paying attention. We swear it never fails. When we bring the disruptive kid up front, at some point the child says, "But they're not listening to me." We just have to look at them and you can see the light bulb pop up. Suddenly they realize what it's like to try to get the attention of a group of distracted, disrespectful kids. They learn to be more respectful when others are speaking—and they encourage their classmates to do the same. This empowers the kids. And in most cases, people who have been traumatized have had their power stripped away from them, so empowering them helps them to heal their trauma.

Right now, as the despair of COVID begins to lift, the future is a mystery. We don't know if a vaccine is going to fully solve the pandemic, or if some variation of our COVID lifestyle is going to grind on, for months, maybe years. We don't know if the Biden administration is going to successfully effect some kind of cultural change in this country, encouraging compassion and kindness between disparate, angry groups. We don't know if those armies of angry White people are going to put down their *Blue Lives Matter* flags and agree to simply listen to other peoples' stories. We hope, but frankly this isn't the way people have ever behaved in the past, so hoping for it in the future can feel futile. Still, our work continues, with a focus on broadening the reach of our work by expanding the horizons of our students and empowering them to believe they have knowledge and ideas worth sharing. This first part of the puzzle—expanding horizons—is key.

CHAPTER FIFTEEN

The One-Block Radius

If you've ever gone to a mindfulness workshop, or hung out with a meditator, you've heard the word *expansiveness* used. There are all sorts of definitions of what exactly this expansiveness is. Some might use it to describe a sense of oneness; others an honesty with one's own self. Well, yes. But there's also another more literal way to describe it. We think of expansiveness as being the ability to open up your emotional, mental, spiritual, *and* physical world, and to move beyond the boundaries and borders that keep you locked in your own smaller social circle, unable to feel compassion for the experience of people in social circles outside of your own.

For those of you who live in a reliably safe neighborhood and aren't in a daily state of fight, flight, freeze, or fawn, this might be as simple as upping your weekly hikes or making the effort for a small moment of adventure to visit new-to-you areas of town. This kind of expansion is completely valid and valuable. However, in a neighborhood like Smallwood, these barriers are life-and-death. We call these barriers the one-block radius, and that radius is the outer limit of safety and security for both kids and adults in the hood. That radius is also the limit of their scope. They feel connected to only that area, and the things they see, feel, and experience are their reality. It's very limiting because of the lack of resources and opportunities there, and leads to feelings of hopelessness, helplessness, despair, and desperation.

We talked earlier in the book about how the old social ties of neighborhoods like Sparrows Point and Smallwood frayed and fractured after desegregation, the War on Drugs, and Bill Clinton's 1994 crime bill. Those social ties never completely disappeared, but they lost a lot of their power. They no longer could hold together whole communities, but they could—more or less—keep a block unified and safe. Over time, those block radii calcified and strengthened into something like a barrier reef. Sure, they keep the island safer, but a whole lot of people drown trying to swim across them. Kids who never left the block grew up to be teens who never left the block, who grew up to be young adults who died if they tried to.

In our early days, when we were still living on Smallwood, we saw some of our kids walking in the hood with a pair of bolt cutters. We knew they weren't going in a good direction. We tried to chase our kids down and get them, but they were young and in shape and waaaaaaaay too fast, and they dusted us and got away. The next day, all our neighborhood kids, including Ra'Mon and his cohort, were suddenly riding around on new bikes. We knew that their parents didn't get them those new bikes. Where did they come from? None of our kids were interested in telling us, even though it was pretty obvious they'd either lifted them from another neighborhood or earned them doing stuff we wouldn't approve of. New bikes are currency for kids like ours. And these new bikes soon got the attention of the kids one block over.

A week later, the kids from one block over moved in on our kids. Ra'Mon, then still a kid, saw his friend's older brother, Mook, get stabbed in his head and his back, and fall, bleeding, into the street. Ra'Mon and his friends thought they were going to die, and scattered.

So we talked to the crew. "What's going on?"

"Some kids stole our bikes."

"Well, y'all never really had no bikes to begin with."

"Well, we stole the bikes, then these kids stole them from us."

Never mind it was only a two-block distance from where the kids who stole the bikes from *our* kids lived. This was an open declaration of war, between two sets of kids living in almost identical circumstances and dealing with the exact same deprivations as each other. In any other world they would be friends. But on Smallwood, the one-block-radius rule meant the kids who lived two blocks away could be their mortal enemies.

For a day or so there was an uneasy quiet, but we knew enough to know that that peace wouldn't last. Mook, the little dude recovering from the stabbing, was hanging out on his steps after getting out of the hospital. He had staples in his head and back. We gathered our kids up just to have a discussion with them and let them know: "You know what happens, violence begets violence. Y'all are going to go beat these kids up—and look, they tried to kill Mook." We told them: "Y'all stole bikes, then they stole them from you. The next thing you know, someone is going to end up dead."

Our kids didn't care. Their guy had been hurt, their bikes had been stolen, and everything—their names, their honor, their integrity (at least in their eyes)—was on the line. This thing was going to end in a bloodbath.

We talked to Tay, one of the leaders in our little guys' crew, and said, "You walk us to the house and we'll nip this before someone ends up dead or in jail." It was only a thirty-second walk, but it felt like the longest walk of our lives. We were feeling nervous energy—we didn't know what we were walking into. But we had to dead this situation; otherwise, a lot of our kids were going to end up deceased or in jail.

The whole way over, our little dude, Tay, alternated between bravado and fear. "I don't want to go, I don't want to go. I'm going to mess them up." We told him, "Just roll with us, we'll handle the talking." The grandmother answered the door, and we got the little boys out of the house, and you could just feel the hate in their eyes, emanating out to each other.

Mind you, this was when they were in middle school, so these kids, ready to kill, were maybe eleven or twelve at the time.

We looked at the grandma, and as calmly as we could, told her, "Look, we need to nip this in the bud. If it goes any further someone is going to end up dead. I just want to let you know that your boy stabbed up our kid. They want to retaliate, but we told them we'd come to talk this out with you."

The grandmother gave us a long look and said, cold as could be, "I know they stabbed them. I gave them the knife and the screwdriver."

254 · Let Your Light Shine

It took being very, very deep in the practice to not want to punch this grandmother in the mouth. She was the one fanning the flames of violence. So, we did something very HLF. "We don't want trouble. If your kids want to join our program, we can get them in." We told her how we were a new organization trying to build community, so the kids from different blocks could be friends, not statistics. Even though we only had the budget to cover our small group of kids, we offered her grandsons a chance to join. And to her credit, the grandmother said, "OK, I'll think about it."

On the way back, Tay was like, "F**k them, we don't want them in our program." Our kids had respected us enough that they didn't go back there and retaliate. They squashed a beef. And we had to show them the same respect and honor their wishes. So, even though we knew that these kids desperately needed intervention, and that it wasn't too late to offer them help, we had to respect our kids and not allow them in the program. If we forced those kids into the program, we would lose ours—possibly forever.

And here's the f**king tragedy of the one-block radius. Both of the young brothers are gone now, lost to the machine that is Baltimore. Those kids were no different from any of ours. If we'd gotten to know them, we would no doubt have loved and protected them as fiercely as we loved and defended Tay and Ra'Mon and all the others in our group. But they were outside the block and outside of our reach—at least then.

And there's another point we take away from this. In her own twisted way, that grandmother was acting as the matriarch of her family, sending the young men off to fight. What was broken about it was that she had never learned how to think through, process, and deal with her stress and trauma. That grandma was in the same state of fight or flight that she'd probably adopted as a hungry child, surviving Smallwood in the '80s and '90s. In turn, her young grandsons had never completed their evolution from adolescence to manhood. Because they had never gone through a positive rite of passage—perhaps like the Ohero:kon that the young people of Mohawk experience. They had never transitioned from the immature masculinity of youth to the wiser masculinity of adulthood. Without traditions and ritual to guide her, that grandmother had no idea how to steer her grandsons toward that symbolic passage into maturity. This lack of ritual has led to a crisis in masculinity in all parts of the world that don't practice it, Baltimore included.[1]

The one-block radius is a double-edged sword. Within that radius—like on the atoll, surrounded by that protective coral reef—everyone knows each other. There's a sense of community and connection. But that one-block radius is a small and limited world. Just as it limits young people's experience of the larger world, it exacerbates their experiences within their block. Small issues and seemingly petty arguments are blown up to be major life events. Without a sense of perspective from engaging with the larger world, our kids see these disputes as the greatest issues within their lives and respond accordingly.

Our parents actively worked to break us out of the one-block radius. Part of it was our practice: the meditation and yoga and breathwork. Part of it was modeling integrity and commitment to the long, slow work of education. Our dad sent us to Friends specifically to get us out of our block radius. We lived in the hood, but our "Friends-block radius" included the children of doctors and entrepreneurs, living in mansions. Cassie also pushed for Friends for that reason and refused to let Ali transfer out of the school because of it. Our ride to school with our dad was one way, but when our mom took us, she would go the long way so that we could drive through Roland Park and Homeland to see all the giant houses and tell us that that was what we were destined for and should be striving for.

In their own way they were trying to create, if not a rite of passage, at least an experience, one that would test us, and push us, and demand maturity and wisdom in their young sons. The mindfulness opened our eyes and our minds, much as the sitting and the fasting does for the young people of Mohawk. The poses and breathwork pushed us beyond the limits of our own bodies, forcing us to contemplate the existence of realities beyond our scope of knowledge. Attending Friends, and being sometimes uncomfortable and out of place, forged our empathy and our sense of kinship with others. And feeling the dirt on our feet or the rain on our faces cracked open our hearts and filled them with love for the natural world beyond the scope of our experience.

We try to increase the scope for our kids, because most kids in hoods only have that one-block radius. We have Black speakers from all walks of life—MDs and entrepreneurs—come in to talk with them. But we also make sure they meet and interact with people from other races. Baltimore is one of the most segregated cities in America, and we want our students to be able to interact with and feel comfortable around all types of people so that when they do get out of that one-block radius, they know how to function. To that end, we take our kids out of the hood, to experience plays and parks and museums and all the stuff that kids with more resources take for granted. Everything we do is, in one way or another, an attempt to get our kids out of their constricted reality.

The one-block radius keeps kids disengaged from the issues that shape their lives. They don't vote or engage with local or national politics. They don't question the fact that gas compressors, waste facilities, or polluting factories are built in their neighborhood or that the only stores they see are carry-outs and liquor stores.

As they grow older, they often learn that they lack physical copies of their birth certificates, don't know their own Social Security numbers, and can't easily get government-issued IDs. As a result, they can't produce the ID to open bank accounts, meaning they are cut off from benefits (such as the pandemic stimulus checks) that are their right.

Low-income people of all demographics are less likely to vote: only 25 percent of eligible adults who earn less than $20,000 a year did in 2012.[2] Older Black people who grew up in the South were purposefully not issued birth certificates to begin with, and were instead merely noted in the next census. This conveniently left them often unable to prove citizenship and register to vote, even in towns where the local—usually White—registrar had known them their whole lives. (There are elderly Black folks still living today who have literally never been able to prove their right to vote, no matter how badly they want to.) Right now, there are still living survivors of the Tulsa massacre. Even though they are in their hundreds, they are still trying to get people to care about what happened to their families and homes.

Other seemingly trivial issues, like school administrators who bar kids in tennis shoes from crossing the stage to collect a diploma, push impoverished Black kids further and further away from having a sense of pride and accomplishment in themselves, something that is so crucial to personal growth (and show an amazing lack of awareness at how many kids only have one pair of shoes to begin with). Our kids struggle to find guidance when they have an idea for their future because their parents don't have experience navigating the bigger world of entrepreneurship themselves. If you have a parent who created their own businesses or was successful in a career, think about how much advice and knowledge you absorbed without even realizing it. Most kids from the hood also don't have parents with the resources to invest in them to make sure they can succeed as entrepreneurs. A lot of our friends from Friends had financial backing from their parents and it helped them create successful businesses. That's one thing that Smitty saw and made sure he was able to give us. This stuff is invaluable, and if you are never exposed to it, it can be almost impossible to succeed.

The one-block radius lives in our kids' minds, even when they venture out of it. Most of the middle schoolers and high schoolers in our programs have never been to Baltimore's Inner Harbor, even as it's considered the most popular part of town. When we were teenagers, we would stand on the hill overlooking the harbor being developed. Even though we had the benefit of going to Friends, we knew on some level that the harbor wasn't for us. Our friends from school didn't understand this. It was natural to them that they would be welcomed in the harbor.

One weekend, a teenage Atman was staying with a friend who lived in Roland Park, one of the more affluent neighborhoods in Baltimore. Together, they walked into a candy store in the neighborhood called Tuxedos. There was a public school nearby, and the store had a rule that public school kids couldn't come in, which was a serious microaggression, but at the time it didn't really register.

They just wanted the candy: sherbet dips, gummy bears, and Lemonheads for Atman's friend, Luden's Wild Cherry throat drops for Atman.* Atman's friend was White, so the shopkeeper gave him service with a smile. Then he saw Atman. "What school do you go to?" Atman said, "Friends," and the shopkeeper said, "You don't go to Friends, get out." Atman, embarrassed, confused, and furious, stormed out of the store, leaving his friend holding a half-filled bag of gummy bears. Here's the thing with this kind of profiling: In the moment you are more humiliated than anything else. You feel like you've done something wrong and been caught doing it. People are supposed to stay in their neighborhood, and you f**ked up.

Atman tried to put the moment out of his mind, and from that moment on he never went to that store again.

Today when tourists think of Baltimore, they think of two things: *The Wire* and the harbor. They don't visit the

---

* Don't knock it till you've tried it.

neighborhood where the former was shot (probably a good idea for their own safety), and young Black children aren't welcome at the latter. Johns Hopkins is building its own city-within-a-city, a few blocks over from the hood, staffed with security and other strategies to keep the influx of highly educated doctors and researchers safe from the locals. That one-block radius holds firm.

CHAPTER SIXTEEN

Connection to the Natural World

There's another element to the HLF story, and that's our deep and powerful love for the natural world. This isn't always an inherent thing for Black folks. And if you think about it, it makes sense. The one-block-radius rule both stifles communities and protects them. Our kids were relatively safe so long as they stayed close to home, but their experiences were limited to those 70,000 or so square feet of concrete, cars, and houses.

These blocks were mostly stripped bare of tree cover: Old "redline" neighborhoods, where most Black folks traditionally lived, have radically fewer trees and green areas than more affluent parts of town. (In the most extreme cases, wealthy neighborhoods have 65 percent more canopy and shade coverage than poorer areas.[1]) As summers get hotter (a heat dome is crushing the West Coast as we write), trees can literally save lives by reducing the heat, adding shade, and improving the quality of life in general.

We understand why Black parents want to keep their kids close: Outside isn't always a safe place for us. (Hell, inside isn't much safer, as we all learned in various ways in the last few years.) But we were lucky to be raised by radicals. Our mom and pop (Andy's too, though we are thinking of Cassie and Smit here) had no time for anything that might constrain their sons. They had zero patience for a world that put up barriers to opportunities and experiences. Friends encouraged us to begin to experience this world, with overnight camping trips and Earth Days that consumed the whole school, and had us participating in community cleanups, observing nature and animals, and appreciating the world outside of our immediate neighborhood.

None of our friends back in Smallwood were spending their school days fishing trash out of creeks or examining different insects they had caught in fine-gauge nets. As kids, we didn't really get this. But as we grew a little older we started to understand that our parents' eagerness to get us out in the forest was unusual to say the least.

There is a long and painful backstory to why many Black Americans avoid wildernesses or national parks: Black people had their deep spiritual connection to nature ripped away by slavery. At least twelve million people were stolen from Africa, kidnapped, and sold into abject misery for generations. Almost two million died during the Middle Passage, crossing the Atlantic. When they arrived in America, they had to adapt to the new climate and environment. Still, our parents and grandparents had a relationship with nature and the outdoors. It was only our generation when kids were taught that nature was dirty and scary, and that food came from the store rather than the ground. Our grandparents' generation would spend time "down the country" and would grow food. The ones who are still around have a wealth of knowledge about nature and farming, but the young people don't see them as a resource and aren't concerned with that information. (The story of what happened to Black farmers' land and rights is another book.)

There is no getting around the fact that the very things that are appealing about nature and wilderness—being alone, being out of communication, finding a rawer and more fundamental connection with Mother Earth—are a liability when White people present a danger, or a potential problem. There is nothing more dangerous to a Black person than a White one who feels irrationally afraid and vulnerable, which can make hiking, camping, or backpacking uniquely risky for Black people. Unlearning this shared cultural experience is the work of a lifetime.

So, decolonizing the wilderness and re-wilding our kids is about two things. The first is throwing off that ingrained fear; the second is reclaiming our power. And Black people have always had power in the natural world, quite literally seeding it with the foods and sustenance necessary for our survival. When we reintroduce our kids to the outdoors, we tell them about the women who wove rice grains into their hair—so they were certain to have a food crop familiar to them—as they were kidnapped away from their homelands. And we think about how enslaved people were not simply victims; they were also creators, reshaping the environment of this new world with small memories of home. The stolen people of West Africa brought crops like millet, sorghum, yams, plantains, black-eyed peas, okra, and taro with them. They were used to eating large amounts of greens and vegetables in their diet back home: They adopted these habits in America, cooking it for themselves and eventually the White slave owners too. These plantation owners benefited from the vitamin- and mineral-rich food, often avoiding the nutritional deficiencies that were endemic in other parts of America and the world. Today, the roots of most "Southern" cooking is at least partially West African. Those Louisiana hot peppers, rice, beans, and starchy stews certainly didn't come from England or France.

Part of our relationship with the natural world is simple appreciation for its beauty. But part of it is also this idea of survival. A 2019 study found that spending *at least* 120 minutes in nature, every week, was essential for our good mental health and well-being. Sitting in your backyard or walking past a park on your way to the market doesn't cut it. To get the full benefit of nature, you have to be in it and fully immersed in the experience.[2] The study found that people who lived in *lower* greenspace areas often spent more time in greenspace, purposefully seeking out parks, beaches, hikes, and other ways to experience nature. In Japan, *shinrin-yoku*, or "forest bathing," is studied and supported by the government. (The term was coined by the Japanese Ministry of Agriculture, Forestry, and Fisheries in 1982.) It is defined as "making contact with and taking in the atmosphere of the forest."[3] Studies demonstrated that spending time in nature (compared to city environments) decreased cortisol, lowered blood pressure and pulse rates, enhanced parasympathetic nerve activity, and lowered sympathetic nerve activity.

More than that, we believe that part of the natural world is connecting with the spirit world, and the spirit of God. If you can't be at peace with God's creation, how can you be at peace with God (whoever she may be)? In the hood, however, we often sabotage ourselves, telling our children that nature is dirty, uncomfortable, or "for White people." All told, when you are living within the confines of the one-block radius, it's damn hard to lose yourself in the natural world.

Radical Nature

By the time we were teenagers we were used to being in nature, hiking deep into the woods or—with Friends—spending days there, wading in streams with our shoes off as we learned about the ecosystem. Sometimes our teacher would send us out to the woods to create structures out of downed tree limbs. Every year, Earth Day was big: The whole school would take the day off to do community cleanups or stream cleanups. All these moments added up to give us a different kind of appreciation for environments outside of our community. We felt like we had a right to be in nature, and it made as much sense for us to be there as it did for our White classmates. Yet, when we came home from school to Smallwood, we realized we were anomalies. The kids on our block had never *left* the block, never mind experienced immersive nature. Yet, even in the hood, nature was around them: Burdock root and mint grew in the vacant lots that had become quiet, almost peaceful, places. There were praying mantises stalking their prey through the rubble, and even red-tailed hawks hunting the pigeon coops. But the kids weren't connected to it, and they didn't notice the life all around them. Once we had kids of our own, at least those in our programs, we realized we had to be those mentors and figure out a way to get our kids to appreciate nature.

Sometimes nature shows her raw power. Every so often a rainstorm would dump water, sweeping down the streets where the gutters were filled with trash, swirling the refuse into the storm drains, and filling the Inner Harbor with junk that would bob along the edges of the seawall until a high enough tide washed it out to sea.

We instinctively knew that there was something not right about this. When our friends from the upper echelons of Baltimore would come to hang out and play action figures, they would have to step over the Utz wrappers, Little Hugs, chicken bones, and vials and needles that littered the block, despite our families' best efforts to keep it clean. Our friends loved being around us, and they never said anything, but we knew enough to feel depressed and angry about the experience of the world around us.

This was probably the first time we explicitly understood the larger idea of what an "environment" is, and how it can affect people emotionally, physically, and spiritually. We were ashamed and angry about the world around us. When we were little kids, Smit bought some land in southeastern Virginia and he'd take us there. We'd stay in a trailer on the property and explore the land and woods by day. He had no time for the one-block radius, and he was damned if he was going to let his kids live within it.

Later, at Friends, the Outing Club, run by Brian Rollefinke and Andy Spawn, would take us camping for real, throwing down a tarp, building a basic fire, and letting us experience life under the stars. It was often cold and wet, and we weren't always happy to be torn away from our teenage lives of video games and music and friends. But these experiences, first with Smit and later at Friends, instilled in us an appreciation for the bigger world.

Today there is no good reason for kids in Baltimore to feel estranged from the natural world: There's green space all over our city, and wilderness not far out of it. But the environment is bigger than this too. Access to the natural world is key for maintaining and developing mental, emotional, physical, and spiritual health. So what happens when an entire city is purposefully cut off from the experience of green, wild spaces?

The Two-Block Rule

The endless amount of trash bobbing in Baltimore harbor was the inspiration for our program to educate our kids about being stewards of the environment. One day, Atman and Ali had the usual group of little guys in the Corolla. Because there were always more kids than space, they were jammed in every which way. Elbows in ears, feet knocking caps off heads. One of the kids reached over to the window—open as always so we wouldn't suffocate—and tossed a soda can out the window. The can bounced down the middle of the street and came to rest by a storm drain. Ali and Atman said nothing, but two blocks later Atman pulled over, made eye contact with the offending kid in the rearview mirror, and told him, "Go pick that up. And pick up another piece of trash while you're at it."

Laughter. Giggles.

"I'm serious."

Disbelief. "It's a soda can. It doesn't matter."

Atman turned off the engine. "Well, it matters enough that we're sitting here till you get that can and bring it back to the car."

Eventually the kid detangled himself from the mess of twelve-year-olds in the back seat, walked as slooowwly as humanly possible back to the storm drain, picked up the can and another food wrapper, and returned to the Corolla. He opened the door, wedged himself back in the car, and Atman turned over the engine. A few blocks later he pulled over at a trash can, and the kid dutifully dumped the can and wrapper into it.

This became the two-block rule. Anytime a kid littered, we would keep going two blocks before sending the kid back to retrieve their trash and a bonus piece of trash. The goal was to teach the kids to mind their own behavior, and to take responsibility for picking up after other people's bad behavior. Our kids embraced this, to the point where one day, one kid threw an apple core out the window and one of his friends said, "Ooooh you're gonna have to walk back and get that." The kid's response: "Shut your dumb ass up, that's biodegradable." We laughed hysterically.

Initially we didn't directly link our trash policy to the one-block radius, but over time, the two-block rule became a huge part of teaching our kids about the bigger world outside of their experience. We realized that the only way we were going to get our kids to know and care was to show them that world, and even more importantly, show them that their actions could affect that world for good and bad.

It wasn't their fault: Littering isn't a thing that people care about in the hood. These kids had parents who didn't know better, and also didn't care. The generations before them probably didn't know about the water cycle and pollution, but they had pride in their community and kept it clean. That sense of pride was gone. Now they tossed food wrappers in the street and figured that *the rain will clean it up for us,* not realizing that the trash would go from the gutters to the Chesapeake Bay.

After we moved out of the hood, we started to realize that city planning was really important—and purposeful. In Charles Village—a vastly more expensive part of Baltimore—there are trash cans on every block, and people use them. In the hood you would see someone standing next to one of the few trash cans and still throw their trash on the ground.

Walking out of your house, seeing trash everywhere, makes you not care about your community. If your community is clean, you want to care for it. When your community is dirty, with used diapers and drug paraphernalia lying on the street, it depresses you on a soul level. Sometimes it's hard to believe that this *isn't* done on purpose.

We realized that educating people about why they shouldn't litter was important for two reasons. The first was the straightforward, care for Mother Earth, granola reason. The second was more radical: If we were going to persuade our kids to care about themselves, then we had to persuade them to care about the environment that surrounded them.

If we wanted to empower our kids to claim their space in the world, and not be shunted aside as just another expendable, nameless Black victim or perpetrator of violence, then they had to believe that they mattered, and that they deserved better.

The next time it rained after the soda can episode, we packed up the Corolla with the same group of kids and drove them down to the harbor. We parked, told them to get out and deal with getting wet, and walked down to the seawall. "Now look." Each one of them poked their head over the stone wall and looked silently down at the harbor, completely covered with trash and refuse bobbing in the stormy water.

The Radish in the Food Desert

Part of what bummed us out about the trash was what the trash was. Flamin' Hot Cheetos wrappers. Little Hug juice barrels. Chick-fil-A bags. It was bad enough that these kids were eating this junk in the first place, let alone that they were tossing the wrappers over their shoulder when they were done. There was also a big disconnect between us and the kids; the three of us were living a vegetarian lifestyle by then. We were in deep with ayurvedic principles, eating onions and ginger and garlic when we felt ill, following a raw diet at times to keep the nutrients of our food intact. Meanwhile, a few houses or streets away, the young people we were trying to mentor were eating foods that were little more than sugar, additives, and artificial flavorings.

Who can blame them? It wasn't like there were many options in the hood. Today, the three most rapidly expanding chains in America are Dollar General, Family Dollar, and Dollar Tree. (This business report came out a few days after news that Jeff Bezos was building a $500 million yacht that came with its own mini yacht to land his girlfriend's helicopter on. We wonder how many small businesses were annihilated to buy that boat. But you know. Capitalism.) These kids were eating the food available to them, though it's generous to call it food. We realized that "environment" means two things: the external environment that you walk through and live in, and the internal environment—or gut biome—that requires just as much loving nourishment as the harbor or the few scraggly trees lining the streets of Smallwood. If we were going to educate our students about how and why to care for the environment, we'd have to start with the one closest to home: the three to four pounds of digestive bacteria that live in each of our stomachs.

You may already understand the emerging science of the gut biome: for the most part, a diverse array of bacterial species, and a large quantity of individual organisms, is a good thing. For reasons that aren't fully understood, a healthy and diverse gut biome keeps our bodies healthy and our minds happy. The gut releases hormones, neurotransmitters, and immunological factors, which in turn send signals to the brain. This "gut-brain axis" affects kids' mental health, and variations in the microbiome are increasingly seen to either cause or exacerbate conditions such as autism, schizophrenia, anxiety, and depression. An optimized gut biome is thus critically important for children, and a conventionally "healthy" diet, plus exercise, are the most important elements to nurturing and preserving a strong gut biome.[4]

The three of us eat plenty of fibrous prebiotics to "feed" our guts, such as walnuts, sunchokes, leeks, garlic, and bitter greens (but to be real about it, we balance out the healthy stuff with plenty of pizza, french fries, mozzarella sticks, and all the other types of vegetarian bar food). These prebiotic foods are full of a type of fiber called inulin, which keeps inflammation under control and may help decrease the risk of cancer, digestive issues, and heart disease. We also eat fermented probiotics, like yogurt, kimchi, and pickles, to restock our guts with the good bacteria. But this stuff takes time, money, interest, education, and persistence (you try finding fresh, organic greens at the corner store), and our kids, and their parents, have precious little of any of this. Instead, they understandably reach for fast food for many of their meals. New research is showing how fast food annihilates the good bacteria in the gut biome[5] and conversely overpopulates the guts with the "obesity bacteria," called bacteroidetes, and contributes to vastly higher rates of colon cancer than in populations that eat less processed food. Amazingly, a study that swapped the diets of African Americans and rural South Africans showed that the gut begins to rebalance itself in as little as two weeks of healthier eating. (The inverse is also true: the South African subjects' gut biomes rapidly deteriorated during the study after two weeks of American-style fast food.)

Smallwood, like most poor neighborhoods, is a food desert. Kids don't eat fresh fruit and veggies like apples and carrots (let alone the "weird stuff" like knobbly sunchokes or bitter chicory) because other than a dried-out orange or overripe banana, they never see them.

And frankly, bad fruit or tough old celery is always going to lose against a ninety-nine-cent Twinkie. So, we came up with a plan to crack open that one-block radius and bring something in from the outside world.

We realized that we might never be able to get a gaggle of eleven-year-olds excited about gut bacteria. But we *could* get them excited about things that they could actually hold in their hands or bite into and taste. Atman—in charge of snacks—ditched the soft apples, desiccated oranges, and mottled bananas and started bringing "weird fruit" to the after-school program instead: Asian pears, dragon fruit, star fruit. Sometimes some papayas. Whatever he could find in that moment that fit our minimal budget. Here's the interesting thing: These kids, who "didn't like fruit," were curious about these strange snacks. *What is that?* quickly evolved into *Give me a piece.* And as soon as they'd try it, they were fascinated. They loved the slippery, tart seeds in the passion fruit. They were down with thin, star-shaped slices of carambola (star fruit). They could have eaten guavas for days. The more they tried, the more they embraced these new flavors: sweet and sour star fruit. Tart kiwis. They dug the mild taste of the dragon fruit. Once these kids had a taste of something more interesting than an overripe Red Delicious, they were sold.

Veggies were a harder proposition. You try getting any kid invested in a head of lettuce or bitter turnip greens. Still, we didn't simply want our kids flying high on fructose, no matter how organic. We spoke to the principal of Robert Coleman Elementary, and they agreed to let us build raised bed gardens in an attempt to spread the joy of vegetables.

The first response from our kids was pretty predictable. "I don't want to get dirty, there are worms in there." But, like most kids, the first time they came out at recess and saw green poking out of the dirt, something shifted. Suddenly all this abstract stuff that we were going on about— "Vegetables are good for you. Eat your greens"—seemed tangible. Now, instead of lagging and dragging their heels, they were running up to the boxes to see what had happened in the twenty-four hours since they'd last visited. The first day the purple crown of the first radish, or the orange head of the first carrot, poked up through the dirt, the kids about lost it. It got to the point where the kids got so excited when the veggies got ripe, they would pop them out of the ground and eat them raw. (Good because we wanted them to eat veggies; bad because it meant we had to constantly replant them.)

Bigfoot

It's not surprising that plenty of the Robert Coleman kids were astonished to see vegetables growing out of the ground. Plenty of their older siblings had been equally astonished to go on group trips with us, into the country, and see cows for the first time. They knew that cows produced milk, but even though they drank milk on a regular basis, seeing the cows that produced it was as strange and unexpected as spotting Bigfoot for the first time. None of our mentees had ever seen an animal the size of a cow, and for a few minutes at least, they were as impressed with the bovines as Martin Lawrence was seeing the pie when he was in jail in the movie *Life*.

Their surprise was touching, even funny on some level. But it was also deeply sad. We'd grown up grumbling through cold and damp nights on a tarp in the woods. As much as we didn't like getting rained on in our sleeping bags, there was something about hearing the foxes and small animals scurrying through the night, or the feeling of warming up around a morning campfire, that brought a meaningful, tangible sense of joy to our lives. Once we had the funds to start taking our students, and later our trainees, camping, we did.

Our workforce development program for senior staff takes place in North Carolina, and we always time it to a meteor shower. We wake up at 4:00 a.m. to drink some of Atman's homemade yogi tea, then practice yoga until the sun comes up. We eat breakfast, and we read and learn from Uncle Will (no longer in his physical form, but still with us in every other way). Then we nap and go for long hikes. After that is evening pranayama and meditation, then dinner and a campfire.

One year Ali kept telling everyone he thought Bigfoot lived in these mountains. We thought Ali was full of it until we heard a loud tree knock while we were all practicing the pranayama exercise sitkari (which the kids call the Bigfoot breath). Ali had a huge smile on his face and said, "See, I told you." We had five more breaths to do after we heard the tree knock, but Ra'Mon refused to let us continue the practice. He had no interest in messing with the old man of the woods.

After a long day of talking, meditating, practicing, and sharing, it was time to look up. The first time a shooting star flew overhead, everyone went, "Whooooo . . . !" Soon the whole group was quiet, reveling in the show.

One year we took the kids on an overnight camping trip to Woodberry. We knew we wanted to create a similarly memorable moment—something that would help break through the tough-as-nails exteriors of these eleven- and twelve-year-olds. Already, they were on edge with the sounds of the campsite. We asked them, "Y'all are not scared of gunshots, but you are scared of crickets??"

Midway through the trip, Andy had to leave for his high school reunion. Now, all day we had been telling the kids about a gorilla that had escaped from a nearby zoo, and frankly we could tell they thought we were full of it.

Later the kids hit their tent. Just as they were falling asleep, the tent unzipped open, and a gorilla's massive, hairy head poked into the tent, roaring. The kids screamed so loud the whole mountain must have heard. Andy (who had snuck back a few minutes before) tore off a gorilla mask, and the kids' fear turned to hysterical laughter.

A big part of us scaring them was to take the edge off being in the woods. They were afraid of nature and we didn't want them to be. We wanted to show them how ridiculous their fear was. They were tough kids in the hood, where there were real dangers, but the new environment of the woods at night scared the hell out of them. We wanted them to feel comfortable in the woods and enjoy their connection to Mother Earth. They were teenagers who'd been working hard all week, out of their element, sometimes cold and uncomfortable. The gorilla mask broke through all that.

Here's the thing: Kids are already wearing masks. *All kids.* Doesn't matter what color they are or what their socioeconomic background is. All kids, tweens, and teenagers have stuff going on in their heads and their hearts that they don't want adults to see. Those masks contribute to that uneasy separation between adolescents and their caregivers (and most caregivers have plenty of their own stuff they need to be open and honest about too). Once you can dislodge those masks, you have a window of opportunity. The world has shifted, just a bit. Those tough kids' perspectives have shifted too. They take their masks off with us and be real, even if they can't be like that anywhere else. The gorilla mask incident allowed them to be like little kids. The rest of that trip they lost their fear and were totally free to connect with nature in so many ways.

Heading Home

A few years later, Ra'Mon was sitting at the very back of the van, staring out of the window, unusually quiet for someone as talkative as Monny usually is. It was the end of another camping trip and he was feeling it. As we merged onto I-95, heading north, closer to the city, he started to sigh. We pulled off the exit ramp toward the neighborhood and saw the junkies on the corner. We saw the trash filling up the gutters, waiting for that next rain storm. We've seen this transition a hundred times, ever since we were kids, but now, hearing Monny's obvious distress, it came home to us just how crazy this was. We were coming from a place where there are apple orchards and fresh running water, just a few hours and half a tank of gas away. Yet back in the hood, nothing had changed.

We'd been in nature, waking up doing yoga, cooking vegetarian meals together, putting our bags of water in the sun during the day so we could wash with warm water in the evening. We pulled off of I-95 onto Washington Boulevard and Monroe Street. We rolled past a kid handcuffed on the street with police officers. There were more and more police officers and police sirens, and less and less green.

The next day, Monny got his tennis shoes stolen off his feet at gunpoint, and he was like, "Man, I don't want to live like this no more." It was a big shock for him to see the environment he lived in from a distance—from outside the radius. He had adapted to a reality that he didn't want to be in. He was at peace in the wilderness. He was "who he was meant to be," but as he got closer to the city, his anxiety crept up again.

Ra'Mon was serious when he said he didn't want to live like this anymore. A few years later, when he was one of our first cohort of new teachers, he took the train up to the Omega Institute for a permaculture immersion course. He'd never been camping by himself before, but he had to stay out there for six weeks and it totally changed his life. Every few days he would call and tell us, "I'm coming home, I'm coming home." It was a lot for him, because he is very social, and he'd never been anywhere where nobody knew who he was. He was way, way outside his radius, and it was an experience. But just like the young people of Akwesasne, he was going through a rite of passage, in the woods, caring for himself, surrounded by strangers during the day and the woods by night. He was experiencing what it is to be fully self-reliant, away from his support system and the familiar world, even just for a little bit. Expanding your world can be painful, it can be scary, but it will also change you, for good.

Once Monny had his kids, he hustled hard to get them out of Baltimore. Today, they live in a peaceful neighborhood with a backyard, and one murder a year. Sometimes, on warm summer nights, he and his son camp out in the backyard, among the pots of mint and herbs that Ra'Mon tends. For him, plants transition into work with children. "Loving plants opened my heart enough that I could love other people. Took me away from hating the world, because the world didn't care about us. Yoga and mindfulness, dealing with plants and children, opening up my heart chakra slowly, slowly, slowly. When my dad got killed, my heart chakra shut down. I was always loving, innocent as a kid. Then you get taught how to hate. No one is born hating anything."

Toward the end of his life, Uncle Will began to come on our early training retreats in the mountains of North Carolina. He was happy to see us passing on our knowledge to the first cohort of kids from the neighborhood. The guys themselves were . . . surprised? After all, Will was old by then, and all his joints hurt. He had shrunk in that old-man way, and he was swimming in those big sweaters and faded jeans that he used to fill out. The bus couldn't make it all the way up to the ridgeline, where our tents were (Uncle Will stayed in a cabin downhill). So we climbed the slope on foot, the young dudes powering ahead, and Will hobbling behind, Yoda-style, rolled-up yoga mat in hand, until he finally made it to the summit.

Then he unrolled the mat. And suddenly that old, limping guy was transformed: He was like Superman on that mat, falling effortlessly into sat kriya for three minutes at a time. His arms pointed straight up, fingers meeting above his head, forearms hugging his ears. He'd do the pose for three minutes, then grant us a minute's rest. He made us all attempt five cycles of this.

The young guys were looking at each other: *What in the hell is going on here?* He blew everybody away. Suddenly these young dudes were seeing the Uncle Will we knew: a mentor, a teacher, a wise elder. Someone with a deep and hard-earned well of knowledge to share. And we were seeing—to our surprise—that Uncle Will had effortlessly fallen into an element beyond the comforting familiarity of his kitchen table.

When we weren't practicing, Uncle Will would talk about the natural world. He'd walk up to the sassafras trees, touching the leaves and bark, smelling the aromatic wood (sassafras used to be the main ingredient in root beer, and it has that same rich, sweet smell), and teach the guys about the plant's medicinal qualities, educating them on how Indigenous people used the plant to treat wounds. (Some modern research has shown the plant has antiseptic properties.) He'd talk about the long needle pine, and how spiritually potent the trees are, especially when they are near bodies of water. We cooked meals out on the fire and ate together. We made huge pots of tea, which we drank all the time. The guys drew up around the fire and listened to the old man. For many of them, he was the first true elder they had ever experienced.

In his own way, Uncle Will was expanding his radius—getting a little uncomfortable and putting his usual routine aside. He was showing us the way nature could help break the one-block radius for all our other kids too.

Today, the three of us still head out to camp on Smit's property in Virginia whenever we can. There's still no electricity or running water. The old cabin fell down years ago, so we throw down the same tarps and tents on the meadow instead. His spot isn't an official dark-sky preserve, but it might as well be. In the middle of the night, the Milky Way lights up the dark, illuminating our campsite and invigorating our souls. If you've ever seen the constellations in the middle of the night, you know how close they can suddenly feel, blotted out by a hand held up in front of your face, revealed a moment later. When you lower your hand and see the constellations in their place in the vast sky above, you remember, *This is vast, endless, eternity.*

When the sky starts to warm up, and we feel the first rays of the sun come up behind the pines, we pull ourselves out of our sleeping bags, stir the ashes of the fire, and do our own practices as the spirit moves us. The wild turkeys, foxes, and rabbits scramble just out of sight, going about their business while keeping a wary eye on the interlopers. We tell them, "No worries, we're vegetarians," and point out the eagles overhead who might actually cause our friends some trouble.

For once in our crazy lives we are completely together. No distractions. Just the three of us, and whatever is brewing in our souls and minds. We can detach from all the other stuff, and actually see and hear each other, in ways we can't when those phones are endlessly going off in our pockets.

Everyone needs the outdoors, but we're going to put it out here that men *really* need the outdoors. Why? Because men aren't taught to nurture their relationships with each other. Even us. We spend our days talking and teaching about love, connection, communication. And we still aggravate the f**k out of each other on the regular. We can go days, weeks even, without talking about stuff other than budgets and programs and travel. The frustrations and stress of what we do is a burden; whenever something goes wrong, it is the three of us who are responsible for solving it. So, getting out in the wild, where we can forget about everything except the very essentials—food, shelter, fire, friends—lets us shed that, just for a couple of days.

CHAPTER SEVENTEEN

Love
Zombies

We see a lot of similarities between traumatized children who are "acting in," by falling into self-harm, depression, and anger, and traumatized children who are "acting out," by aiming their raw feelings at the world, rather than themselves. We've talked a little about what gets a child to that place, and how meditation, breathwork, and yoga can pull them back from the edge. Of course, our practices are one part of the puzzle. We purposefully based ourselves in the school system for a few reasons. Some practical: That's where the kids are. And some bigger-picture: Educators are often the first line of defense when it comes to protecting a troubled child from negative outside influences. (Although, conversely, those closest to the solution are also furthest from the power to solve the problem—as true in education as it is in anything else.) For a kid who has almost no weak ties to rely on, a teacher may become the most significant influence outside of their home life, however functional or dysfunctional that is. Often, "problem kids" who act out in class are acting out to get the attention of the one reliable adult in their life. They aren't looking to cause a problem so much as they desperately want the attention and validation of the only adult who regularly pays them any attention at all.

A basic mindfulness program can give these kids a sense of control over their lives. Parents, caregivers, and adults also need to model good mental hygiene and understand how our brains are affected by the information and ideas we allow into them. We mentioned earlier how brains love to follow the same well-worn paths. This is partly because our brains eat up 20 to 25 percent of our body's energy, literally burning calories as we observe, interpret, and interact with the world. It makes sense for the brain to conserve energy where it can, by using shortcuts and establishing heuristics instead of calculating a new response to the same inputs on a daily basis. (If you have a loved one addicted to online or cable news, either left or right leaning, you can see this in action.)

We want our kids to know they deserve the good stuff in life as much as any other more privileged child. Kareem and Asia are a brother-and-sister duo, and two of the first kids we worked with. Every day after school they waited their turn for a ride in the Corolla to the YMCA for the after-school program. Every day. Their story is as rough as any kid we've worked with. We were able to offer them that hope, and both of them grabbed it and didn't let go.

If you ask Asia and Kareem now what they remember and value about their experience, yes, they'll talk about the yoga and meditation (something they both still practice), but what really lights up their eyes and geeks them out is reminiscing about the winter snowboarding trips we took a few kids on over the Christmas break. Burton Snowboards sponsored these trips, and sent two amazing teachers, Matt and Shawn, to run the program, something we are eternally grateful for. Still, these expeditions were nothing fancy. We'd rent a van, stuff as many twelve- and thirteen-year-olds in it as it would safely hold, and head for the slopes for the day. On the way home, we'd stop for KFC, passing around a greasy bucket and napkins as the windows of the van gently steamed up with the smell of sweaty kids, chicken, and biscuits. Here's the thing. Part of those trips were just to get the teens out of the city, reward them for their hard work and ever-improving behavior, show them something new, and push them to do something that felt outside of their abilities.

A snowboarding trip is something other than just a day trip, though. It's cultural currency. Kareem ended up going to a primarily White high school and later college. His fellow classmates had, for the most part, comfortable and moderately to very privileged upbringings. Most of the teenagers he was meeting at freshman orientation considered a snowboarding trip, or summer break to Europe, their due, or at the very least an experience so normal and expected that it was unexceptional. For Kareem, being able to talk about snowboarding— maybe share a funny story about a hard fall or an epic run—was a way to connect with people he might otherwise have had very little in common with. It gave him a shared point of reference with teenagers who had almost no other shared life experiences with him. By the time his new peers realized just how different Kareem's upbringing was to theirs, they were friends.

In 2019, when *Hamilton* was being performed live in DC, a wonderful friend, artist, illustrator, and donor, Leah Pearlman, gave us enough tickets to take most of our teachers and a few students to see the play and have dinner afterward. Again, this experience was more than simply a fun evening out; it was cultural currency, and it served two purposes. It reminded our kids that they have equal claim on the good stuff of life. That art, nature, knowledge, and beauty are their right, just as much as they are anyone else's right. If literally everyone is talking about Lin-Manuel Miranda, or singing "My Shot," why shouldn't our kids too? And second, as Kareem and Asia found out, it was a way to join a bigger conversation that they might not have had access to otherwise.

Love Zombies

All of this is about one thing. If we just get our kids through their school years and then say, "See ya," we haven't done our job. Consistency and long-term commitment are everything when you are working with deeply traumatized people. Like Smit said, "It's not enough to earn a check, you need to *be* the check." For us, this means empowering young people to take on the mantle of mindfulness and teach it themselves, earning dollars and building self-respect.

There is nothing more powerful than having valuable knowledge and being paid to share it. Right now, our newest teachers are going through teacher training. A lot of them are fifteen, sixteen. Their students will be their classmates. Their stomachs are in knots and their palms are sweating. They don't know if they can do it. But in a few weeks they will find out they can. Most privileged kids have had these moments already. Their parents have pushed them into enrichment activities like music camps or other after-school activities. They've absorbed the lesson that they matter, and that their words are powerful. They will fight for their rights and demand fair treatment over the course of their lives. Our kids? Not so much.

And here's another part of the story: HLF was, and is, blowing up. We were turning down contracts because the three of us were doing everything. Right when things were getting good, we saw a future where they fell apart. So, for the last few years we have actively developed our teacher training, stepping back from being in the classroom ourselves, and empowering our original few generations of students to take over the work for themselves.

It's not a magic cure. A lot of our kids still feel pulled between life in the streets and life as a teacher. They come and go. But something that never leaves is the knowledge that they've developed over the years of attending our different programs. Like Laila says, "It feels like I have learned something and I have this tool within me that I can share with somebody else and pass on to the next generation. So right now in my life I don't know what I want to be, who I want to be. Mindfulness is a practice, yoga is a piece of it. I feel like that side of my life, if I were to lean into it, I would be content with it. If I was to make that my living—I could be content with it because I've been dealing with it my whole life. It makes me feel better to take what I've learned in my pain and suffering and pass it on."

Kareem started teaching when he was eleven. "Teaching allowed me to be seen. Asia and I would have fallen through the cracks. There's a tradition in our community where you just hang out on the stoops. At times, gangs were really big. Gang activity was hot. So, HLF kept us focused." By teaching—standing up in front of his peers, directing their activity, helping them, guiding them—Kareem and our other teacher-students get a chance to experience themselves in a different way, as leaders.

So, as you work within your community, remember that you are passing on that role as teacher. Give them authority, give them autonomy. Let your child guide *you* through a meditation or sequence of poses. Ask them what they think, and listen with open ears. If you are lucky, you will hear that moment when the student becomes the teacher.

This is the last—and maybe most important—lesson from Uncle Will. A teacher is never more than a conduit for the knowledge. The information doesn't die with him but is passed on, a flame kept alive by the commitment and belief of both teacher and student. Something we were about to learn the hard way.

CHAPTER EIGHTEEN
Will's
Last Day

Uncle Will had the ability to endure. And he endured seventy-eight years of a not-easy life. He molded his life into what he wanted it to be. His son Oba would say that Will smiled in the way a man smiles when he has control and mastery of his life, his economics, his family. He slipped up sometimes, but he was man enough to say he made a mistake and he would do better next time. Just seeing him constantly work between being a father, a yoga teacher, and a hustler, it made sense to call him the ultimate tough guy.

Death is supposed to be a sad thing: Most people fear it. But Uncle Will made dying look easy. He always told us that Death was an angel who got a bum rap. Death is a friend as much as it is an enemy. And he lived those words in that final hour of his life. He waited until all of us—his partner, Dee Dee; his daughter Malika; and his youngest son, Oba; and the three of us—were with him. We each touched his hands and feet, and when Uncle Will was ready, he said, "Take this m****rf***ing mask off of me and let me go." And we did.

His death looked easy and beautiful because he always taught us not to fear death. It's the living that hurts. Death takes you out of that suffering. He had some problems with his body when he died, and he was in pain.

But when he died . . . his final breath was the sweetest sound we had ever heard. Oba says that his last exhale sounded like someone in relief, and that at first he didn't understand it. Eventually he realized that the last breath was his last lesson: The m****rf****r died smiling. His last lesson to us was: "Look, I'm dying here and it's fine, it's not scary."

The outbreath was a beautiful sound. He waited for everyone to get there and then he just went on ahead.

Oba and Will were close. Like, really close. Still, Oba says that he doesn't feel sad when he thinks of him. Like us, Oba always thinks of him as something that is still present. His energy is eternal, it doesn't dissipate, it doesn't disappear. When you miss a person, you go within yourself and there they are.

We all feel Uncle Will around us every day. Even for stuff that he's not here to experience, we know how he would feel and we know what he would say. Oba hasn't skipped a beat with him: Will hasn't gone anywhere. Like the saying goes, "A man isn't truly dead unless he is forgotten." Uncle Will would never take ownership of the knowledge; he was always a mirror, just reflecting it back to where it came from. If you came to him with results and said he had taught him, he would say, "Nah, that's you, give it to you and God."

For us—well, Uncle Will's death didn't hit us in the moment, but it came hard afterward. Anytime we went over to Dee Dee's and sat in that kitchen, around the table, it was a struggle. He wouldn't want us to be sad, but let's be real.

He was our mentor and our best friend and he wasn't there anymore. Those long kitchen jam sessions, drinking bang and Heineken, and staying up to dawn just chanting and singing, "Om! Om! Om! Om! Om!" and laughing, were done. Ali lasted ten minutes in the kitchen the first time he went over. Emotionally he just couldn't deal with it.

The living shouldn't lament the living or the dead. But those are easier words to say than believe. Uncle Will had gone to a different plane, but he had spent enough time on the physical plane to give us all the concepts we needed. We wouldn't be lost and we wouldn't need to call on him. We would understand the deeper concepts, and if we didn't, we had each other to reflect those ideas back like a mirror.

Losing Will was hard for us. It was even harder for Dee and Oba. Yet Uncle Will left us with a mission, something we know he would want us to do. He gave us the tools to fulfill the mission. In essence, he created us as the first love zombies, the first people empowered to take what we had learned and share it widely.

Will's physical self is gone, but we feel every facet of his spirit with us every day. The Panther in him wouldn't want us to ever stop fighting for justice, for peace, for joy. The yogi in him would smile at the kids, chanting mantras in their heads and unwinding their trauma, one meditation at a time.

And the uncle and father in him would—we are sure—smush us all in for one last, amazing, everlasting, cosmic hug.

Acknowledgments

Caroline Greeven

Stephanie Tade

Sara Carder and the entire
  TarcherPerigee team

Lydia Santiago

Enrique Santiago

Asuman, Amar, and
  Ananda Smith

Megan Armbruster and Family

Nora Bucke and Family

Valerie Mitchell

Titi Trina

Ms. Marcy

John "Tron" Bolden

Smith Family

Sifford Family

Nelson Family

Evans Family

Santiago Family

Gonzalez Family

Classy Fellas

North and Pulaski Family

Southern Bulldog Family

Althea "Dee Dee" Borders

The Holistic Life Foundation
  family

The Involution Group Family

Old Mill Family

Madison, Wisconsin, Family (Abraham Lincoln Elementary School)

Robert W. Coleman Elementary School YOUTH

Divine Life Church of Absolute Oneness Family

Nashville Family (Tay, Joe, Jafee)

Sifu Jeff Finch and the Stage 4 Family

CVP (Charles Village Pub) Family

Friends School of Baltimore Family

Jim Gimian and Barry Boyce

Congressman Tim Ryan

Phil Leaf

Mark Greenberg

Zanvyl and Isabelle Krieger Fund Family (Karen, Betsy, Brooke, and Jen)

Sharon Salzberg

Dinabandhu and Ila Sarley

Charlie Hartwell and Maureen Pelton

Karen Weber

Vance Benton

Tamar Mendelson

Maria Kluge

Jennifer Buffett and Stephanie Hartka

Michael Craft

Seane Corn

Bessel van der Kolk and Licia Sky

Dan Harris

Leah Pearlman

Elizabeth Lesser

Sat Bir Khalsa

Dan Siegel

Victor, Lynne, and Vicki Brick

And all other loved ones, friends, and supporters

Notes

Introduction: I'm Not a Teacher, I'm a Reminder

1. Valeria Pelet, "Puerto Rico's invisible health crisis," *The Atlantic*, September 3, 2016, https://www.theatlantic.com/politics /archive/2016/09/vieques-invisible-health-crisis/498428/.

2. A Negro Nurse, "More Slavery at the South," *The Independent* (New York City), vol. 72, January 25, 1912, 196–200, Documenting the American South Collections, University Library, University of North Carolina at Chapel Hill, 2001, last modified September 10, 2002, https://docsouth.unc.edu/fpn/negnurse/negnurse.html.

Chapter One: Wipe the Dust Off and Let Your Inner Light Shine Out

1. Addison Kliewer, Mirand Mahmud, and Brooklyn Wayland, "'Kill the Indian, save the man': Remembering the stories of Indian boarding schools," *Gaylord News*, n.d., Gaylord College of Journalism and Mass Communications, University of Oklahoma, accessed April 9, 2022, https://www.ou.edu/gaylord/exiled-to-indian-country/content /remembering-the-stories-of-indian-boarding-schools.

2. Rosalyn LaPier, "Canada's Oka Crisis marked a change in how police use force," *High Country News*, July 21, 2020, https://www.hcn.org /articles/indigenous-affairs-canadas-oka-crisis-marked-a-change-in -how-police-use-force.

3. "Sovereign citizens movement," Southern Poverty Law Center, https://www.splcenter.org/fighting-hate/extremist-files/ideology /sovereign-citizens-movement.

4. "Baltimore residents' priorities sharply at odds with proposed city budget," Baltimore Justice Report, Open Society Institute-Baltimore, June 18, 2020, https://www.osibaltimore.org/2020/06/baltimore -residents-priorities-sharply-at-odds-with-proposed-city-budget/.

5. *Baltimore Sun* Editorial Board, "Why can't Baltimore's top cops live in the city?" *Baltimore Sun*, February 10, 2020, https://www .baltimoresun.com/opinion/editorial/bs-ed-0210-police-residency -requirement-20200210-l5uxjtbm4nbrrgkggk7y52oy4y-story.html.

6. Justin Fenton, "Baltimore Police plainclothes units now in uniform, marked cars," *Baltimore Sun*, September 18, 2020, https://www .baltimoresun.com/news/crime/bs-md-ci-cr-police-plainclothes-ordered -into-uniform-20200918-7wj5nyxqefcv3cciompireneeq-story.html.

7. Laura Newberry and Howard Blume, "Some Black parents see less bullying, racism with online learning and are keeping kids home," *Los Angeles Times*, June 8, 2021, https://www.latimes.com/california /story/2021-06-08/black-parents-see-less-bullying-racism-with -online-learning.

8. Alfred Edmond, Jr., "Segregation was never good for Black people. Not even a little bit," *Black Enterprise*, April 25, 2018, https:// www.blackenterprise.com/black-people-were-not-better-off-during -segregation-not-even-a-little-bit/.

9. Gillian Brockwell, "Florida seeks to block uncomfortable themes in schools. History is full of them," *Washington Post*, February 9, 2022, https://www.washingtonpost.com/history/2022/02/09/florida -history-discomfort/.

10. Olivia B. Waxman, "How the U.S. got its police force," *Time*, May 18, 2017, https://time.com/4779112/police.-history-origins/.

11. Jonathan M. Pitts, "In its day, Baltimore county's Turner Station was a beloved African-American enclave. Now some seek a revival," *Baltimore Sun*, February 2, 2019, https://www.baltimoresun.com /maryland/baltimore-county/bs-md-turner-station-20190124-story .html.

12. Roshan Nebhrajani, "Liberty City: From a middle-class black mecca to forgotten," *New Tropic*, March 13, 2017, https://thenewtropic.com /liberty-city-history-moonlight/.

13. Lindsey Norward, "The day Philadelphia bombed its own people," *Vox*, August 15, 2019, https://www.vox.com/the -highlight/2019/8/8/20747198/philadelphia-bombing-1985-move.

14. Danielle Paquette, "Ghana to Black Americans: Come home. We'll help you build a life here," *Washington Post*, July 4, 2020, https://www .washingtonpost.com/world/africa/ghana-to-black-americans-come -home-well-help-you-build-a-life-here/2020/07/03/1b11a914-b4e3 -11ea-9a1d-d3db1cbe07ce_story.html.

Chapter Four: The Path

1. Rhonda Y. Williams, *The Politics of Public Housing: Black Women's Struggles Against Urban Inequality* (Oxford University Press, 2004), 201.

2. "1966–1976: After the Unrest," Baltimore's Civil Rights Heritage, https://baltimoreheritage.github.io/civil-rights-heritage/1966-1976/.

Chapter Five: A Man's Man's World

1. "Power of the good mind," *Indigenous Values*, https:// indigenousvalues.org/haudenosaunee-values/power-good-mind/.

Chapter Six: The Holistic Brain

1. R. M. Sapolsky, "The influence of social hierarchy on primate health," *Science* 308, no. 5722 (2005): 648–652, https://www.science.org /doi/10.1126/science.1106477.

2. "CVS pharmacy emerges as symbolic flashpoint of Baltimore riot," *Los Angeles Times*, April 28, 2015, https://www.latimes.com/nation /la-na-cvs-pharmacy-baltimore-riots-20150428-story.html.

Chapter Nine: Mantras and Mudras

1. Susan Moran, "The science behind finding your mantra—and how to practice it daily," *Yoga Journal*, March 20, 2018, https://www .yogajournal.com/yoga-101/sanskrit/mantras-101-the-science -behind-finding-your-mantra-and-how-to-practice-it/.

Chapter Ten: The Child's World

1. Joshua Ceballos, "Environmental Groups Liken DeSantis'
   Anti-Protest Bills to Fascism," *Miami New Times*, January 12, 2021,
   https://www.miaminewtimes.com/news/desantis-anti-protest-bills
   -opposed-by-florida-environmentalists-11799261.

Chapter Eleven: Shedding Trauma, Finding Self-Love

1. Eva Selhub, MD, "Nutritional psychiatry: Your brain on food,"
   Harvard Health Publishing, March 26, 2020, https://www
   .health.harvard.edu/blog/nutritional-psychiatry-your-brain-on
   -food-201511168626.

Chapter Twelve: Mindful Moment

1. Erica L. Green, "Why are Black students punished so often?
   Minnesota confronts a national quandary," *New York Times*, March
   18, 2018, https://www.nytimes.com/2018/03/18/us/politics/school
   -discipline-disparities-white-black-students.html.

2. "Black children five times more likely than White youth to be
   incarcerated," Equal Justice Initiative, September 14, 2017, https://eji
   .org/news/black-children-five-times-more-likely-than-whites-to-be
   -incarcerated/.

3. Zach Beauchamp, "How broken policing is breaking our democracy,"
   Vox, April 23, 2021, https://www.vox.com/2021/4/23/22394495
   /police-democracy-weaver-lerman.

4. Samantha Michaels, "Black kids are 5 times likelier than White kids
   to be locked up," *Mother Jones*, September 17, 2017, https://www
   .motherjones.com/politics/2017/09/black-kids-are-5-times-likelier
   -than-white-kids-to-be-locked-up/.

Chapter Fifteen: The One-Block Radius

1. Anthony Patrick Curtis, "Warriors of the Skyline: A Gendered
   Study of Mohawk Warrior Culture" (2005), *Theses, Dissertations and
   Capstones*, Paper 52, Marshall University, Huntington, WV.

2. Daniel Weeks, "Why are the poor and minorities less likely to vote?" *The Atlantic*, January 2014, https://www.theatlantic.com/politics /archive/2014/01/why-are-the-poor-and-minorities-less-likely-to -vote/282896/.

Chapter Sixteen: Connection to the Natural World

1. Ian Leahy and Yaryna Serkez, "Since when have trees existed only for rich Americans?" *New York Times*, June 30, 2021, https://www .nytimes.com/interactive/2021/06/30/opinion/environmental -inequity-trees-critical-infrastructure.html.

2. Mathew P. White et al., "Spending at least 120 minutes a week in nature is associated with good health and wellbeing," *Scientific Reports* 9, no. 7730 (June 2019), https://www.nature.com/articles/s41598 -019-44097-3; Jim Robbins, "Ecopsychology: How immersion in nature benefits your health," Yale Environment 360, January 9, 2020, https://e360.yale.edu/features/ecopsychology-how-immersion-in -nature-benefits-your-health.

3. Bum-Jin Park, et al., "The physiological effects of Shinrin-yoku (taking in the forest atmosphere or forest bathing): evidence from field experiments in 24 forests across Japan," *Environmental Health and Preventive Medicine* 15, 1 (2010): 18–26, doi: 10.1007/s12199 -009-0086-9. PMID: 19568835; PMCID: PMC2793346.

4. Megan Clapp et al., "Gut microbiota's effect on mental health: The gut-brain axis," *Clinics and Practice* 7, no. 4 (Sept. 15, 2017): 987, https://www.ncbi.nlm.nih.gov/pmc/articles/PMC5641835/.

5. Stephen J. D. O'Keefe et al., "Fat, fibre and cancer risk in African Americans and rural Africans," *Nature Communications* 6, no. 6342 (2015), https://doi.org/10.1038/ncomms7342.

Index

About the Authors

Ali Smith is co-founder and executive director of the Holistic Life Foundation (HLF). Ali was born and raised in Baltimore, Maryland, and is a graduate of the Friends School of Baltimore and the University of Maryland, College Park, from which he received a BS in environmental science and policy. He is a pioneer in the fields of yoga and mindfulness in education as well as trauma-informed yoga and mindfulness. Ali has taught in seven countries on three continents. Co-founder and longtime director of development of HLF **Atman Smith** is a native of Baltimore. Atman attended the University of Maryland, College Park, from which he graduated with a BA in criminology and criminal justice and was a letter winner for the men's basketball team. He is also

a co-owner of the Involution Group and co-creator of the Spiritual Strategic Plan. Co-founder of HLF **Andres Gonzalez** is a certified health coach through the Institute of Integrative Nutrition. He received a BS in marketing from the University of Maryland, College Park, and an MBA from the University of Maryland, University College, and has over twenty years of experience providing yoga and mindfulness to populations all over the world.

Rebekah Elly